PROCEEDINGS

OF THE

NATIONAL BAPTIST

EDUCATIONAL CONVENTION,

HELD IN THE

FIRST BAPTIST CHURCH OF PHILADELPHIA,

MAY 28th, 29th, and 30th, 1872.

OFFICIAL EDITION.

NEW YORK:
SHELDON & CO., BROADWAY.
BOSTON: GOULD & LINCOLN.
PHILADELPHIA: BIBLE & PUBLICATION SOCIETY.
1872.

PREFATORY NOTE.

THE Second National Baptist Educational Convention was held under the auspices of the Philadelphia Baptist Ministerial Conference, the Board of the Pennsylvania Baptist Education Society, and the Board of Trustees of Crozer Theological Seminary. By a Committee appointed by these bodies, of which the Rev. George Dana Boardman, D. D., was Chairman, a generous hospitality was provided for the members, and provision was made for reporting and publishing the Proceedings. The Official Edition is published entirely at the expense of this Committee, under arrangements kindly and competently made by the Rev. L. Moss, D. D. This edition being published, the types by the further liberality of the Committee, are made over to the American Baptist Educational Commission, for the publication of an edition for general circulation, at the cost of presswork, paper and binding. The Official Edition is so designated on the title page.

SEWALL S. CUTTING.

NEW YORK, August 1, 1872.

DELEGATES IN ATTENDANCE.

MAINE.

Colby University.—Rev. D. B. Cheney, D.D.; Hon. William E. Wording, LL.D.
Baptist Education Society.—Rev. C. M. Emery.

VERMONT.

New Hampton Literary and Theological Institution.—Rev. D. C. Bixby.

MASSACHUSETTS.

Newton Theological Institution.—President Alvah Hovey, D.D.; Rev. Alva Woods, D.D.; Rev. W. H. Eaton, D.D.; Rev. J. Upham, D.D.
Northern Baptist Education Society.—Rev. G. W. Bosworth, D.D.; Rev. R. C. Mills, D.D.; Rev. C. W. Anable, D.D.; Rev. A. J. Padelford.
Pastors' Conference.—Rev. James S. Dickerson, D.D.
American Baptist Missionary Union.—Rev. J. N. Murdoch, D.D.; Rev. William Lamson, D.D.
Worcester Academy.—Prof. Samuel S. Greene, LL.D.
Baptist Social Union of Western Massachusetts.—Rev. R. J. Adams, Rev. C. H. Spalding.

RHODE ISLAND.

Brown University.—Rev. Samuel L. Caldwell, D.D.; Prof. John L. Lincoln, LL.D.
Baptist Education Society.—Rev. Henry C. Graves, Rev. G. Bullen.
Baptist Ministerial Conference.—Rev. N. M. Williams, D.D.; Rev. J. T. Smith.
Baptist Social Union.—Rev. J. C. Stockbridge, D.D.; George B. Peck, A. W. Godding.

CONNECTICUT.

Baptist Social Union.—Hon. Francis Wayland.
Baptist Education Society.—Rev. Robert Turnbull, D.D.; Rev. E. Lathrop, D.D.; Rev. E. Cushman, Rev. A. L. Freeman.
Suffield Literary Institution.—Principal E. Benj. Andrews.

NEW YORK.

Baptist Education Society.—Samuel Colgate, Rev. J. Peddie.
Madison University.—President E. Dodge, D.D., LL.D.; Prof. N. L. Andrews, Rev. T. D. Anderson, D.D.
University of Rochester.—Prof. A. C. Kendrick, D.D., LL.D.
Rochester Theological Seminary.—Rev. E. G. Robinson, D.D., LL.D.
American Baptist Home Mission Society.—Rev. J. F. Elder.
New York State Pastoral Conference.—Rev. E. T. Hiscox, D.D.; Rev. G. F. Pentecost, Rev. C. P. Sheldon, D.D.; Rev. G. H. Brigham.
Cish Academy.—Rev. J. Hendrick.
American Baptist Educational Commission.—Rev. S. S. Cutting, D.D.; Rev. Edward Bright, D.D.; W. A. Gellatly.
Manhattan Baptist Social Union.—J. F. Wyckoff, William Phelps, Smith Sheldon.
Brooklyn Baptist Social Union.—James D. Reid.
By Special Invitation of the Convention.—Rev. Thomas J. Conant, D.D.

NEW JERSEY.

Peddie Institute.—Principal H. A. Pratt.

South Jersey Institute.—Principal H. K. Trask, H. J. Mulford.

Ringoes Seminary.—Principal A. B. Larison, C. W. Larison.

New Jersey Baptist Education Society.—Rev. Henry C. Fish, D.D.; Rev. J. T. Brown, D.D.; Rev. William Hague, D.D.; Rev. H. F. Smith, Rev. Charles Keyser.

PENNSYLVANIA.

University of Lewisburg.—Prof. George R. Bliss, D.D.; Rev. W. Shadrach, D.D.; Rev. A. K. Bell, D.D.

Crozer Theological Seminary.—Rev. Henry G. Weston, D.D.; Rev. George D. B. Pepper, D.D.; Rev. Howard Osgood, D.D.; Rev. J. Wheaton Smith, D.D.

Philadelphia Committee of Arrangements.—Rev. George D. Boardman, D.D.; Samuel A. Crozer, Rev. Lemuel Moss, D.D.; Rev. J. G. Walker.

Baptist Ministers' Union.—Rev. Howard Malcom, D.D.; Rev. William P. Hellings, Rev. G. Frear.

Baptist Education Society.—Rev. J. H. Castle, D.D.; Rev. G. M. Spratt, D.D.; T. J. Hoskinson.

Bible and Publication Society.—Rev. Benj. Griffith, D.D.; Rev. J. M. Pendleton, D.D.

Kingston Academy.—Rev. A. J. Furman, J. Frear.

Mount Pleasant Institute.—Rev. B. F. Woodburn.

DELAWARE.

Wyoming Academy.—Principal O. F. Flippo, Rev. G. W. Folwell.

VIRGINIA.

Richmond College.—Rev. Barnas Sears, D.D., LL.D.; Rev. A. E. Dickinson, D.D.; Prof. H. H. Harris.

Richmond Female Institute.—Principal C. H. Winston.

NORTH CAROLINA.

Wake Forest College.—President W. M. Wingate, D.D.; Rev. J. Mitchell, D.D.

SOUTH CAROLINA.

Furman University.—President J. C. Furman, D.D.; Rev. J. A. Broadus, D.D., LL.D.

Southern Baptist Theological Seminary.—President James P. Boyce, D.D., L.L.D., Rev. C. H. Toy, D.D.; Rev. T. G. Jones, D.D.

TEXAS.

Waco University.—President R. C. Burleson, D.D.

IOWA.

Central University.—President L. A. Dunn.

Des Moines University.—Rev. J. A. Nash.

CALIFORNIA.

Baptist Educational Convention.—President Mark Bailey.

WISCONSIN.

Baptist Educational Commission.—Hon. James R. Doolittle, LL.D.; Rev. O. O. Stearns.

ILLINOIS.

University of Chicago.—President J. C. Burroughs, D.D., LL.D.; Prof. William Matthews, LL.D.

Baptist Union Theological Seminary.—President G. W. Northrup, D.D.; Prof. E. C. Mitchell, D.D.; Rev. G. S. Bailey, D.D.

Illinois Educational Association.—Rev. C. Thomas.

North-Western Baptist Education Society.—Rev. H. L. Wayland, D.D.; Rev. D. H. Cooley, Rev. J. Gordon.

MICHIGAN.

Kalamazoo College.—President Kendall Brooks, D.D.; Hon. C. Van Husen.

Baptist Education Society.—Rev. A. Owen, D.D.; Rev. J. Donnelly, Jr., Rev. F. B. Cressey, Rev. L. H. Trowbridge, Rev. R. E. Manning.

OHIO.

Dennison University.—President S. Talbot, D.D.; Rev. E. Thresher, Rev. J. C. Fernald.

Baptist Education Society.—Prof. F. O. Marsh, Rev. R. Jeffrey, D.D.; Rev. Marsena Stone, D.D.

Granville Young Ladies' Institute.—Rev. D. Shepardson.

DISTRICT OF COLUMBIA.

Columbia College.—President James C. Welling, D.D.; T. U. Walter, LL.D.

WYOMING TERITORY.

Wyoming Institute.—Principal D. J. Pierce, Rev. E. E. L. Taylor, D.D.

PROCEEDINGS

OF THE

BAPTIST EDUCATIONAL CONVENTION.

FIRST DAY'S PROCEEDINGS.

MORNING SESSION.

The Convention met in the First Baptist Church, Philadelphia, on Tuesday, May 28, 1872, at 9.30 A. M., and was called to order by SAMUEL COLGATE, Esq., Chairman of the Executive Committee of the American Baptist Educational Commission. Rev. S. S. CUTTING, D. D., Secretary of the Commission, read the call, as follows :—

A National Baptist Educational Convention is hereby called, to be held in the First Baptist Church in the City of Philadelphia, on such a day in April [or May] next as may hereafter be announced, to be continued through three days, at which time topics of common interest to the cause of Education will be discussed, and such action as the Convention may please will be taken in reference to the organization of the educational work of the Baptist denomination in the United States, for the promotion of its common interests.

All Theological Seminaries, all Universities and Colleges, and all Academies connected by their Boards of Management with the Baptist denomination, all Baptist Education Societies having their territorial boundaries coincident with States, or embracing more than one State,—to which Seminaries, Universities, Colleges, Academies and Education Societies this call shall be sent,—are requested to appoint delegates to this Convention, in the numbers of four each from Theological Seminaries, Universities and Colleges, and two each from Academies (of whom one-half shall be from Faculties and one-half from Boards), and four each from Education Societies. State Pastoral Conferences, or other local organizations of equal authority, will be invited by special requests, to secure a representation of Pastors, to the number of two from each State. The general Missionary Societies of the denomination and the Social Unions, are requested to send four delegates each.

This Convention is called in grateful acknowledgment of the extraordinary interest and influence of the Convention of 1870, in recognition of an unprecedented and profounder concern for every form of higher education in the Baptist denomination, and in the devout hope of bringing into greater unity and efficiency this important department of our denominational work. This Convention, like that of 1870, "is called in general and not in special interests, its design being to move, if possible, the Baptist denomination to greater interest in every form of education."

SAMUEL COLGATE, *Chairman of Executive Committee.*
S. S. CUTTING, *Secretary.*

NEW YORK, January 2, 1872.

The following Committee on Nominations was appointed:

Rev. J. WHEATON SMITH, D. D.
Prof. E. C. MITCHELL, D. D.
Pres. KENDALL BROOKS, D. D.
Rev. S. L. CALDWELL, D. D.
W. A. GELLATLY, Esq.

The Convention joined in singing the hymn,

"The starry firmament on high,"

after which, prayer was offered by Prof. George R. Bliss, D. D.

In behalf of the Committee, the Rev. J. Wheaton Smith, D. D., reported the following nominations:

President.

HON. FRANCIS WAYLAND, Conn.,

Vice Presidents.

Hon. JAMES R. DOOLITTLE, LL. D., Wisconsin.
Pres. JAMES C. FURMAN, D. D., S. C.
Hon. C. VAN HUSEN, Mich.
Col. MORGAN L. SMITH, N. J.
Pres. R. C. BURLESON, D. D., Texas.

Secretaries.

Rev. WILLIAM H. EATON, D. D., N. H.
Prof. C. H. WINSTON, Va.
Rev. D. H. COOLEY, Ill.

The report was adopted, and these officers declared elected.

The Hon. Mr. WAYLAND was conducted to the chair by the Rev. J. WHEATON SMITH, D. D. and President JAMES P. BOYCE, D.D., LL.D.

The PRESIDENT: GENTLEMEN OF THE CONVENTION:—I thank you for assigning me to a position which, received at the hands of such a body of educated Christian gentlemen as I see before me, is a most enviable honor, and to the discharge of duties which your courtesy and the harmony of your deliberations will not permit to be difficult. I certainly cannot err in assuming that such courtesy and such harmony will characterize and dignify your discussions. For even if it be remotely possible that any root of bitterness could, under any circumstances, spring up in a Convention so largely under clerical control—(and I vaguely remember to have heard of the *odium theologicum*)—yet it is the great good fortune of this assembly to be called to consider a question, the paramount and pressing importance of which is conceded by all. For my own part, I may be suffered to say that I should do violence to my early training, and to the more mature convictions of later years, if I did not sympathize wholly and heartily with the object of this Convention, with the public spirit which it is expected to create, with the practical results which it is intended to accomplish. I gather from the circular—bearing the signature of our able and indefatigable Secretary—that we are called together, at this time and place, to consider, in the light of such information as our ablest educators will give us, by what best methods our denomination is to be elevated to a higher and still higher plane of Christian education. With this end in view, with the counsel and co-operation of so many men of wisdom and experience, with the blessing of Divine Providence, which we need not hesitate to invoke upon such an undertaking, we can scarcely fail to reach results of the highest utility to our denomination, and of permanent service to the cause of enlightened and progressive Christianity. [Applause]

Dr. CUTTING read a communication :

A COMMUNICATION FROM THE AMERICAN BAPTIST EDUCATIONAL COMMISSION TO THE SECOND NATIONAL BAPTIST EDUCATIONAL CONVENTION.

THE American Baptist Educational Commission, now in the last year of its existence, proposes to surrender to this National Baptist Educational Convention, the care of that department of educational work in which it has been engaged. In making this surrender it offers some record of its doings, with intimations in respect to future service, which have been suggested by its own experience and by currents of manifested opinion.

The Commission was called into existence for the two-fold object of promoting in the Baptist denomination a wider popular interest in the higher forms of education, and likewise a more adequate increase of the Baptist ministry. Originally its operations were restricted to the States of New York and New Jersey, but it was foreseen that its inquiries and influence could not be hemmed in by State lines, and provision was therefore made in its constitution for a possible enlargement of the sphere of its work. Its organization arrested immediate attention throughout the denomination, as giving expression to the sense of common needs, and as furnishing a rallying point for workers in a cause which had been hitherto carried forward with no mutual stimulus and help, and in only disjointed and fragmentary ways. The solitary worker in Minnesota, as that State was merging into existence and moulding into form the institutions of society which were to determine its character, had been chilled and weakened by the consciousness that his more favored brethren in New York knew nothing of the struggles of his special labors, and even the most favored laborers of different States performed their tasks without the cheer and enlightenment of mingled-sympathies, and the knowledge of each other's methods. In Missions, Foreign and Home, in Publication and Bible work, we had been wiser. There we had sought and found unity. To all these departments of Christian service we had given the force of a general and concerted movement; but in respect to education, that cause which in important respects is fundamental to the permanent success of all others, which addresses itself so intimately to our families and our congregations, to our relations with other branches of the Christian family, and to the social character and prospects of our time, we were living utter strangers to this great source of power and progress. The Commission was hailed therefore as the germ of the promise of better things. Applause from every quarter echoed back its organization. Its few publications,—for it had no treasury to make these publications many,—were received widely with avidity, and the services of its Secretary were in requisition from the most distant States.

It was influences and facts like these which led to the calling of the National Educational Convention which met at Brooklyn, in April, 1870. That Convention, memorable for the extent of country and number of institutions represented, for the character of its members and the importance of its deliberations, was memorable likewise for the influence of its proceedings on the cause of higher education both within and without the Baptist denomination. The question of organizing permanently our educational work, in respect to its common interests, was then brought up for consideration, eliciting a discussion in which the consciousness of the need of an educational centre, as a source of enlightenment and stimulus and help, was a fundamental and pervading conception. As however any organization under the limited powers of that Convention could, in the judgment of many, be provisional only, it was deemed wisest to make the Educational Commission itself that provisional organization, by the enlargement of its sphere, and by instruction as to its duties, leaving the question of more permanent organization to another general Convention, clothed distinctly with authority to that end.

In conformity with this expressed wish of the Convention of 1870, the Commission assumed a national character and functions, and proceeded to perform the specific duties enjoined. Among these duties was the calling of local conventions of similar character, which were held at Worcester, Chicago, and Richmond, in the year 1871. All these illustrated the power which a general movement imparts to every local interest, and at all these Conventions the desire was expressed that another National Convention should be called, to take into consideration and to promote the common interests of education in the denomination. It should be added that a Convention, after the model of our own, called independently by Southern brethren, was held at Marion, Ala., in April, 1871; this the Secretary attended by invitation, meeting there a fraternal welcome.

In noting the results which have been accomplished by labors now in their fifth year, it is to be borne in mind that the specific purpose of the Baptist Educational Commission was *to act upon opinion.* Results must therefore be largely indirect, and be so intermingled with those of other coöperating causes as to be incapable of distinct statement and estimation. They are to be seen more in general progress than in particular facts. This view was taken into account in the formation of the Commission, and constituted the movement in a special sense a work of faith. Those who are engaged in it entered upon their work as seeing that which is invisible. Its purpose was, if it were possible, with the Divine blessing, to arouse and move, with a new energy, the denomination on the fundamental questions of better education and an increased ministry. It has found its rewards, not always in the exact lines contemplated, but, in the aggregate, in just that awakening and movement, more widely manifested than could have been reasonably looked for.

Looking back between four and five years upon the cause of education, as its facts then presented themselves to the thoughtful observer, we find certain characteristic and depressing features. Perhaps it was the fact most noticeable and most depressing, that while, whether of our ministry or our laity, a comparatively few foreseeing, large-hearted and liberal men, were engaged in building up institutions of higher learning, amassing in them, in some instances, large sums of money, and while in many of these institutions instruction was offered not exceeded in quality by those of any existing schools of higher learning in the country, there was not in our congregations a corresponding appreciation of such learning and interest in it, crowding those institutions with our young, and with candidates for the ministry of our churches. The difference between these two currents of thought and feeling, between the enlightened individual zeal and the general popular indifference, was most palpable, menacing some of our institutions themselves with arrested development or decay. Another fact closely allied to this, in part explaining it, but not the less unfortunate, was the fact that under the great and pressing need of our churches for an educated ministry, our characteristic denominational interest in education, and especially in its organized forms of action upon public opinion, through our Education Societies, had come to be an interest in ministerial education *almost wholly*,—and we were already suffering, suffering sadly, and more and more, from the attempt, unconscious and unintended, to divorce the education of the ministry from that of the laity. Though less forgetful of the education of our daughters than of our sons, we were striving to fill our pulpits with educated men, without the advantages to denominational character and usefulness, of thoroughly educated classes in our congregations to occupy the higher spheres of industrial, commercial and professional life. It increased the evil that we were doing this at a period characterized by superficial and materialistic popular views of education, which are to find their best and only correction in the higher educational motives and processes which spring from the distinctively Christian mind. And finally, there was the patent fact, already referred to, of the isolation of workers, their interests local, their aims local, learning little from each other's experiences and helping each other not at all by the power of communion of spirit and of aggregated force. The denominational press, as was most natural, shared the common lack, working nobly towards local interests, but wanting the inspiration and power which can come only from higher enthusiasm and broader purposes, in the minds on which it expends its force.

Such was our condition. In less than five years we have witnessed a change great and remarkable. It is not yet time to see a large number added to the students in our institutions of learning. Such an increase comes with the slow growth of opinion in the great mass out of whose homes they proceed. And yet even in this respect the change has been striking and satisfactory. Many of our colleges have increased materially the number of their students, and in our theological seminaries the aggregate increase has been the surprising and cheering one of more than twenty-five per cent. In many instances the labors of the Commission have stimulated and led young men to processes of education. At different times and in marked instances their labors have promoted large gifts to funds for the support of students, and the Commission has had its full share of influence in stimulating the liberality which within five years has augmented so very greatly the funds of our institutions of learning. But not in any or all these forms, so reducible to statements, have its most satisfactory results appeared. They appear rather in that progress of opinion out of which the more tangible fruits are to be gathered in the years to come. The local Conventions of 1871, the great Convention of 1870, and this similar present assembling, would have been deemed, and would have been in fact, impossibilities in 1867. Discussions of education in our Associations and our State Conventions, and the action taken thereon, have assumed a breadth and an intelligence, and are distinguished by a force, hitherto unknown. Proofs are multiplied of an awakened sense of pastoral responsibility in respect to education, which is the best pledge of advancing opinion and feeling among the masses of our people. To no one thing have the efforts of the Commission been more steadily directed than to the engagement of Pastors in the work of promoting intelligent views of education, and of doing this as an indispensable element of faithful pastoral duty. Evidences of this awakened pastoral and public interest have reacted upon our institutions themselves, taking from teachers the sense of isolation and neglect, and inspiring them with the joy and the vigor which spring from conscious companionship and support. And our press, which is the mirror of our denominational life, coöperating in this good work in a manner which surpasses praise, exhibits alike in what it gathers from the facts of our condition, and in the discussions which it sets forth, an advance so great, in compass of views, in intelligence and earnestness, as to be little less than a revolution. All these manifestations of opinion are marked moreover by the consciousness of working in a common cause, and every local interest is deriving strength from the general movement. To one who has access to means of information embracing the whole field of the denomination, no one thing manifests itself more conspicuously than the pressing of the public opinion of the denomination towards education, including now, as before, the education of our ministry as the crown of our work, but including more than ever before the education of the greater mass of our sons and daughters. It seems to be discerned that a denomination of Christians, no matter how primitive and how pure its forms of faith may be, which, in an educating age, is not an educating denomination, will be doomed, and doomed most justly, to make its educated classes a perpetual overflow into denominations in better accord with their personal character and sympathies, and in an equal ratio to keep in perpetual dwarfhood its own influence and power. Under this consciousness our people seem ready to start on a new career. They will not forget that to preach the gospel, to organize churches to be the homes of faithful souls, and the means of still wider diffusions of truth, is indeed the first and fundamental duty. But they will remember that evangelization blossoms in education, and requires it as the condition of its own augmenting power, and that therefore the next duty is *to educate the young* in all the fulness and completeness possible to their various spheres and destinies. Our growing numbers, which in a hundred years have raised our members in communion from fifteen thousand to fifteen hundred thousand, show us to have been an evangelizing body. The spirit which rules this hour would make us not the less an evangelizing body, but rather the more. It would, however add to our faith knowledge,—it would make us preëminently an educating body, doing this in our Lord's name and for the comprehensive ends of his kingdom, making our sons and daughters strong for his service, and illustrating to the extent of our responsibility, the bloom and the beauty of Christian society and civilization.

It is under circumstances like these that the American Baptist Educational Commission surrenders into the hands of this Convention its uncompleted work. Grateful that it has been permitted to do something toward awakening an educational interest in the denomination and bringing that interest into unity and augmented power, it leaves to this Convention the question whether more and better shall be done in similar directions. If the call for a permanent organization in behalf of the common interests of education in the denomination, which has uttered itself in many quarters, is really an expression of denominational sentiment, it will find an expression here, and your wisdom will dictate the method, the ends and the leadership. Your action will be historic. You will determine the desirableness and possibility of the working together of independent churches in a great cause fundamental to their prosperity and usefulness. You are the representatives of 18,000 churches and a million and a half of members in communion. You are the representatives of an adhering population variously estimated at from five to seven millions. How can you best awaken and sustain in all these churches, and in this great population, such an interest in education as shall make strong your institutions of learning, as shall fill them with your sons and daughters, and render the name which in Christ's service you bear, honorable among the forces which carry forward the cause of Christian education for our country and for mankind? These are your problems. Our great movements in education have proceeded hitherto from organized denominational action. And in the good providence of God, this Convention is assembled just where that action was taken. There have been with us, previously to the present, two epochs in education, and the distinguishing feature of both was that the denomination moved together. The first of these epochs takes for its date 1764, when Brown University, proceeding from the counsels of the Philadelphia Association was founded by a movement which extended from New England to Georgia. The second takes its date just fifty-three years later, when in 1817, under the leadership of that great light of our churches, Dr. Richard Furman, of South Carolina, at the first Triennial meeting of the Baptist General Convention, held in the city of Philadelphia, were instituted the measures which gave us the next in order of our institutions of learning, and the fresh impulse of all our later educational efforts. In the first decade of a second century we find ourselves assembled in the same city, and in the midst of a new epoch, in which an interest in education, transcending by far that of any previous period, manifests itself from ocean to ocean, and from the cold boundaries of the North to the endless summer of our southern borders. The epoch is distinguished likewise by a vast increase in our numbers and our wealth, and in the array of our scholars and devoted friends of education to lead a new and glorious movement. All other of the great denominations are organized for their educational work, and propose to seize it with a new energy. They have caught inspiration from the example of our Educational Commission, and will watch with fraternal solicitude our further activity in the common cause. The question of the responsibility of this Convention, at such a crisis, is respectfully submitted, with a prayer for that divine Wisdom whose counsels may be trusted to save us from error.

This paper was referred to a Committee on the Organization of our Denominational Work in Education, to be hereafter appointed.

ADDRESS OF WELCOME.

In behalf of the Baptists of Philadelphia, the REV. GEORGE DANA BOARDMAN, D. D., Pastor of the First Baptist Church, addressed the Convention as follows:

MR. PRESIDENT:—In accordance with the instruction of a Committee of Arrangements, appointed by the Philadelphia Baptist Ministerial Conference, the Board of the Pennsylvania Baptist Education Society, and the Board of Trustees of the Crozer Theological Seminary, it becomes my pleasant duty to extend to you, sir, and to the Convention you officially represent, assurances of our warmest greeting. We welcome you to our city, so rich in the inheritance of denominational and educational memories. We welcome you to the meeting-house wherein worship a church once presided over by a MORGAN EDWARDS and a WILLIAM ROGERS with a fidelity and a success which have become historical. We welcome you to our homes. Nor are these words a mere formality. The welcome is in our hearts, as well as on our lips. It is our joy and our pride that you are with us. And among the many pleasant reminiscences connected with this, the second session of the National Convention, our hope and trust is that not the least pleasant reminiscence will be that it was held in Philadelphia. [Applause.]

REV. BARNAS SEARS, D. D., LL. D., delivered the opening address, on the following subject:

INSTITUTIONS OF LEARNING ESTABLISHED BY CHRISTIAN DENOMINATIONS CONSIDERED WITH REFERENCE TO PRESENT AND PROBABLE SYSTEMS OF PUBLIC INSTRUCTION.

INTELLECTUAL distinction is partly the gift of nature, and partly the result of culture. The former comes without our bidding; the latter depends on us. But let no one suppose, that there is in men a certain amount of knowledge divisible into two equal parts—the one original, the other acquired. Man is created without any knowledge save, perhaps, that of his own existence; but with capacities for all knowledge. The difference between the savage and the philosopher is not in their nature, but in their culture. They stand upon the same earth, and look into the same heavens—but with what different eyes! The one sees but little more than does the faithful dog by his side; the other analyzes and classifies all the dust and rock beneath his feet, and reads their history from the creation; and, by the use of instruments of his own invention, gives us the mechanics and the chemistry of the heavens.

Observe now the training of the eminent scholar, as contrasted with that of the undisciplined barbarian. Besides what he learns incidentally, from instinct, from experience, imitation and tradition, he masters the accumulated knowledge of the past—the wisdom and the science of his own age—by a life-long application to study. He passes his childhood in the elementary school, his boyhood in the academy or high school, his earlier youth in the college, his later youth in the professional school. He then spends a few years in travel and study abroad, and is finally settled in his chosen profession, where he slowly and laboriously rears the fabric of his greatness. Ten or twenty years of enthusiastic and intense study give him a name and a place in the world of letters.

But soon he dies and his knowledge dies with him. Humboldt dies, and his successors must begin where he began. La Place dies, and Le Verrier must learn astronomy as he learned it. Sir Humphrey Davy dies, and Faraday must become what he is to be, by his own efforts. Heeren and Schlosser die, and Mommsen and Curtius must study ancient history for themselves. Macaulay dies, and Froude must examine the British, French and Spanish archives for himself. Webster dies, and some one else,—I know not whom,—must study and learn to interpret constitutional law. And so it is in all the other departments of learning.

Knowledge is not hereditary. Each generation of men is to go through all the arduous work of acquisition for itself. It is as if wealth, instead of being accumulated to be transmitted in families, departed at the same time with its possessor, leaving each son to begin where his father began, and to go through the same process of slow acquisition. And yet there is an important difference here. The generations of men do not succeed each other, as the leaves of the forest in successive years; but society is progressive, and from age to age knowledge is ever on the increase. Such could not be the case, if every generation did not transmit to posterity all its treasures of knowledge by careful instruction. This is the great argument for education. Civilization itself is dependent for its progress on the knowledge and discipline furnished by the schools.

Taking now all that has thus far been said for granted, and accepting, as I am sure you will, with me, the theory of the necessity of education, let me next inquire, what are the several parts to be included in a complete system of education in its most comprehensive sense. There is here an established but invisible order of things, much broader and deeper than any formally recognized by us, binding together all our organizations for forming the character of the young, into a higher unity.

It is like the vital principle of the human body, which unites all its organs into a complex whole. The parts of this system are:

1st. Religious education in the family, the church and the Sabbath-school;

2d. Elementary education in the public schools;

3d. Higher education in the academy, the scientific school, the college, and the professional school;

4th. General education acquired in business, in society, and by general reading.

These parts are all so connected with, and dependent on each other, that no one can be omitted without detriment to the whole. As they all presuppose each other, every part becomes defective when standing alone.

1st. RELIGIOUS EDUCATION.

This is confessedly the most important of all. No education without religion is complete in itself, sufficient for the wants of the individual, or safe for society. But while the subject of religious instruction is plain and simple at first view, it is, in some of its aspects, one of the most difficult, and one in respect to which there is great jarring and confusion in the public mind. I do not here refer to the mysterious nature of the subject or to the abstruse character of some of its doctrines, but to the difficulty of adjusting the rights of conscience so as to produce peace and order and the highest public good. As a man's relations to his God are the most important of all, his religious interests transcend all other interests, and consequently he cannot allow any claims of society to interfere with them. As a parent he has to give direction to the religious education of his children.

Can the public schools be made to supply this want? In part, and only in part. We should attempt to introduce into these schools only what properly belongs there. Evidently they should be Christian schools. There is no good reason for making them heathen schools. All our civilization is Christian. The genius of our public institutions is Christian, without being sectarian. Inasmuch as education includes moral training, Christian morality ought to be the ruling spirit of the school. It is the teacher's great power. Take from him that, and you deprive him of the means of disciplining and moulding the character of his school. Wherever both teacher and pupil attempt to follow the golden rule, and the Lord's prayer and David's psalms of praise are repeated daily, with other similar exercises, there the best schools will be found. But the moment sectarian instruction is introduced the good effect ceases and evil enters. Men of another faith will complain that injustice is done to their children. No State in the Union could be induced either to recognize an established church, or to give to any one denomination the control of religious education in public schools. But ethical and devotional Christianity is common to all sects, and this is what the youthful mind specially needs. Further religious instruction is indeed necessary, but this can best be given in the family, the Sabbath-schools and the church, where the work is not put into incompetent hands as it might be in the public schools. When these three parties all perform their proper functions, then the objection frequently made to public schools, viz. the insufficient provision for religious instruction in them, falls to the ground of itself. These two kinds of education are counterparts of each other, the one supplementing the other. Indeed, both processes go on simultaneously. The child passes six hours in the school daily, and the remaining hours at home under domestic training, and five days in the week at school, and one at church and in the Sabbath-school.

But some have said, if this be the case, let us give up the public schools altogether, and let us depend on private and parochial schools, which shall have such a religious character as we prefer! Then each denomination must have separate schools in every village in every part of the State. There will be neither money enough to support, nor pupils enough to supply each school. Large numbers, nearly one-half, who need instruction most, will be excluded by their poverty. Those who will be able to attend the school, will do it at double the necessary expense, with half the advantage of the other system. Moreover, we cannot have good schools in this way. They cannot be well graded, as their numbers will be small, and the stages of their advancement various. The teachers cannot be properly selected, as they are self-appointed, and the choice between them will be limited. The schools will not be properly organized, nor will the most improved systems be adopted, because the teacher must have regard to economy. The whole matter of public supervision and control will of course be surrendered. Besides all this, private schools very often fail to give a religious training. In them there have always been found teachers unfit to have the care of youth.

2d. ELEMENTARY EDUCATION IN THE PUBLIC SCHOOLS.

We may safely assume the position that universal education has become a necessity. There is no other way of meeting the present demands of society. The arguments, now so familiar, need not be repeated here. Every one knows, that our peace, security, and prosperity depend on the instruction given to the young. Such being the fact, it is plain that provision must be made for public, free schools. No other schools can extend their benefits to the whole population. Private schools reach but a part—often only a small fraction of the masses of the people. These schools are *designed* only for the few who *can* pay. The teacher cannot afford to give away his time and labor. Money-making is an essential part of his policy; and in all questions regarding the improvement of the school, that consideration turns the scale—too often alas against the interest of education. In the public school that consideration does not operate at all. The simple aim is to educate all, and to educate them well—economically, of course, but not for pecuniary profit.

Endowed schools are equally limited in their operation. England has expended millions of money on such schools, and has accomplished much for the education of the few. But how is it with the masses of the people? Her statesmen have, for half a century, been justly alarmed at the dangerous character of her ignorant population; and the government has been compelled, for self-preservation, to devise measures for humanizing this fearful accumulation of misguided force, which it can no longer control. It has no peril to fear so great and threatening as this Titanic power of associated and organized ignorance, which has laid in the dust one of the proudest thrones of Europe, and which, like a spectre of night, stalks abroad in the lands with bold strides and defiant mien.

Contrast this with what Prussia has done and become in the nineteenth century. Overrun, pillaged and plundered at the beginning of the century,—with a fugitive king and court, a ruined nobility and gentry, and an impoverished peasantry, it began in the day of its greatest humiliation and weakness the work of moral reconstruction by establishing schools for the elevation of the people, teaching them self-reliance, social order and patriotic sentiments, putting the best talents in the country in the departments of public instruction, and making its whole system of education a model for all Europe, and its entire population the most intelligent to be found in all the world,—and what is her rank among the nations of Europe to-day?

And now look at France, of whose conscripts it was found, one-third could not read or write: whose laws make the school age of children only from seven to thirteen years. Half priest-ridden, and half atheistic, with a populace that knows just enough to give organization to a mob, breaking with all the past, sundering all the moral ties of the present, and looking with total indifference to the future, she lies in ruins, like Herculaneum and Pompeii, her corruption but half concealed by the *debris* that covers her.

Hear what her minister of education said just after the catastrophe: "The unexampled misfortunes which have befallen the country, should teach us the lesson, never to be forgotten, that the only power which makes a nation invincible is the intellectual and moral power. This we must restore." Another minister of state said in no friendly tone: "The empire has systematically kept the great mass of the people in ignorance, in order to make them convenient tools of despotism." We should be blind indeed if, from the recent history of these three great European states, England, Prussia and France, we were not to derive any lessons of wisdom. Need I refer to Spain and Mexico on the one hand, and to Switzerland and Sweden on the other as illustrating the same principle? We must either educate the whole population, or the scenes which have imperilled the interests of society in some parts of our country within the past few years, and which threaten us still, will be repeated and multiplied till our political fabric shall fall upon our heads. There are but two ways in which a people can be governed,—by reason and by force; by the former when they are intelligent; by the latter when they are ignorant. We must choose between the two: there is no middle course.

Disband our public schools, as some would blindly do, and thousands of children will be turned into the streets to be trained in the school of vice and crime, to make work for the police courts, and to fill the houses of correction at a cost vastly exceeding that of educating them for usefulness and honor.

General education must be provided not only for the people, but through the people. They need to be enlightened on the subject and aroused to a sense of its importance. A sound, vigilant, and ever-active public sentiment needs, first of all, to be created. Where a state has advanced so far as to put forth its whole energies, and to appoint its wisest and best men to direct them, a powerful influence is exerted upon the masses of the people. The entire population, under the guidance of the best lights of the age, concentrates and puts forth all its power for its own improvement and elevation.

We have now reached that point in our discussion, where the higher schools come in for consideration, for the support of which we cannot rely on the public school fund, but must rely on voluntary associations and private munificence.

We do not take into account State universities, agricultural colleges, and normal schools, which may be regarded as exceptional or, at least, isolated cases, but confine ourselves to those classes of institutions which are supported by private munificence.

Completeness of treatment would require me here to pass in review all the schools for special and professional education outside of the system of public instruction, but the occasion on which we are met, calls for the discussion of those schools only in which the Christian church has a particular interest, namely the academy, the college, and the theological seminary.

The utility of each of these has been called in question: the first because of the general establishment of high schools; the second because colleges belong to the past rather than to the present and the future; and the third because candidates for the ministry would learn better how to perform their duties from a pastor who is in the work, than from professors who are withdrawn from the sympathies and the society of the living world.

In attempting to show that there is still a necessity for *academies*, I shall not say a word in disparagement of public high schools, but on the contrary shall plead equally for both. While encouraging the former in every way, and aiding in their ample endowment, we ought undoubtedly to join with our fellow-citizens in supporting public high schools wherever the population is sufficient to justify it. They are a great public blessing. Our patriotism alone should be a sufficient motive; for by this means only can the generality of people receive that degree of culture, which shall elevate them and bring them into intellectual intercourse with the better part of mankind. This grand result can never be reached by private schools or endowed institutions. They act indeed most beneficently, but they act upon the few. The history of education in England for six centuries demonstrates this, as we have already seen. Consider the number of such establishments and the enormous amount lavished upon them, and tell me if the degradation of the common people in England is owing to any want of schools of this description. These institutions have done a noble work, and are justly the pride of the nation; but one thing they have not done, and cannot do:—they cannot widely diffuse higher education and make it the heritage of the people generally.

But we should encourage the multiplication of public high schools for a reason that comes nearer to most of us, because they furnish the means of cheap education to all our children, so that every one of us, who lives in towns of sufficient population, may raise his family to a respectable degree of intelligence, and afterwards, perhaps, have the means of sending them abroad for the purpose of pursuing higher studies.

But all this does not militate against the utility and even necessity of endowed literary institutions. Public and private schools have different functions, and supply different wants. The true policy of a state is, to multiply its high schools as far as possible, carrying the precious boon of knowledge to the very doors of the people. The true policy of endowed schools is to resist the tendency to multiplicity as fatal to their success, and to seek concentration and strength. The very fact that they are, or ought to be few in number, that they are to be boarding establishments for pupils that leave their homes, that they are often outside of a city, or in a small town, or even in a retired place in the country, shows that they do not in any way interfere with the public high schools.

Now there is a large number of people who live either in rural districts or in small villages where there are no high schools. Our common school system, excellent as it is, works better in large than in small towns. There is less wealth in the country. Schools must be organized for smaller numbers of children. Consequently the local taxes must be high, or the schools very ordinary in their character. Only schools of a common grade will exist, and often nothing but primary schools. The population will not furnish children enough for several schools of different grades, and the wealth of the place will not afford money enough to supply houses and teachers of a very high order.

What shall that large class of families do, that find themselves in these circumstances,—residing, where none but the poorer class of public schools exist? If they are what they should be, they cannot deny their children a good education. They cannot give enough of their own time, to instruct their children properly, even if they have every needed qualification. They cannot afford to employ private tutors; and even, if they could, that would not answer the purpose. Nothing is left but to send their children from home to some good school for their education. Shall they send them to towns which have high schools? They will not be received. The school committees have no right to give free education to any but its own citizens; and the law does not contemplate the payment of tuition by children coming in from other towns.

There is therefore need of a class of schools—few indeed but well endowed, organized, and equipped,—where such persons as I have described, can place their sons or daughters and find what they want.

Again, there are in all our large cities families of wealth, which desire to remove their older children from the gaieties of city life, and from the entanglements of unprofitable society, and to place them in some safe retreat for study, and the formation of a pure and strong womanly or manly character, where a sound education will be given, accompanied by all good influences upon the heart and life. The public high school does not meet the wants of this class.

There are other persons still, who wish their children to have a religious as well as intellectual training under teachers of known Christian excellence and skill in moulding the character of the young. In the public schools there must be a certain compromise in matters of religion. The Bible, Christian morality and devotion properly belong there. But we cannot go beyond these: and the use of these depends partly on the character of the teacher, and partly on the sentiment of the community. A parent, whose time is very much occupied with business, or who distrusts his own power to instruct his older children, may be eager to put them where he is sure that their spiritual interests will receive, in the form most approved by him, all that attention and direct and positive influence, which he would desire. We cannot decide for others, how far home education and home influences shall be depended on. All those,—and they are numerous,—who wish to provide for the education of their more advanced children under the choicest influences, and are able and willing to bear the expense of sending them where they will be suitably cared for, ought, I think, to be able to find such a place among their own people.

The high schools in our largest cities may give instruction of as high a grade and of as good a quality as can be desired; but in the majority of towns they will only make moderate provisions for the higher English studies and for the elements of ancient and modern languages. Their aim is rather the wide diffusion of knowledge than profound acquisition. They seek to train the great mass of the youth of a place for practical life, and to start the few who aspire to it on their career for literary distinction. If they call forth the slumbering intellect into activity, if they impart a taste for literary pursuits, if they turn the faces of boys born for study towards the college and university, and make it possible for the sons of the lower classes to pass from them directly to the halls of science and learning, they accomplish their legitimate work.

But how many there are, scattered all over our whole country, who have determined to give their sons as good an education as the best institutions can furnish. Our people are becoming wealthy. They can afford to consult not merely their convenience, but the intellectual wants and interests of their sons, who, they fondly hope, will one day rise and give lustre to their families.

One of this class will naturally apply to educated men for information and advice in respect to the best schools; and will send a thousand miles to find one rather than put up with one of lower rank near his own door. He will give his patronage to a school of his own religious denomination, if it be as good as any other; but when you appeal to his public spirit and denominational pride in order to induce him to sacrifice the education of his son, the idol of his heart, to help keep alive a languishing academy that is on your hands, he will be too much of a logician for you. He may have contributed to the funds of this impoverished school, he may even belong to its board of trustees, and yet the parental instinct will rise superior to all other considerations, and he will say to you, in the anguish of his heart perhaps: "When you ask a charity, I can cheerfully give it; when you desire my personal services, they are at your command. These I can well afford to contribute to a good public object. But when you ask me to sacrifice my child, and to place him at a school where I know he cannot acquire the best discipline and scholarship, when you beg me for conscience' sake to deny him the means of education which others enjoy, and thus doom him to a life-long inferiority, either my conscience or something else within me as holy, cries out against the unpaternal character and inhumanity of such a sacrifice. I can do more for my own people by educating for their service a man of the highest order of scholarship, to fill with honor a station of public usefulness, than I can by adding one to the number of those who pay their quarterly bills, waste their spring-time of life under unskilful tuition, and spend the rest of life in lamenting their mistake."

Such debates and conflicts occur as matters of fact almost every day somewhere. In the course of my life I have seen many a man who has cursed the day when he was made such a victim by the advice of brethren; I have seen, and still see, others, who, by broader views of duty and of policy, were sent to the best institutions for the sake of the choicest culture, and we are all reaping the benefit of such a course to-day.

While a people are poor and oppressed there is an excuse for not having literary institutions of the highest order. Our fathers did all they could, and did nobly. But that day has passed long ago. What we need now is not power; but wisdom to direct and concentrate it. We need large plans, wide co-operation. Let there be an interchange of views and fraternal consultation in regard to our common interest. Let there be a wise calculation as to the number of institutions needed, and the places where they should be maintained; and then let us work upon a general plan, giving unity and vigor to our action, and we shall all be the stronger and the better for it. Support and strengthen academies where they are really needed. Surrender those that cannot prosper, and transfer the money and labor uselessly expended on them to such as have the principle of vitality in them. Then the anxieties and struggles of many noble minds will be ended. The apparently diverging lines of duty and of interest in patronizing schools will coincide, and the friends of education among us will all be moving in one direction. A spirit of enterprise will take the place of despondency, and a generation will spring up after us that will take up our great religious enterprises and carry them far beyond what our feeble faith will now allow us to believe.

We need a high order of academies furthermore, that they may become nurseries to our colleges. If we fail to have them, we shall thereby reduce the colleges to the necessity of admitting classes of students who are not duly prepared, or of confining their instruction to a number too small for the support of an able faculty. The danger will be that all other considerations must yield to the inexorable demands of pecuniary necessity. The standard of scholarship must consequently descend towards that of the academy. The well-prepared student from a good academy may even find himself degraded in the Freshman Class of an impoverished college.

If it be said that the colleges, with their various courses lately introduced, have a place for everybody, we reply that if this is really so, nothing could more effectually show the worthlessness of the whole system. The college must, in that case, either impose upon a mature professor, with a full salary, a task unworthy of his high literary attainments, which could be performed much cheaper and better at another place, or employ a subaltern grammar master, and thus set up a miserable opposition to the academy, to the serious detriment of both institutions. A position of such degradation to a student in an inferior college class is little adapted to inspire in him a love of letters, or to add to the reputation of that school of learning which shelters under its wings the dupes of such puerile absurdities. I never knew an institution which tried the experiment whose officers did not privately express contempt for it.

We must, then, have good academies for the sake of the colleges, and the latter must be distinct from the former, and not ungratefully ruin them by descending from their own level and thus interfering with them.

These academies must in turn know their proper sphere and keep within it. If they descend below it, they perform an unnecessary work for which better provision is made in the public schools. If they have a foolish ambition to rise above it, they undertake a work for which they are not properly qualified. What can be more absurd than for one man, without proper assistants and appliances to profess to do the work of a whole college faculty, and by a few extra recitations in languages, mathematics and philosophy to pretend to give a liberal education? In attempting thus to teach the liberal arts and sciences he diminishes the attendance at the college by retaining those who should resort thither, spoils the scholarship of the pupil, who becomes nothing but a sciolist, and makes himself ridiculous.

But by whom shall such academies be founded and supported? It must be done by a body of public-spirited and influential men, voluntarily associated for this purpose. And there is generally found no bond of union for enlisting men in the enterprise so strong, so permanent and reliable as that which unites a Christian denomination. Other associations for the support of academies are held together by too slender a tie. They rest on compromises, and are too negative in their character. There is a want of a single overpowering motive for contributing funds and conducting the affairs of the school with diligence and care. A corporation made up of heterogeneous materials, with a vague and feeble interest in common, will be likely to do little more than meet once a year and pass formal votes. Such a corporation will lack vitality and power. Nor will it be any better if the academy is a private establishment, owned or controlled by one man. It will be variable in its character, and be subject to all the chances and changes of individual fortune; and at best it will be conducted in the interest of the proprietor.

But perhaps some one will say, Why not avoid all this expense and trouble, and depend on the schools of other denominations for the education of our children? You may do so, if you are willing to confess in this manner that you are less intelligent, public-spirited and enterprising than they; if you are willing that they should be nobler than yourselves, and, with justice, more highly appreciated and honored. Do not excuse yourselves from doing your part because others are willing to do it for you. Why not throw yourselves into their position? Why not go forward yourselves and establish schools for your own benefit and that of the public?

We now come to *Colleges*. On this and the remaining topics I shall be brief. The college gives to a liberal education its character. To furnish this in the best manner is its sole aim. In it alone does the academy realize its object. The latter is introductory chiefly, and serves merely to prepare the student for his college course, and would lose much of its object if he were to proceed no farther. The little Latin and Greek usually taught there, embracing only the elements of languages, would have little value if not followed by a thorough study of classical authors, as the means of mental discipline and culture.

So the professional school loses much of its solidity and strength, if it do not rest on the basis of a liberal education. The aim of the college is to cultivate the mind in a general way, by disciplining all its faculties, to make young men strong in intellect, to give them acute, polished and well-balanced minds. If this disciplinary work is well accomplished, the mind may afterward be applied to any subject, to the study of any profession or art, and it will be able to work with ease, precision and power. Our reformers in education are constantly overlooking this fact. They seek what they call practical knowledge only, as if the development of the reason did not belong to the realm of practical knowledge. Knowledge is indeed acquired at the same time, but not so much for its own sake as for its use in disciplining the mind, and in storing it with those facts and general principles which are the key to unlock all the treasures of knowledge.

If we examine what schools have given the stamp of intellectual greatness to men distinguished in public life, we shall find that it is not so much the special or professional school as the college or university devoted to general learning. In looking for the record of the student life of the men that have most adorned the pulpit, the bar, the bench, the parliament, the cabinet in England, we do not go to the practical or professional school, but to those old renowned seats of learning, Oxford and Cambridge. So in our own country, we resort to the triennial catalogues of the colleges to trace the literary parentage of our great men. And what college cannot boast of such? And what a long list of worthies does the history of some of our older colleges present!

I will dismiss this topic, with the remark that our colleges need two things especially: better trained entering classes, and larger endowments. The former can be attained only by elevating and improving our academies; the latter, by concentrating all our strength upon a smaller number of colleges.

THEOLOGICAL SCHOOLS.

The seminary is the crowning literary institution of the church, to which the academy and the college are preparatory. It gives a practical direction and completion to ministerial education. The Christian denomination which neglects to provide for an educated ministry dooms itself to weakness and insignificance. Intellectual superiority is power, and gives influence everywhere. United with piety, it gives the ministry and church a controlling power in the formation of public sentiment in matters of morality and religion.

If you would have an efficient ministry, select young men whom God has designed for the work: furnish their minds with discipline and knowledge; then educate them for their calling:—let them be thoroughly grounded in Christian doctrine; in order to do this, give them a critical knowledge of the Scriptures; let them learn God's teachings in the external and internal history of the church for eighteen centuries; let them receive instruction and counsel from one mature in the knowledge and experience of ministerial and pastoral duties; and then let them go forth in God's name, and put on the armor which their fathers are putting off.

To say that a young man can learn these things better by living with a pastor than at a seminary is like saying that one can become a better civil or military engineer by practicing the art with another than by studying mathematics. All professional education is two-sided, theoretical and practical, and the latter element is founded on the former. Both are necessary. What sort of Hebraists and biblical interpreters should we have, if our pastors, weary and exhausted with parochial labors, were to do all the teaching? How would our young ministers be prepared to grapple with the fundamental questions which a secret or an avowed infidelity is industriously forcing upon the public attention every day? They are set for the defence as well as the proclamation of the gospel. Surely this is not a time in which the church can dispense with her heavy artillery, when that of the enemy is pointed against her from every hill-top.

Who are the men that now stand on the walls of Zion, with sword girded on, and spear and shield in hand? Who are the chosen champions of the church, and the defenders of your faith? Who translate your Scriptures, write your commentaries, prepare your books, and contribute the strong articles to your reviews? Who discuss the fundamental religious questions of the day, both in great assemblies, and in the weekly religious press? There is but one answer,—the ripest scholars and the ablest men that can be found. The labors of this class of men, their power of working in centres of influence with superior energy, and of diffusing sound views of truth with masterly skill, cannot be dispensed with.

Our seminaries are a safe-guard against erratic opinions, and are a general bond of unity and peace. Our safest men are at the head of them, and if a young man has his crotchets, they will be kindly but affectionately taken out of him by his teacher or his class. Look at our leading schools, north and south. east and west,—their professors, and the great body of their graduates, and see what they are doing for the Church of Christ. They are here, and almost everywhere. Not a note of discord; no taint of heresy; no schism, no strife. What a beautiful spectacle! What a blessing! We have never had such harmony, peace and prosperity as we now have under the double tide of light and love going forth from them.

Men sometimes talk about recluses in our seminaries! Give us men such as certain reverend doctors that I could name, if they were not present. You can hardly take up a newspaper that does not speak of their burning words of eloquence and wisdom at Ministers' Institutes and various public meetings. Recluses in this bustling age are as rare as ghosts. Our theological students are in the very midst of a busy world. They are in society, in Sabbath-schools, in mission stations, in popular assemblies. If they do not acquire a knowledge of the living world, it will not be because they are not sufficiently in it. We are all moving so much and so fast that this sort of objection is antiquated.

4th. EDUCATION AS ACQUIRED IN BUSINESS, IN SOCIETY AND BY GENERAL READING.

It would be foreign to the purpose of this Convention to enter into a particular discussion of the topic now named. I can only indicate the line of thought here intended. After receiving a training in the schools a young man is greatly influenced, I might almost say controlled, by his business relations, the society in which he moves, and the literature which he reads. If these are characterized by honor, integrity and truth, he will be likely to receive their impress. If they are not so, the reverse will take place. What would a true picture of our times be in this respect? Is it not an age of Mammon worshippers, unfavorable to honest dealings? What deception, what false dealing in trade! What recklessness and wickedness in speculation! What corruption in places of trust!

If we pass to a view of the intercourse of society, we find the same evidences of deterioration. The undue love of wealth, of power, of distinction—the fires of ambition, and the desperate struggle for ascendency, make sad work with the social virtues. It is a materialistic, sensual age; an age of vulgar display and low-bred self-assertion. The love of pleasure among our youth,—frivolity and show in the one sex, and dissipation in the other, give little promise of good for the future.

Our fashionable and popular literature is both the creature and the creator of this derangement of the social order. Our declining morals encourage the press to open the flood-gates of corrupt and corrupting influences. When will good and intelligent citizens unite in putting the brand of infamy upon books which teach Parisian morals, and upon those vile issues of the daily and weekly press, which parade before our families the details of every crime that can be named? On this, and the two preceding points, there is a Herculean task for Christians and all the friends of humanity to perform. Is it already too late? Has this tide of corruption, like a crevasse in the lower Mississippi, worn a channel so broad and so deep as to defy all attempts to stay the flood?

For the education which society gives to each new generation—for its business habits, its manners and its literature, it is itself responsible. Let each one take to himself his share of responsibility, and bravely do what he may for the good of his race.

Thus I have endeavored to sketch an outline of a general system of education, so far as it comes within the scope of this meeting. The more particular discussion of some of the topics embraced in it, is reserved for others, who have been selected for the purpose, and who will do them ampler justice.

The Convention adjourned to half-past two o'clock, P. M.

TUESDAY AFTERNOON SESSION.

The Convention reassembled at half-past two, P. M. The proceedings were opened with prayer, by Rev. Dr. J. C. FURMAN. The following Committee of Arrangements was announced by the Chair:

Rev. GEORGE D. BOARDMAN, D. D.
Rev. G. S. BAILEY, D. D.
WILLIAM A. GELLATLY, Esq.

A notice was read inviting the Convention to visit the Hall of the American Baptist Historical Society.

Pres. WESTON: I have the honor, in behalf of Crozer Theological Seminary, of inviting the Convention, at such time as may be expedient and convenient for them, to visit our Seminary. In making the arrangements for the present session, we thought it might be pleasant for the members of the Convention to make an excursion into the country,—and we should count it a very high honor if the Convention should think it was a part of its duty, in the discharge of its practical work, to visit this, the youngest of our theological institutions, and to give us a token of fellowship by breaking bread with us.

It was voted that the invitation be accepted, and that the arrangements be referred to the Committee of Arrangements.

A paper was then read by Pres. KENDALL BROOKS, D. D., of Kalamazoo College, on the question:

HOW, AND TO WHAT EXTENT MAY COLLEGES ESTABLISHED FOR THE EDUCATION OF YOUNG MEN, AND ADJUSTED TO THAT END, BE MADE, BY THE TEACHING WHICH THEY OFFER AND BY THEIR APPARATUS OF INSTRUCTION, TO SERVE, WITHOUT DAMAGE TO THAT ORIGINAL PURPOSE, IN THE EDUCATION OF YOUNG WOMEN.

[A young man representing himself as connected with the Philadelphia newspaper press applied to Dr. Brooks for the temporary use of this manuscript, and never returned it. All efforts to find him proved unavailing, and these Proceedings are therefore printed without that important paper. It was the first draft, and Dr. Brooks was unable to command the time to reproduce it.]

Dr. CUTTING proposed the following, which was adopted:

That in the discussions arising on papers, reports, and matters of business, members be restricted to seven minutes; and no member shall speak more than twice on the same question, except for the purpose of explanation or inquiry, without consent.

An order of Proceedings having been printed for the consideration of the Convention, the Committee of Arrangements proposed its adoption, providing, however, that the Convention shall meet on Thursday afternoon, at 2 o'clock, and adjourn at 4, to enable the Convention to visit the Crozer Theological Seminary. The report was adopted.

The following is the order referred to:

ORDER OF PROCEEDINGS.

TUESDAY.—MORNING.

9 to 10—Organization of the Convention.

10 to 12 : 30—Opening Address, by Rev. BARNAS SEARS, D. D., LL. D., to be followed by Oral Discussion.—Subject, Institutions of Learning established by Christian Denominations, considered with reference to present and probable systems of Public Instruction.

AFTERNOON.

[*The papers named below are limited in the call of the Convention, to* THIRTY MINUTES, *and are to be followed by oral discussions, which are expected to be limited by the Convention.*]

2 : 30 to 3 : 45—How, and to what extent, may Colleges, established for the Education of Young Men, and adjusted to that end, be made by the teaching which they offer, and by their Apparatus of Instruction, to serve, without damage to that Original Purpose, in the education of Young Women?—Pres. KENDALL BROOKS, D. D., Kalamazoo College.

3 : 45 to 5—Methods and Uses of Classical Studies.—Prof. A. C. KENDRICK, D.D., LL.D., University of Rochester.

5 to 5 : 30—Communication from the Executive Committee of the American Baptist Educational Commission.

EVENING.

7 : 45 to 9 : 30—Education, a Development of Christian Life, the Supplement and Support of all Evangelization, and therefore Due in its Highest Practicable Forms, to the whole body of the Ministry and Laity.—Pres. SAMPSON TALBOT, D. D., Denison University.

WEDNESDAY.—MORNING.

9 to 10 : 30—Causes which hinder the Increase of the Ministry.—Rev. R. C. MILLS, D. D., Salem, Mass.

10 : 30 to 12—What is a Theological Education?—Prof. G. D. B. PEPPER, D. D., Crozer Theological Seminary.

12 to 12 : 30—Report of the Committee on Organization of the Educational Work of the Baptist Denomination.

AFTERNOON.

2 : 30 to 3 : 40—The Moral Elements of the Teacher's Art.—Prof. N. L. ANDREWS, Madison University.

3 : 40 to 4 : 50—Methods and Limits of Beneficiary Aid.—Prof. H. H. HARRIS, Richmond College.

4 : 50 to 5 : 30—Reports, and Miscellaneous Business.

EVENING.

7 : 45 to 9 : 30—The relative claims of our Institutions of Learning on the Public Benefactions of our Churches.—Pres. A. CASWELL, D. D., LL. D., Brown University.

THURSDAY.—MORNING.

9 to 9 : 30—Reports and Miscellaneous Business.

9 : 30 to 11—The place of Theological Science in the Sciences comprised in a Liberal Education.—Prof. C. H. Toy, D. D., Southern Baptist Theological Seminary.

AFTERNOON.

2 : 30 to 4—On Limiting the Number of our Institutions by our Power to make them Strong. —Rev. T. G. Jones, D. D., Nashville, Tenn.

4 to 5 : 30—Reports and Discussions.

EVENING.

7 : 45 to 9 : 30—Reports and Discussions.

RESERVED TOPICS,

For Discussion or Reference to Committees.

1. The Library as an Incentive and Aid to Teacher and Pupil.

2. Methods of Religious Instruction and Influence in our Schools.

3. Preservation of Endowments by Legal Safeguards.

4. Influence of American Colleges on the Public Life of the Nation, as measured by the actual character of the Education of Public Men.

5. The extent to which it is desirable to add Special or Professional departments or Schools in our colleges, to the range of instruction required in a comprehensive and well proportioned Liberal Education.

6. Can Denominational Colleges be well sustained without Denominational Academies as their Base?

The discussion of the paper read by Dr. Brooks was in order.

Dr. BROADUS: I am unwilling to be entirely silent on a subject of such great interest and importance. I have long felt it a great hardship that young women of superior abilities and elevated aspirations should not be permitted in certain cases to receive the instruction given to young men. I lived many years at one of the chief universities of the country, and remember to have been acquainted with cases of young ladies who lived for years and years within one or two hundred yards of the hall where most admirable lectures were delivered, and although they were very anxious to hear them, they were denied that privilege. Especially were they anxious to hear the lectures upon Bible history and kindred subjects. I have, therefore, a certain amount of sympathy in favor of giving them that privilege, if it can be done. And yet, I do not know—it may be an old-fashioned feeling, it may be timidity, it may be an idea that ought to be banished from one's mind at this time of day,—I do not know. I wish somebody who has seen the thing done would tell us how the ladies themselves like it, and tell us whether students are really as attentive to their lectures when ladies are present.

I was a student once, sir. A person cannot always tell in a hypothetical case, but I have a feeling that in my case—especially if certain young ladies of the community had been present, I should have had more wandering thoughts than would have been desirable, not to say wandering eyes. [Laughter]. I do not know. I am afraid. We ought to have institutions in which there should be opportunity for the more aspiring of our young ladies to have kindred studies. I have known a few young ladies who had the taste, the capacity, and the desire for such studies. But whether it is not best to have separate institutions for them—I rose to suggest that,—I don't know whether it would be. I rose to say that I do not feel sure—for unless somebody should say that, it might go forth that we were all in favor of the co-education of the sexes.

Dr. BLISS: It seems to me very important to receive testimony, if we can, on this interesting subject. I quite agree with the remark of the gentleman who preceded me, that it would be well to know how the thing has been done. I consider it a question of interest and importance, whether young ladies may participate in the general course of studies in our colleges with advantage to them, and without harm to the progress of the work that we are now doing. I have had a slight degree of experience in reference to this matter, of which I desire to speak. In the early days of the institution with which I am connected [the University of Lewisburg] before the establishment of a separate institution for the instruction of young ladies, we had young ladies reciting with our classes. I have myself heard their recitations, extending on through the Sophomore and Junior years. I am able to testify to the capacity of young ladies to participate in the studies of young men in college up to that degree on about equal terms. But there was one difficulty that we always experienced, and that was in having them speak out in recitations what, all things considered, it was supposed they had in mind. The instructors of that day, if they were present—one or two only are now in the land of the living—would recollect, I think, as a permanent feature of those exercises, the difficulty experienced in having the young ladies speak audibly. I should be glad to know whether that is a general difficulty.

My impression is that a considerable part of the study that we considered most important and essential in the college course is not essential, and is scarcely proper for the generality of young women. Yet, that is an impression which I would gladly surrender to testimony of another kind. I do think it would be an excellent thing where institutions for young women and colleges are near together, that more ample opportunities should be afforded the ladies to participate in the studies of the young gentlemen in particular lines, while the main life of the institutions should be entirely distinct. I cannot think it is likely that within any short period of time to come arrangements can be made for the living together in the same buildings, or in the same vicinity, of large bodies of young ladies and young gentlemen, with safety to the general interests of both sexes. But I am extremely desirous of hearing testimony in regard to this matter, and should rejoice to see some one institution putting the thing to the test.

Pres. BURLESON: Mr. President, I am here as a learner, having been twenty-five years of my life in one of the frontier states of the extreme South. I am here to learn, and what I may suggest will be merely in the direction of drawing out some one to instruct me on these points. In the institution that I represent, Waco University, for the last seven years we have practised the co-education of the sexes. And in reference to the remark of Dr. BROADUS—the difficulty which he suggests about wandering eyes and wandering hearts—I would suggest whether it is not *distance* that lends enchantment to the view? [Laughter].

Dr. BROADUS: If the Doctor will allow me, I will say that I should not wish myself to be disenchanted. [Laughter].

Dr. BURLESON: I would ask the Doctor if he kept his mind always steady, even when the young ladies were absent from the school-room? [Laughter].

The venerable father, (Dr. Bliss) inquires for experience. I find in the last seven years we have had less love-making and more hard study than I had previously witnessed when the sexes were in distinct neighboring institutions. That has been our experience, and I think it has been the experience of every one who has examined the facts in the case.

While I am up I will suggest another point—and this is a subject in which I am profoundly interested. I want to hear others on this subject. My point of anxiety has been that while co-education might improve the young men in morality it might make the young women somewhat less feminine. I find that seven years' experience, if it demonstrates anything, demonstrates that it improves men in manliness and women in modesty. But I am here to inquire, and I drop out this suggestion to elicit testimony.

Pres. BROOKS: It is a very small experiment with us (at Kalamazoo College) for the number of young women connected with the college classes has been very small. The experiment has been tried in just about the way indicated in the paper. No change has been made, but there are three courses of study, and any one admitted to college may enter on either of those courses. One of them, a full classical course, a second, omitting Greek or Latin, and a third, omitting both, and substituting other studies in their place. There have been, all along, a very few young women connected with these classes, and the influence has been far more favorable than we supposed it would be. The general influence upon the manners of both sexes, and upon their character, has certainly been favorable. I have no hesitancy at all in testifying that the general appearance of all in the recitation room, and in their deportment, is better than what we ordinarily expect in a college for young men only. I am quite sure of that. In the class that graduated a year ago—our classes are all small—there were eleven members who graduated, of whom three were young women. They were the first who received a regular degree. Two of them were in the Latin [and] scientific course, and the third was in the scientific course; neither of them having any Greek. But I think that the recitations of at least one of these young women were as good throughout the course as those of any other member of the class. The class was a good one as a whole. The scholarship of the young women was of a high order, and I think their presence in the recitation room, after the young men became accustomed to it, was no interference with attention, and exerted only a favorable influence upon both parties. I give this testimony because experience is called for, and perhaps I ought to give it.

Rev. A. C. KENDRICK, D.D., LL.D., of the Rochester University then, the hour having arrived, read a paper on

THE METHODS AND USES OF CLASSICAL STUDIES.

If on a theme that has been so prolific of discussion, I can hope to offer little that is new, yet I remember that our present object is not novelty but truth, and truth less for speculative than for practical purposes. The duty of education presses anew upon each generation, just as if nobody had ever educated, or been educated, before. Each successive generation, therefore, must have its own living convictions of, and living interest in, the great truths and principles with which it deals. The moment that a system, whatever its original excellence, becomes stereotyped and fossilized; the moment that it becomes a mere matter of tradition, and is adhered to, not as supplying the felt needs of the present, but as a bequest, no matter how intrinsically precious, from a buried past, it becomes a *caput mortuum*, and the sooner it is decently inurned, and replaced by a system grounded on conscious wants and living convictions, the better. This is our apology for perpetually rediscussing principles and systems of education. They reach men not as mere abstractions, but through living agents, and each successive relay of educators must be fired afresh with the spirit, and trained anew in the methods of their work.

But not only are the same truths to be reiterated for each generation, but the principles themselves, or rather their modes of application, undergo material changes, and give scope to ever fresh illustration. "Tempora mutantur, nos et mutamur in illis." Under the essentially unchanging types of humanity, its specific variations from age to age are countless. The altered conditions of society, the discovery of new sciences and the enlargement of the old, change the relative value of old arguments, and necessitate fresh examinations from new points of view. Who thinks of confining our discussions of Christianity to the forms of argument which a century ago were deemed sufficient and decisive? The march of science and philosophic thought has forced upon us objections to the authority of Moses, to the inspiration of the Scriptures, to miracles and atonement, which never visited the dreams of our fathers, and may possibly never visit the dreams of our children; but which, at all events, demand to be looked in the face, and compel the champion of the gospel to enter the field clad in other panoply than that which bucklered him a hundred years ago.

So with the subject before us. Classical study stands in a multitude of new relations. The new fields of enterprise and avenues to wealth thrown open to young men render them less patient, than formerly, of years of apparently unpractical, and merely disciplinary study. The modern languages, with their vast and growing stores of literature, challenge increased attention; and especially Physical Science, exulting in her youthful energies, and loaded with the spoils and crowned with the laurels of a thousand victories, enters the domain of education, and looks down with haughty contempt upon the merely prescriptive claims of its ancient occupants. How then stands now the question with classical study? We look the subject in the face, and ask, What are we going to do about it? To set aside, or abridge, or radically modify, or simply enlarge, improve and strengthen our courses and methods of classical culture?

My own conviction is unweakened of the high value of linguistic and classical study, and of not merely the desirableness, but the absolute necessity of retaining for it its time-honored place in our system of education. The "education that we need" is, I believe, with modifications important but not fundamental, still substantially the same that was demanded and instituted by our fathers. The ground of my conviction I can, of course, but briefly develop.

The value of the study of language as a means of discipline has not been, and can, I think, scarcely be overstated. That language is a necessary instrument and condition of consecutive thinking seems beyond dispute. It follows, therefore, that he who has the completest mastery of language will, other things being equal, have completest control of the processes of thought. Thought and speech mutually and most powerfully interact upon each other, and as thought is continually struggling to embody itself in language, and is thus enlarging the boundaries of expression, so each new linguistic attainment, each polishing and perfecting of our powers of expression, is a sort of clearing of the channels, and removing of the obstructions of thought. A powerful language is thus an invaluable auxiliary, or rather an indispensable condition, to powerful thinking. A great thinker, with a rude and barren language, is a giant in chains. The language will fetter and dwarf him, or with supernatural might he will bend it to his needs, and will flood it with a richness and power before unknown to it, and throw it centuries forward in its path toward perfection.

With such relations between thought and language, the function of the latter, as an educational and disciplinary power, must be potent and manifold. All working in language is working in thought; all analysis of words is analysis of ideas; every verbal discrimination is a discrimination in the spiritual essence which it embodies. To be thoroughly educated, therefore, in language, is to have a culture which penetrates to the very interior, and has taken up and moulded the vital elements of the soul. True, this is after all but a half culture; complete extensively, it is very incomplete intensively. The process, to be perfect, must be reciprocal. We must go not only from language to thought, but we must work back from thought to language. We must study the science in its terminology; but we must also study the terminology in the science. The two processes mutually complement and round out each other. Here you have the primal, impalpable, spiritual substance; there you have the secondary, palpable, yet scarcely less spiritual embodiment. Take them apart and put them together; set them over against each other in their marvellous relationship, and you are dealing with and solving the fundamental problem of education. And peculiarly healthful and wide-reaching is the discipline of learning a foreign language. Memory, judgment, imagination, nice tact and discrimination, all are brought into constant and rapidly alternating exercise, and are effecting a harmonious and symmetrical development of all the faculties of the soul. Strength, precision, quickness, elegance, all are the natural and necessary product of such study.

This latter feature of the discipline of linguistic study—its bearing, that is, on the æsthetic element of our nature, permit me to emphasize. For educational purposes we may roughly analyze the mind into three faculties: the rational, the æsthetic, the moral; the intelligence that takes cognizance of truth, the taste that takes cognizance of beauty, the conscience or moral sense that takes cognizance of right and goodness. Practically these three elements define the province and limit of education. In the perfection of these is the perfection of humanity. A reason disciplined to the clear perception of truth; a taste cultivated into an exquisite sense of beauty; a conscience delicately sensitive to right and virtue, will nearly realize our ideal of human excellence. And over against these subjective faculties God has set their appropriate outward objects: for the reason, the whole realm of objective truth; for the taste, the whole realm of objective beauty; for the conscience, the whole realm of objective right and goodness.

To the second of these I now ask a moment's attention. I surely need not argue before this body the importance of opening that deep well-spring of beauty that God has deposited in the human soul, and whose objective counterpart he has so lavishly diffused over the whole realm of nature and art. To be in our magnificent world without a deep sense of the beautiful, and a quick sympathy with its myriad forms of manifestation, is to be pitiably mutilated, arrested and blighted in one of the divinest possibilities of our being, and the God of the beautiful robbed of one of the divinest elements of our homage. For the culture of this faculty we have the beautiful in nature, in art, and in literature. But of these, as an instrument of artistic culture, the last is incomparably the most potent, as evoking so much more fully and variously than the others, the hidden harmonies of the soul. Language is an art; in its lower and rudimentary forms, a useful art; in higher and more perfect forms, and especially as embodying itself in literature, a fine art, and of all the fine arts beyond comparison the most elegant and refining. Sculpture freezes into the marble, painting spreads warm upon the canvas, one single striking phase of thought or of passion. But language starts with them on their first emergence into consciousness; runs step by step with them through all their stages; sinks and swells with all their varying life and power; catches their most fleeting hues; runs its lines along their subtlest distinctions; glows with all their fire and shines with all their splendor; and puts livingly before us every line and phase of the soul's wondrous existence. Nothing is so marvellous as speech except thought, and it is doubtful even if speech be not the more marvellous of the two; seemingly scarcely less spiritual and impalpable than the thought which it embodies, and yet embodying it in forms which abide when paintings, statues and pyramids have mouldered into dust. Put then the choice works of art over against the choice works of literature; the sculptures of Phidias and the paintings of Apelles over against the imaginative creations of Homer and Sophocles; traverse the galleries of Rome, Florence and Dresden, and then turn and wander in thought along those vaster halls filled with the creations of the immortal masters of history and philosophy, of eloquence and song—and tell me in which does the spirit of beauty move with freest step, clothe herself with richest drapery, and luxuriate in her most congenial element? From which will the spirit catch the most of that inspiration of the beautiful which will be to it a fountain of perennial enjoyment, and which softens, mellows, harmonizes, tinges with transcendent loveliness all the faculties of the soul?

Excuse me for dwelling so long on a topic which after all, is but incidental and subordinate. My main point in favor of unrelaxed and high classical study is that it is the natural basis and support of all liberal studies, and of all high education. This may be variously illustrated. First, the basis of the study is language; and language we have already seen to be the most immediate product, a sort of *objectiving* and spontaneous embodiment of the mind. We have then the spiritual nature in some sort incarnated in the word; and it is in words, first of all, that we study that wondrous essence, the human soul. Language is the immediate gateway to the philosophy of mind.

Again, as language is the creation of the mind, expressing its ideas and emotions, the aggregate of these ideas and emotions makes up the aggregate of speech. And this is true alike for individuals and for nations. Irrespectively, therefore, of the value of its literature as literature, the life of a nation lies imbedded in its language. Study its words, ascertain their compass and depth of significance, and when you have mastered these, you have determined the range and depth of its ideas. The character of the nation, its social habits, its political institutions, its moral and religious ideas—all lie embedded in its language. The words which it used, in their extent, import and complexion, tell the story of its position in the social scale; the height to which it had risen, or the depth to which it had sunk.

But again, and yet deeper than this. Language, apart not only from its literature, but even from the special significance of its words, has a distinct life and organic character, stamped by the individuality of the people that produced it. The language as such, as a vast physico-psychical structure, has an objective and independent existence, and in its character as an organism, in its richness or meagreness, in its strength or feebleness, in its delicacy or coarseness, in its complexness or simplicity, in its gravity or lightness, in its naturalness or artificiality, and in a thousand subtle and indescribable points and features, reproduces the character of the people that gave it birth. Thus in the mere analysis of speech, apart from all special meanings, we have a most powerful instrument of deeper national analysis—a mirror in which the national mind stands all unconsciously, but most curiously reflected. Who can fail to see in the Greek and the Latin, the Hebrew, the Sanscrit, the German, the French, the Italian, and the English—in the very structure, mechanism and complexion of their tongues, the salient features of the national mind and character? Just as the national mind lies below the language, so the language lies below all the special productions of its literature. In fact, all these special productions are but undulatory heavings—I had almost said rising and bursting bubbles—on the surface of the vast ocean of its organized speech, and symptomatic of the depth and power of the element from which it sprang. Homer and Sophocles, Pindar and Aristophanes, Plato and Demosthenes, are but the natural and necessary products of the genius that enshrined itself in the Greek tongue. That tongue is a creation more marvellous, more indicative of the matchless endowments of the Greek mind, than temple or statue, or than even its sublimest individual productions in eloquence or poetry. Given such a language—and the genius that originated such a language—and all the rest follows of course. They who are skeptical about the extraordinary excellence of the Greek literature, should set themselves to solve the deeper problem of the Greek language. We should not be surprised to find the man who had constructed a musical instrument of unmatched power and delicacy, afterwards drawing out of it some corresponding harmony: the wonder would be that he did not.

And the same principle applies, though certainly in an unequal degree, to the sister classical tongue, the Latin. Cicero, Horace and Tacitus are but the offspring and exponents of their own almost unrivalled language. On these two tongues God laid the burden of recording and transmitting almost the whole earlier life of the race. They are worthy of the high prerogative. The Latin, stern, rigid, sonorous, moves with the stately and majestic tread befitting the speech of the organizers of empire and the lords of the world. The Greek, light as the breeze of summer, yet solid as one of its own temples; kindling at a breath beneath the fiery inspirations of Homer, and surging with exhaustless life under the diviner inspirations of Plato; dancing light as air through the boundless harmonies of Aristophanes, and launching forked thunderbolts from the flaming hand of Demosthenes; with infinite complexness and infinite simplicity; more graceful than the French, more vital than the German, softer than the Italian, and more masculine—almost—than the English, the Greek has not, in all earth's utterances, had its peer or rival, and we may well suppose never will have, until our regenerated earth shall catch the melody of the speech that is syllabled by the immortal lips of the sons of the resurrection.

But beyond all this, languages are the formal depositories of the records of a nation's life—alike its outward life and its inner. All other memorials of its achievements sink to nothing besides those embraced in its literature. In this, we have the materials for all our historical and philosophical researches. The record of all human history, of all progress and revolutions in thought, of all political and social changes, of all moral and religious ideas, stands embodied in the written documents of the race. The student of humanity must be conversant with the literature of humanity. And as this fact is too obvious to require illustration, it is equally so that the past is the parent of the present; that we are at the apex of an inverted pyramid of civilization, upon which presses down the weight of all the centuries that have preceded us. I spoke near the beginning of my paper of a "buried past." I recall the expression; there is no buried past. The past re-lives in the present; the present roots itself vitally in the past. Bengel's celebrated Biblical aphorism but concentrates at a single point a principle admitting a much wider application: *Novum Testamentum in veteri latet; Vetus Testamentum in novo patet.* We trace our modern institutions back to the middle ages; we study the Mediæval in the light of those of Greece and Rome; we follow these in rudimental forms to still remoter ages. Who can comprehend our system of jurisprudence, of the civil and canon law, our forms of theological doctrine, our philosophical thinking and terminology, without following them back step by step, through the written documents of many centuries and many languages? The seeds of all our philosophy and most of our science, the germinal principles of nearly all our culture, lie scattered over the wide domain of the past. And the different lines of knowledge interlace each other, so that to start upon one line of investigation inevitably forces us upon another, and still another, till we find ourselves sedulously exhuming entire antiquity. Now will the mind of man allow itself to be shut out from these vast realms of knowledge? Is the career so splendidly begun to be at once arrested? Are we to be lulled into an ignominious repose by the contemptible sophism that education should deal with the practical rather than the speculative, with fact rather than theory, with the present rather than the past? May we not state just the reverse of this as the real province of education?—that it is to deal with the speculative rather than the practical, with theory rather than fact, with the past rather than the present? For the speculative will generate the practical; theory will originate, explain and reproduce fact; and the past, as it has poured its life into, so it clears up the problems of the present.

Now to all this vast range of study, historical, philosophical, religious, the Greek and Latin tongues stand in a central relation. The intrinsic excellence and power, the wonderful organic perfection of the languages themselves, commend them as intrinsically most deserving of study, and rich in various and salutary discipline; the quality of their literature corresponds largely to this admitted superiority of the languages, while the wide space in history filled by the nations that spoke them, their extraordinary significance for all that allies itself to the progress of the race, urge for them a still mightier claim, which it is utterly impossible should be postponed to that of any or of all others. For the million centuries of the Darwinian period I grant their worthlessness; but over the Mosaic era—since man became *man*—they pour an illumination which withdrawn—how great would be the darkness! They throw their light at once backward and forward. They link themselves, on the one hand, with the peoples that lie on the Eastern border-land, in the first gray dawn of the world's civilization, and on the other they blend themselves with the institutions and languages of modern Europe. Of history, philosophy, science, and religion—set aside the Hebrew Scriptures—ninety-nine hundredths of what is valuable, in the early annals of the race rests in their archives. Their acquisition puts into the scholar's hand the key which unlocks to him directly vast realms of knowledge. Besides this, it is his natural introduction to the languages of the East, on the one hand, and to the modern dialects of the West, on the other. They reach out one hand to India, and another to

Italy, France and England, and link them in a sisterly embrace. Half of our English speech, Teutonic as it is, is imported from the classical tongues, while the chief dialects of Southern Europe are simply daughters of the Latin.

The classical tongues then, again, are the natural gateway to the modern languages. That these tongues must enter largely into our courses of education is conceded. It is idle to argue either for or against them; they do their own arguing. They push their way into our halls of learning, and if they do not find a place, will make one. Why, then should not the ancient tongues retire gracefully before them? Why should not the beautiful mother give place to the more beautiful daughters, and get her to a convent? Why not bring our youth to drink of the copious streams of modern learning, and leave the ancient well-heads to their grass-grown solitude and obscurity? I have already answered the question. The thing is neither desirable, nor possible, nor necessary. It is undesirable, because we cannot afford to lose the vast body of literature and learning embraced in the ancient tongues; to forego the knowledge of those admirable tongues themselves, and the stern and healthful discipline imparted by the mind's wrestling with so entirely unwonted, and yet so splendidly developed linguistic organisms. It is impossible, because we cannot learn the modern languages thoroughly and philosophically—and this, true of them all, is pre-eminently true of the Romanic dialects—when we have dissevered them from the ancient stock. It is unnecessary, because in a well-organized system of education, they can all be competently mastered. The modern tongues are learned not only most thoroughly but most economically of time and labor, through their Latin parent. Partly by virtue of this connection, partly by their great affinity in structure with our own, partly by the strength for linguistic study acquired in the stern grapple with the ancient tongues; they really need compel the sacrifice of scarcely an iota of the latter. Almost any good student of the classics could, with modern facilities of acquisition, in his six or seven years' course of education, master fairly one or two of the modern tongues, even without special provision for them in our College curriculum. Much less, *with* that provision, need he materially lessen his classical acquisitions in order to taste the beauties of Pascal and Schiller. And the knowledge thus acquired is *knowledge*. The student masters the languages in their roots, traces out their affinities, and converts his facts into principles. It is preposterous, then, to treat the ancient and modern tongues as mutually antagonistic or independent. They will not be dissociated. Abandon the ancient, and the study of the modern would soon cease altogether, except for purposes, from an educational point of view, contemptibly superficial. Every attempt at a generous and scientific acquaintance with them will drive the student back upon the ancient, as their natural parents and expounders. The classical tongues throw their broad ægis over the modern, and take them under their protection. So long as those are cultivated, these cannot be neglected. The spirit that keeps alive the study of the one, will lead their votaries to the mastery of the other; and both will dwell side by side in unity; the ancient tongues giving depth, philological significance and dignity to the modern; the modern rounding out the study of the ancient, and opening out their currents into the oceanlike expanse of our later civilization.

I scarcely need add, that for theological studies there can be no manner of question; their irremovable basis is classical study. The history of Christianity has settled the matter; the providence of God has removed it from the pale of discussion. So long as the documents of his faith stand written in Greek or Hebrew, so long will he who remains a stranger to them pluck out the right eye of his knowledge, and cut off the right arm of his power. An able writer in a secular British Quarterly two or three years since expressed the sentiment that, whatever other reasons might or might not exist, for the study of the Greek language, the single purpose of reading the New Testament in the original was, for every intelligent Christian gentleman, a sufficient warrant for the expenditure of all the time and labor required for a mastery of the language. In my judgment he was right. And if this reason be valid in the case of the lay student of the Bible, how imperatively does it hold of the formally constituted and professional expounders of the Bible, and champions of the faith for which the Bible is their sole voucher and authority. What pitiable imbecility—what moral poltroonery for them to abandon their high vantage-ground, and consent to take at second-hand the records of their faith! I am, of course, far from maintaining that every individual preacher should be a student of the original Scriptures; much more, a proficient of the classics. I speak simply of the general drift and tendency of Theological studies, of our organized education, and of the spirit which should pervade our halls of Theological learning.

But now, how are we to adjust and reconcile the claims of kindred or rival studies? Shall we seek to thrust the same dose of classical attainment down all throats, irrespectively of different tastes and capacities of digestion? One of the first features of our educational system must be freedom and flexibility; a clear perception of what is ideally the best education, and a spirit of ready adjustment to practical exigencies. For such as cannot get the highest education, we must provide the best possible under the circumstances. We must emulate the wisdom of the ancient sage who told a man staggering under a heavy sack of gold to pour out the most of it, and carry what he could. We will not lay too heavy a burden even of gold, on inadequate shoulders. Our system shall be a full bag of gold; we will deal out to each one what he can carry.

Taking as a standard our present average scheme of College study, we shall have partial course students, regular scientific students, and regular candidates for the Bachelor's degree. Of the partialists we require nothing but good recitations in the exercises which they attend. They stay as long as they will, and go with our blessing when they must.

On the scientific students, with their fuller course of French and German, I would make imperative at least a year's study of Latin, and at least a term's study in Greek. The Latin partly for its touch of sterner discipline, but chiefly for its aid in studying the modern languages, including our own. The object of the single term of Greek would be chiefly to bring its light to bear on our scientific terminology, and I scarcely need add that the instruction should be specially adapted to the end proposed.

For the candidates for full College honors, the standard of admission being kept rigidly up to the highest point now fixed in our best Colleges, I would make the established course compulsory to the end of the Sophomore year. After this by sporadic options, or by regularly constituted distinct courses, nearly equivalent, I would give students an opportunity to meet their special tastes, capacities, or needs, and while all get a fair modicum of classical acquisition and culture, enable a smaller number to reach a good classical training, and a smaller number still to explore the deeper mysteries of classical philology and literature to qualify themselves for chairs of high instruction, or for becoming the Bopps and Grimms, the Max Müllers and Grotes, of American scholarship.

Of course, this is but a very vague and superficial indication of the way in which our educational problem is to be solved. Solved it must be, and that by compromise. Three grand separate, if not opposing forces, knock at our gates, and demand admission. Physical science, the modern languages, the classical tongues, all urge claims which are imperative. It is the old problem tripled; three irresistible bodies striking against three immovable bodies—and what shall be the solution? The answer is not far to seek; they will all yield and they will all abide. A certain fundamental course for nearly all, and elective affinity and special circumstances determining the crowning stages of the course.

But we must have no bigotry in education; no conventual exclusiveness; no physicist looking down with contempt upon the explorer of the musty records of antiquity; no classicalist throwing back an equally irrational contempt on the researches of material science. All our workers in the grand school of knowledge; all deciphering their several leaves in God's great book of the universe; all adding in their several spheres to the growing treasures of the ages; all across their respective boundaries may reach welcoming hands, and bid one another God speed in the rivalship of high and generous learning. The motto of our system must be strength and flexibility; strong in principle as bonds of fate; in application and adjustment

"As broad and liberal as the easing air."

I pass to some features in the *methods* of our classical study. And first, we must have competent instruction. Any system will be dead and valueless in hands not competent to work it. The teacher of the classics must *know*, and must have that reflex knowledge which makes him know that he knows. All our departments of learning are suffering from sciolistic instruction; but in none, perhaps, has there been so deplorable an incompetency as in our classical teaching. Thorough scholarship is at the bottom of all good teaching.

Secondly, the method must be *living*. The teacher must go into the lecture-room burning with enthusiasm. He must open his book lovingly, and make the author live upon his lips. By reading the original text, by writing upon the blackboard, by oral and written exercises in reciprocal translation, he must, as far as possible, reproduce the methods by which nature taught him his mother-tongue. The process should be free, vivacious, natural, many-sided, with all the variety and flexibility of life. He must address his instruction alternately and almost equally to the eye, the ear, and the tongue. The tongue must utter the words, the ear must hear them, the eye must see them; through each several avenue the language must reach the mind, each making its peculiar contribution to the collective impression. Language proper is *speech*, exclusively a thing of tongue and ear. It becomes related to the eye only when passing over into its second stage, in which the eye takes the joint products of tongue and ear, converts them by magical transformation into visible symbols, and sends them with lightning rapidity to the mind. This sorcery of ocular action it would be treasonable ingratitude to disparage; we reap too largely the fruits of the beneficent miracle. But it may push its office too far, and wrest language too much from the organs which are its rightful proprietors.

It is unfortunate that the method which, in the production and original acquisition of language nature employs but incidentally and exceptionally, should in the prevalent process of linguistic study have become the chief and almost exclusive one. This vicious method should be reformed. In the modern languages the exigencies of the case compel the needful corrections. In the ancient tongues the teacher should do his utmost to restore the method of nature. He should remember that no language is learned thoroughly until tongue, ear and eye have concentrated their united forces, and lodged it in the mind as the single marvellous resultant of their compound action.

Thirdly, the teacher must give to the study a real character, by bringing it into connection with all valuable knowledge; not, of course, to the sacrifice of grammatical exactness, and thorough linguistic drill, but by opening frequent glimpses into the field of practical knowledge with which the study stands connected. History, Criticism, Philosophy, general Literature, all should open their treasures, and demonstrate how vital are the affinities between the study of words and the study of things.

Most splendidly has classical study redeemed itself from the charge of mere verbal barrenness which has sometimes too justly been made against it, a charge that has found its support in the niceties of the Porsonian school and the verse-making requisitions of the English Universities. The minute criticism of words, the nice adjustment of particles, has allied itself with a broad and generous study of things. Every form of learning has been brought to bear on the interpretation of the text, and the text thus interpreted, has been made in return to lend its aid to practical research, and its scattered lights made to converge on the manifold questions of legislation, history, commerce, art, science, philosophy, and religion. Classical literature has thus stepped into the front rank of the sciences of investigation and progress. I need but mention the names of Boeckh, K. F. Hermann, Wachsmuth, Ernst Curtius, Mommsen, Grote, Max Müller, and a hundred others, to remind you how splendidly fruitful classical researches have been made in the hands of modern investigators. And when the light from India broke upon Europe at the opening of our century, the classical scholarship of the Continent gave hearty welcome to the new revelations. With the rapidity of magic the study of the Greek and Roman tongues widened itself out into the broad fields of comparative philology, and under a series of able men has achieved results which may call forth the marvel even of this marvellous age. The votaries of physical science point to their grand achievements, and demand that dead languages shall no longer cumber the ground which they would cultivate into living fruitfulness. We admit the utmost of their claims for their favorite pursuits: what they affirm regarding the relative barrenness of ours we emphatically deny. Rapid as has been the progress, marvellous as have been the achievements of the material sciences, their rapidity of march and fertility of results have been fully matched in the career of philology. There have been no greater wonders of our time than the achievements of linguistic science. None has responded more sensitively to the spirit of our modern inquiry; none has contributed more munificently to those *spolia opima*, those trophies of the omnipotence of scientific method, that adorn the temple of our modern civilization.

Glance a moment at its achievements. It has exhumed the long-buried monuments, deciphered the enigmatical records, and filled up large lacunæ in the annals of Egypt and Assyria. It has read, and edited, and translated and interpreted the sacred books of India and Persia. It has disentangled the complicated affinities of most of those nations that have given to Asia and Europe nearly their whole political and intellectual life; followed their wanderings from the parent homes and their successive separations from the parent and from affiliated stocks; and thus proved itself the best auxiliary, and almost parent of ethnology. It has investigated their languages with a skill and patience which have enabled it to follow Persian and Indian, Greek and Italian, German, Sclave and Celt, back to their primitive Bactrian home, and has gone far toward the work of constructing a Grammar and a Lexicon of a language of which we have neither the name, nor the alphabet, nor one line of any immediate record, but which we may know with moral certainty was spoken in substance, when Indian, Goth and Greek slumbered, in the loins of a common ancestor. It has thrown its light upon the classical tongues; broken down the barriers by which they were walled in from the supposed Babel-like jargon of the countless Barbarian dialects; compelled them to own the common sisterhood of speech; and reciprocally to receive a flood of light from, and pour a flood of light upon those tongues with which a century ago they were scarcely supposed to stand in the most distant connection. In establishing this vast family of languages, it has penetrated into the hidden laws of speech, alike physical and metaphysical; has routed a whole legion of superficial etymologies that had squatted on the classical domain, and replaced them by another set established by wide and careful induction; it has thus gradually created a science of language as rigorous in its laws, as severe in its methods, as fertile and reliable—though less palpable to the popular eye—in its results, as are any of the boasted sciences that signalize our remarkable age, and is approaching with adventurous yet cautious step and flaming torch the very cradle of speech, and discusses at least intelligently that problem of the origin of language, which was so long the football of wild and fanciful conjecture. And turning back its steps on the classical sections it has rewritten their history in the light of the new researches, with often decisive and always interesting results. Meantime, there is scarcely a point in the vast circumference of human knowledge which it has not touched, and on which it has not thrown some valuable light. No doubt there is much that is yet unsettled and crude; much that further researches will prove to be premature and erroneous. But in these defects it is not alone; and on the whole we may challenge any science to show a prouder record, or stronger claims on the grateful admiration of the age.

This indicates the final feature of the method of classical teaching which I would mention, viz., that it must be conducted in the light of Comparative Philology, and in relation to the established principles of linguistic science. Those principles a higher scholarship cannot ignore. It must take the Greek and Latin out of their classical isolation; shed upon them the light of the researches of Bopp, Pott, Leo Meyer, Schleicher, and that prince of Philologists, Geo. Curtius, and other names scarcely less illustrious. I do not say that every Greek and Latin scholar must go deeply into these researches. But I do say that the accomplished teacher of our day must have largely mastered them, be prepared to throw his eye over the broad domain of general language, and bring Indian, Greek and Italian, Sclave, Goth and Celt together on the grand platform of a common heritage of speech. In the real scholar this broadening of his field will only awaken a deeper enthusiasm. I may be permitted to add, however, a caution; that the classical scholar do not merge himself in the mere linguist; and that the splendid literatures of Greece and Rome be not lost sight of in the dry search for verbal affinities—a search in which literature as such sinks into secondary importance.

I have thus indicated what I conceive to be the relations in which classical study stands to the educational demands of our age. In my judgment those relations were never more important; nor could the study of the Greek and Latin tongues ever with more injury have been abandoned or relaxed than at the present moment. Never did they stand in so central a relation to the whole system of liberal study; never were they more sternly demanded, than for the researches in history and philosophy in which our time is so prolific. The question of classical studies among us is simply a question of the existence of high education; it is more, it is a question of the type of our civilization. If mind is to be merged in nature; if there are no higher studies than those whose text is a piece of chalk, the skull of a baboon, or the law of natural selection, then there is little place for linguistic and classical studies. But if the study of man and of God is still the highest study, and is to secure its share of the energies and devotion of our many-sided age, then I have no fear for the destinies of classical learning. The student of theology, of philosophy, of humanity and of general literature, is driven back upon it as his most effective and almost indispensable instrument. It is the natural nurse and mother of all liberal learning. All that is elegant in art and literature, all that is profound in philosophical and historical research, attaches itself instinctively and clings with a life or death grapple to that range of studies of which language is the grand instrument, and the classical tongues are pre-eminently the fountain-head. Linguistic study is the "graded Nilometer" by which we shall measure the sinking or swelling of the tide of liberal learning in our colleges and country, and for myself I have no serious apprehensions as to the result. I am enough of an optimist to believe that society is neither stationary nor retrogressive. Amidst the enthusiastic cultivation and splendid achievements of physical science, there is a perpetually enlarging number of those whose studies are linking themselves with the higher interests and destinies of humanity. Ours is not a superficial nor unthinking, nor on the whole materialistic age, however it may at times appear such to a cursory view. God is marshalling the moral forces of the world to deeper and intenser action, and in this state of things those studies that are most appropriately called the *humanities*, it is hardly possible should be neglected.

Dr. CUTTING: I will venture to make one suggestion in reference to the paper which has just been read to us. A few days ago, in announcing the successor of Dr. ROBINSON in the Theological Seminary at Rochester, the New York Tribune made the mistake of introducing the name of the Rev. Dr. KENDRICK. But it did not make a mistake when it spoke of him as "poet, divine, and philosopher." [Applause].

The suggestion I wish to make is that in the publication of these proceedings no part of the paper omitted in the reading shall be omitted in the printing. [Applause].

Dr. H. L. WAYLAND: We have with us a gentleman who, in regard to the study of Latin, holds a position not dissimilar to that occupied by Dr. KENDRICK in reference to Greek. I am sure it will give us all pleasure to hear a word from Prof. LINCOLN, of Brown University.

Prof. J. L. LINCOLN: I hardly thought my friend over yonder,—my former pupil too, would call upon me thus abruptly—I will not say rudely, because it was done in so kind a manner. I am sure I do not wish to say anything further after this subject has been so fully and admirably discussed in the paper to which we have listened; but before Dr. Wayland called upon me, I was about to rise, simply to express my hearty thanks, sir, as a member of this Convention, and as a classical teacher, for this most earnest and eloquent plea for classical culture, to which we have listened from Dr. Kendrick. I am sure that we have all listened with delight to those words of his, and the sentiments which they have so admirably embodied. As we listened to those sentences which echoed that language he has loved so long, and so well illustrated, we must have felt that it was with a singular fitness and grace that this plea for classical culture and classical education should have come from one who has been so long versed in ancient letters, by most intimate and most genial acquaintance with them, and who is fitted as few men are, to make a defence of classical studies, if any defence of them needs to be made, on account of his own life-long, most admirable and most fruitful services in the cause of classical education. I confess, after all that it has been my great delight to listen. I felt as Dr. Wayland called upon me so suddenly, that I could rise and say only in those words that have come down to us from over the water, which I remember as uttered by some one who once followed on the hustings Edmund Burke, "I say ditto to Mr. Burke." For that is really all I have to say this afternoon; that I most heartily respond to every word so full of eloquence, which has been uttered in our hearing; and I am very glad, sir, that the writer of the paper has not contented himself simply with dwelling on those copious and eloquent illustrations of the imperishable, intrinsic value of the ancient languages and of ancient literature. But he has also told us how they ought in study, in education, and in all our institutions, to keep pace with these moving, progressive times in which we are living. I was glad to hear him say that we must preserve these languages in our institutions. I thought, sir, as he uttered those sentences there was nothing which more fitly demonstrated the value of ancient languages and literature so rich and so worthy of universal study, nothing so proved their value as the many efforts which have been made to kill them without success; efforts, I might add alike from the friends of these studies and from their foes. Sir, I only hope that all of us will take to heart the words that have been uttered. I have often thought that it was a singular fate of these old classical studies, that everybody acknowledges their worth, their value, the greatness of these ancient writers, and the great variety and extent of their services, everybody acknowledges these things, and in most instances one might almost say, there the whole thing ends. If we would only, as friends of education, take to heart these words and appropriate to ourselves what we have listened to, and try, really, sincerely, and honestly to carry them out, then it would be to some purpose, that we have been delighted as well as instructed this afternoon. But the difficulty is, that, with regard to classical literature, and, it seems to me, with regard to this whole subject of classical study, there is too much that is only theoretical and too little that is really practical.

Dr. BLISS: If it were discussion simply, that was desired upon the paper which has been read, I should feel it incumbent upon me to sit still. I so fully agree with all that has been said, that I could not think of discussing the paper; but my great interest in the subject, leads me to say one word with reference to the practical importance of that line of study in our system of liberal education. As I have listened to the tones of this voice, my memory has been led far back over a period of thirty-four years. It occurred to me, to say with reference to this subject, that these studies are perhaps generally regarded as an unfruitful portion of our system of education. As there are, perhaps, twenty or thirty persons here who have gone through that instruction, under the voice which we have heard to-day, I would like to know whether there is one man of them all, who, whatever he has to object to, in what was done for him, complains that he shared in that course of instruction in the ancient languages? I do not believe there is one. For myself, looking back over it as candidly as possible, it seems to me that there was no portion of the course, that there was no line of study more abundantly fruitful in promoting general culture and in the promotion of capacity for whatever God had blessed them with, than those particular studies, which were conducted by Prof. Kendrick. [Applause].

Dr. T. G. JONES: I was regretting, sir, that circumstances which I could not control prevented me from leaving the city in time to be here at the opening of this Convention, to hear the papers read which preceded this beautiful and eloquent one, to which we have just now listened. I did not intend coming in here to say one word, but I felt constrained to rise in my place and congratulate you on having heard a paper so eloquent and forcible, urging a matter of so great moment as that of linguistic and classical study. We live in a utilitarian and mechanical age; we think of philosophy as Macaulay spoke of it in his critique upon Lord Bacon, as the fruit of something outward and palpable, and material. We do not think enough of the æsthetic, the poetic, and the metaphysical. I rejoice that so able and so cultivated a gentleman has taken a position so high in favor of these things. We constantly tend to the physical sciences rather than the metaphysical, among which the linguistic studies have their place. This is a very material age, and, although one gentleman who preceded me thought that no advocacy or defence was needed of linguistic and classical study, I think that in the general mind, advocacy of that study is needed because of the tendency in almost all of us to the physical rather than, to speak broadly, metaphysical, involving languages. Why, sir, there is not anything that tends more to train the mind than linguistic study. There is not anything that tends more to furnish and adorn it. There are some studies which do eminently discipline the intellect, but they do not at the same time adorn and finish it; but linguistic study, while giving a training, I will say it, sir, with emphasis, in my judgment even equal to that given by mathematical studies, furnishes the intellect and adorns it as that class of studies can never do. I was particularly delighted, sir, with that part of the paper read in which language is represented as setting forth the people. Oh, it does, sir, as nothing else can. It gives the highest thought, and the nicest, subtlest discrimination to the intellect that it is possible to give. When you have got the real measure of the language of the people you are prepared to judge of the people. I say, that one fact, sir, is of immense force in favor of the study of language, the study of the individual through his language. His language will tell tales of him. Study the people in their language and in their literature, and, sir, you will know the people as otherwise you may never know them.

The PRESIDENT announced the following Committees:

On Academies as the Base of Denominational Institutions of Learning.—Prof. J. L. LINCOLN, LL.D., Prof. H. H. HARRIS, Rev. O. O. STEARNS.

On the Connection of Special or Professional Schools with Colleges.—Pres. E. G. ROBINSON, D.D., LL.D., Prof. John A. BROADUS, D.D., LL.D., Pres. E. DODGE, D.D., LL.D.

On Libraries in Institutions of Learning.—Rev. S. L. CALDWELL, D.D., Prof. C. H. TOY, D.D., Prof. W. MATHEWS, LL.D., Rev. WILLIAM HAGUE, D.D.,

On the Relation of our Colleges to the Education of Women.—Pres. A. HOVEY, D.D., Pres. R. C. BURLESON, D.D., Rev. H. L. WAYLAND, D.D., Prof. G. R. BLISS, D.D.

On Colleges and the Public Life of the Nation.—Pres. JAMES C. WELLING, LL.D., Hon. JAS. R. DOOLITTLE, LL.D., HORATIO GATES JONES, ESQ.

On the Increase and Education of the Ministry.—Pres. JAMES P. BOYCE, D.D., LL.D., Pres G. W. NORTHROP, D.D., JACOB F. WYCKOFF, ESQ., Pres. H. G. WESTON, D.D., Pres. L. A. DUNN.

On Enrollment of Delegates.—Rev. H. C. GRAVES, Rev. G. W. BOSWORTH, D.D., Rev. B. F. WOODBURN.

On the Organization of our Denominational Work in Education.—SAMUEL COLGATE, ESQ., SAMUEL A. CROZER, ESQ., Rev. EDWARD BRIGHT, D.D., Prof. E. C. MITCHELL, D.D., Pres. W. M. WINGATE, D.D., Principal D. J. PIERCE, Rev. WILLIAM LAMSON, D.D., Rev. R. JEFFREY, D.D., Hon. C. VAN HUSEN, to which were subsequently added, Rev. E. E. L. TAYLOR, D.D., and Pres. J. C. BURROUGHS, D.D., LL.D.

To Introduce a Resolution on the Decease of the Hon. William Kelly.—Prof. A. C. KENDRICK, D.D., LL.D., Pres. J. C. FURMAN, D.D., Prof. HOWARD OSGOOD, D.D.

The Chairman of the Committee on the Organization of our Denominational Work in Education, proposed the reading to the Convention of a paper on Organization prepared by the Rev. S. S. CUTTING, D. D., which paper was accordingly read.

ON THE ORGANIZATION OF THE EDUCATIONAL WORK OF THE BAPTIST DENOMINATION.

It was said by Morgan Edwards, a man remarkable among our earlier ministers for the share he bore in our educational efforts, that Baptists were more agreed as to the *credendi* than as to the *agendi* of their order. And yet scattered along our history are multiplied proofs that our common faith has many times pressed us to act together in the cause of education. Much of this associated action has been more or less local. Of this character was the service rendered by the "Religious Society" of Charleston, S. C., formed in 1755, by which Samuel Stillman was aided in his preparations for the ministry. Of this character likewise was the far greater service rendered by the "Charleston Baptist Education Fund," instituted in 1791, under the presidency of Richard Furman, combining the representatives of a considerable number of churches, and acting with great liberality and efficiency down to the period when, a quarter of a century later, its distinguished leader became the leader of a far greater movement. The annals of the Philadelphia Association have no more interesting feature than that which was exhibited in their care for the Academy of Mr. Eaton at Hopewell—the little school which rendered its great service between the years 1756 and 1767. "This infant seminary of learning," said our fathers in 1762, writing to the Baptist ministers of London, "is yet weak, having no more than twenty-four pounds a year for its support. Should it be in your power to favor this school in any way, you will be pleased to know how. A few books proper for such a school, or a small apparatus, or some pieces of apparatus, are more immediately wanted, and not to be had easily in these parts." But the little bud was ready for the blossoming. James Manning had gone from this Academy to the College at Princeton, and was now ready, under the instruction, and in fulfilment of the hopes of the Association, to proceed to his greater work in the cause of education. The movement of the Warren Association which gave us the eldest of the Education Societies represented in this Convention to-day, had its origin the same year (1791) which called into life the Charleston Baptist Education Fund. In 1812 was formed in Philadelphia the Baptist Education Society of the Middle States, and collections were made which enabled Dr. Staughton to commence those early labors in instruction which were destined, as we shall see, to more signal enlargement under a later and wider impulse. Of this earliest of our strictly theological schools, the venerable Dr. Greenleaf S. Webb, of New Jersey, now more than four-score years of age, is the still surviving pupil. In 1814 the Boston Baptist Association proceeded to form the Society which fifteen years later took the title Northern Baptist Education Society, the title under which, in the fifty-eighth year of its honorable service, it sends its delegates to the counsels of this Convention.

This enumeration of the dates of organized local action in the Baptist denomination, in promotion of the cause of education, might be brought down without difficulty to the present year. There is scarcely a State in the Union which has not an organization or organizations of this character, and out of these have grown the greater number of the institutions of general and of sacred learning whose delegates are here assembled.

We are not then strangers in any part of our history to organization for educational purposes. Local organizations have been always inseparable from our progress. But that which is more important to our present designs is the fact that this progress is distinguishable by epochs, marked by the organized movement of the whole denomination. The first of these epochs may for convenience take the date of 1764, the year of the founding of the College of Rhode Island, now Brown University. The Philadelphia Association, in whose counsels the College originated, was itself the chief organization of American Baptists. The New England churches were unassociated, and the Charleston Association was the only body then organized south of Philadelphia. But the Philadelphia Association has no claim to the founding of Brown University, except that of leadership. It rallied the denomination,—it appealed, to use the language of the day, to "the Continent," and the Baptists of the Continent moved together. South Carolina and Georgia gave to the first funds of the University more liberally than any other section of "the Continent," excepting Rhode Island only. By a movement less thoroughly one of the denomination, there is no reason to believe that the College could have been established.

The second epoch in the educational work of American Baptists, marked in like manner by the organized movement of the denomination may take for its date the year 1817, when, at the first Triennial meeting of the Baptist General Convention, held in this city, the President, Dr. Richard Furman, brought forward the "Plan of Education," as the result of which the sphere of the Convention was made to include educational operations. Three years earlier, however, at the very first assembling of American Baptists, when, to use their own language, brethren who had never met before, and had never expected to meet on earth, found "mutual and unutterable pleasure" in interviews which anticipated heaven, it had been seen that education must be associated with evangelization, and they had included the subject of education with that of missions in their address to the Baptists of the United States. This address, issued in May 1814, was followed in July of the same year by the responsive action of the Baptist Education Society of the Middle States, already mentioned as formed in 1812, which now took the name of "the Baptist Education Society of the United States of America," and to the names of trustees from Pennsylvania, New Jersey, Delaware, Maryland, and New York, added those of Baldwin and Bolles from Massachusetts. The action of 1817 was therefore but the ripened expression of anterior sentiments and impulses. Between 1814 and 1817 John M. Peck and James S. Welch, the latter still surviving in vigorous old age, had been pupils of this enlarged school, and presenting themselves to the Convention of 1817 as candidates for missionary service beyond the Mississippi, they lent the force of an incarnated argument to the educational aspirations of that body. The Convention now entered on its educational work. The trumpet tones of Luther Rice's voice, as in his wonderful journeys he traversed the country from New England to the Gulf and to the Mississippi, preaching the crusade of missions, proclaimed at the same time and with equal success, the crusade of education. Education societies sprung up side by side with Missionary societies, and the same reports which make records mingling the contributions of South and North and West in the service of evangelization, make records likewise mingling the contributions of South and North and West in the common cause of learning. It was a movement of the whole denomination, animated, earnest, and fruitful. Out of this zeal came the Columbian College at Washington, with its theological department, giving to us as first-fruits and earnests, Knowles, and Stow, and Cushman, and Neale, three now in heaven, and the last still with us to-day. And granting that the removal of the Theological Seminary of Philadelphia to Washington was a great mistake, granting that the misfortunes of the College wrecked the immediate hopes of the general movement at the point of its concentrated working, its permanent fruits exhibited themselves with astonishing rapidity in every part of the country. The local interest which the general movement had excited may be traced in all those institutions which were born of the faith and zeal of the men of that period. Waterville* and Newton in New England, Hamilton as an original centre, and as gathering into itself the interests and hopes of the Seminary in New York city, of which John Smitzer remains the only surviving pupil, Dennison and Shurtleff in the West, Georgetown, Mercer, and Wake Forest in the South, all are monuments of the stimulus given to education by the movement of 1817, and even Rochester and Chicago, Greenville and Crozer, and all, indeed, of our later institutions, are but after fruits of the same great educational awakening.

These epochs then vindicate abundantly the attempt to move American Baptists together in the cause of education. Indeed, their history shows that affinities profounder than their conscious purposes, incline them to move together in this cause. In 1814 they met in Convention under a call which had reference to missions only; so assembled they were led by ways they knew not to combine for purposes of education in 1817. Just a half century later, in Oct. 1867, in the dawn of this new epoch, in the remarkable Conference held at Poughkeepsie, out of which grew the Educational Commission, it probably entered the thoughts of no man that then and there was the commencement of a movement embracing the whole denomination, but it can now be seen that the path to the Convention of 1870, and to this of 1872, was natural and direct. The representatives of the denomination came together at the first call, in an assembly such as their annals had never exhibited, with purposes and hopes dimly apprehended, but yearning for something to lend power to the cause, and they are assembled to-day, with equal character, under similar impulses, with the burden of a great practical problem brought into more distinct apprehension, but a problem still. Can we organize the cause of education in the Baptist denomination as advanced now to its vast numbers, and its wide territorial extent? Can we so move together, that invading the free development of no special interest, we can make all special interests stronger? Can we by any united action raise education, both for our ministry and the mass of our people, to a higher place in our denominational activities? Can we do anything to direct and keep the rise of institutions of learning with the spread of our population and the growth of our churches?

* Waterville, chartered in 1813, gave no instruction till 1818.

To help in the solution of the problem which these questions express, we may gather up the suggestions which have been made in respect to the ends of a denominational organization for purposes of education.

1. We may organize for the collection and diffusion of information. To know what others are doing in a common cause, and to use that knowledge, as it can be made to bear on our own work, are always a help to success. The worker in Wisconsin is wiser and stronger when he knows what his fellow-worker is doing in Alabama. It was one of the effects of the organization of 1817 to collect and to diffuse just this information. Whatever was done by our brethren anywhere in the cause of education, found record, limited and imperfect to be sure, but better than we have had since, in the American Baptist Magazine, the common organ of the denomination, and became an inspiration and an aid. With a higher average intelligence, with better facilities of intercourse, with more abundant means, we can organize now, for the far better collection and the far better use of all facts relating to our common work.

2. We may organize for the stimulus to be given to the cause by local and general meetings of educators and friends of education, for the discussion of all questions relating to our educational work. We can thus enlighten, and guide, and make potent our public sentiment, creating a higher enthusiasm and broader purposes in our leading minds, imparting a new tone to pastoral instruction, raising to its proper place the question of our future ministry, awakening in the minds of parents a higher and wiser interest in the education of their children, and so by God's blessing make our institutions stronger, and the instruments of a wider and better work. We can thus do our part, as one of the chief bodies of American Christians, to keep Christian education in movement by the side of public education; if we are faithful to our trust we can do our part to keep Christian education always in advance of public education, and in a condition to lend to it the powerful force of its own better inspiration and ends. It will be a dark day for our country and the world if education, as to its character, its methods, and its purposes, however it may be advanced as a public interest, is suffered to pass from the profoundest and most earnest deliberations and counsels of distinctively Christian men.

3. We may organize for purposes of advice in reference to the establishment and maintenance of institutions in the rising States. True, the advice which proffers no help is not likely to be highly valued, and yet there would be a moral force in the action of a living and earnest denominational organization, which would do much to save us from blunders such as sometimes have done us so much dishonor, and have so retarded the cause of education in important States.

In reference to so much as has now been named, we might perhaps accomplish what is necessary or practicable, by the establishment of a bureau of education in one of our present great organizations. The objects of such a bureau would not be remote from those of the Home Mission and Publication Societies, and there would be considerations of economy in favor of such a connection. But so far as manifested opinions indicate the drift of denominational wishes and aspirations, something beyond this may be required.

4. We may then organize for the aid of institutions rising with rising States. The minds of many of our people have been turned with remarkable interest to the operations of the Society for Promoting Collegiate and Theological Educa-

tion in the West. Established thirty years ago by the Congregationalists o New England and New School Presbyterians of the Northern States, but now Congregationalist in its character and operations, it has quietly, under many discouragements, but with great efficiency, performed a wonderful work—to be as immortal as the human mind. Commencing with aid to four Colleges and one Theological Seminary, all in great straits, and some in desperation, it has seen all these advanced to competence;—it has taken others upon its bounty which have risen to independence of its aid;—it has others now upon its hands advancing to independence;—and itself among the leading means which have made the local Congregationalism of New England western, it proposes to make it national by planting a New England College in any State of the Union where its services in education are required. The net resources of all the institutions originally taken on its bounty were $300.000. It has expended on those institutions and their successors about $850.000, and has seen the net resources of all its beneficiaries taken together, rise to about $3.000.000. Its plans admit neither waste nor failure. It takes up no doubtful institution. It leaves none half able to take care of itself. Its coöperation is pledge of character and success. It was forced to confront objections at the beginning, just such as we should have to confront in a similar attempt. "If you succeed in carrying money to the West," it was said, "you will impair the resources of struggling eastern colleges." In point of fact eastern colleges have grown strong on the educational spirit which this Society has done so much to evoke. "You will reduce the West to paupers," it was said, "by supporting their colleges without their own exertion." In point of fact the great charity has been so administered as to stimulate Western zeal, and the West has established its own colleges by this stimulus. The grand result is that to-day Christian education in the West has its strong seats in the Colleges which this Society has nurtured. There they stand, and there they will stand forever,—seats of Christian learning, fastened so far as human foresight can penetrate, to an evangelical faith, by the prayers and consecration from which they have proceeded. The tone of public institutions may rise or fall with the average public sentiment,—it may be devout or skeptical with changes of teachers and of times,—but these colleges will stand, the sources of the lofty inspiration of Christian training and the sources of a Christian literature, till He shall come again to whom they belong. The letter of Lyman Beecher which narrates the circumstances of the birth of the Society is grander than an epic. It glows with a prophetic rapture, and when the old man's sun went down, the Western sky was already crimsoned with the glories which he had anticipated. It would be difficult to find a great work more thoroughly born of prayer and faith, or one to which the rewards more certainly and more rapidly came.

Can we go and do likewise? Wisconsin needs this work, Minnesota needs it, Iowa, Nebraska, California, need it, and there are south and south-western States old and new, which need it. Work for a century invites us, and work to endure forever. Our name will perish, and ought to perish, if we fail to do our part in the great work of Christian education, for the ages and the uncounted millions of the future. We may organize for such a work, taking it up humbly at the first, helping only as we make all things strong as we go, and giving to the work increasing proportions under the light of God's providential guidance.

It is the plan of the College Society to expend no money on buildings.

These must be erected at local expense. When a preparatory department is established, and is sufficiently advanced, this Society makes its prosperity sure by granting the small sums necessary to supplement the adequate support of instruction. It stimulates the local endowment by the hope of help from without when local means have done their utmost. In so far it might give us useful lessons by its experience. There is another feature which might be added with advantage in case of an organization by us for similar ends. The organization might become the guardian of funds to prevent the possibility of loss or waste. It might hold the funds given under the patronage of the organization in trust, until the strength of the local organization should become assured, and make them ours under conditions to guard them forever from perversion. In such case liberal friends of education, desirous to give their money for the establishment of Christian Schools, and unable to make the necessary examinations as to the questions of wisdom and safety, might have in the endorsement of a wise Board set apart to that duty, and in the guardianship of funds by men of reputation, skilled in finance, the necessary conditions to inspire and reward their liberality.

An organization in this totally passes from the region of sentiment to that of intelligent and necessary work. The Secretary of the Western College Society, watching with fraternal interest, the Baptist movement in education, has remarked of this movement that it needs the College Society's work to supplement it, and that the College Society needs for its supplement a movement like this of the Baptists. It was wisely said. We have been engaged in awakening sentiment,—it is time to put that sentiment into action, and to give to the cause of education among Baptists such complete form as shall press our whole people towards education, inspiring with hope and joy our teachers, making our institutions in old States strong, building up new ones with rising States, filling them with our sons and our daughters, and encompassing and consecrating them with our prayers. The present question is that of attempting this work in the name of our divine Master, looking for success in his blessing.

On motion, the paper read by Dr. CUTTING was referred to the Committee on Organization.

Adjourned to 7.45 P. M.

TUESDAY EVENING SESSION.

The Convention reassembled at 7.45 P. M., and was opened with prayer by Rev. J. C. STOCKBRIDGE, D.D.

President SAMPSON TALBOT, D.D., read the following paper:

EDUCATION, THE DEVELOPMENT OF THE CHRISTIAN LIFE, THE SUPPLEMENT AND SUPPORT OF ALL EVANGELIZATION, AND THEREFORE DUE IN ITS HIGHEST PRACTICABLE FORM TO THE WHOLE BODY OF THE MINISTRY AND THE LAITY.

The two great forces in operation for the improvement of mankind are Education and Religion. Can these forces act together? or rather can they do their work apart? It is certain that in some respects they are closely related. Education has its spiritual side, as Religion has its educational or natural side.

Taken together they are in some sense supplementary to each other. Religion in education is not less important than education in religion. We would no more separate the spiritual life from intelligence than intelligence from the spiritual life. The two were not made to exist side by side or separately, but to constitute the one continuous life.

Religion is in part natural. As meeting and blending with the religious instincts, as standing in relation to reason and nature, and as based on a revelation to be received into human thought in order to be a revelation, it is natural; as a body of revealed truth and a divine spirit of life, it is supernatural. So on the other hand intelligence, as constituting a rational community between God and man and as leading up toward the Divine, bears a spiritual aspect. The highest thinking of mankind has led up toward God; religion, not atheism, has been the consummation of the philosophy and moral history of our race. Hence as men dishonor revelation when they seek to cast doubts on its profound reasonableness, so they dishonor reason when they seek to disconnect it from its correlation with the divine.

The subject of this paper requires me to show that education is connected with the development of the Christian life, and, consequently, with the progress of the Kingdom of God in the Earth. The Christian life as here to be treated must be taken not in respect to its divine origin and support, but in respect to its natural basis; that is, in so far as it exists as a fact in the present fixed order of things.

Is religion capable only of a partial application to human nature, or is it a true world-power, a spirit able to take up and contain in itself, all the forces of individual and social life? Is anything that is human alien to it? If so, then education and religion never can be wholly joined. This question therefore first demands investigation.

There is a certain conception of religion which we may call the ascetic. It holds that human nature must be driven out before the divine can be fully received; hence, that the divine must be received and must exist in man only in a mechanical manner. It holds that this world belongs to the wicked one, and that the Christian, having renounced his service and his works, has resigned all right and participation here, except the necessary one of living for a while on the territory of a foreign power, to the proprieties and customs of which he is unable to conform. The ascetic view of religion withdraws man from the common life of the world, makes his existence a toilsome work-day, and leaves him nothing but to wait in patience for death. But there is another conception, which is expressed in the words of Paul: "God hath not given us the spirit of fear, but of power and of love and of a sound mind." This finds in Christianity elements that are capable of universal application, and claims this world for Christ. In the language of a recent utterance: * "The ideas which Christ made manifest on the earth are capable of endless expansion to suit the wants of men of every age; and they do expand, developing into forms of larger import and wider application in direct proportion to that progress of mankind of which they are both root and sap."

It must be that He who became man is the truest friend of man, that his doctrine is concerned with whatever concerns mankind, and that his Spirit is

*Rev. Stopford A. Brooke.

the only perfect educator of ours. This conception of the relation of Christ to humanity, flows at once from the great first truth in philosophy that God created man in his own likeness, and that, therefore, the mind of man and the constitution of nature must be in correspondence, and both must be simply reflections of the creative mind; and from the great first truth in religion that God was made flesh and dwelt among us, and that, therefore, the divine and human in him meet and mingle. The distinction between God and man is shown by both these great truths not to be one of opposition. God lacks not all that is in the human,—man lacks not all that is in the divine. The Son of God was also the Son of man. He is all divine and all human according to the point of view from which we contemplate him. True, the divine in him was not humanized, the human in him was not deified; but they flowed together in his one conscious life. It must follow, therefore that the life of Christ, the theanthropic life, received into the soul of man, will produce a development on the side of the human as well as on the side of the divine. The humanity of Christ himself while he was on earth did not probably have free development, was not fully unfolded in all its powers, since his life was a peculiar one because of his peculiar mission; but this limitation we cannot consider permanent. And thus the reverse of our subject is true, that religion is the development of the human life, the leading out of human nature into its completeness. But for this very reason must it not also be true that education is the development of the Christian life, since in respect to each we have to do not with an abstraction, but with a living process? We do not forget that religion itself is a principle of redemption, not of education, and is carried on by the power of Christ in the Soul, not by the natural powers of the Soul. Hence the education of the simple human, mere human culture, however perfect, does not constitute an appropriation of the divine, nor can ever become a substitute for this. How then shall we state the relation between Education and the Christian Life? Shall we say that education by effecting the growth of humanity, thus supplies the ground for a fuller appropriation of the Christian life? This would be true, but inadequate; for it considers the Christian life only in its source or divine origin, not as a fact in the human soul. The spirit of Christ, received into the life of man, must become human, that is, it must enter and manifest itself in a living process of renewal; it must become part of the development of the human life in a manner conformable to human nature. Thus Paul says: I live, yet not I but Christ in me, still it is I that live. Is this humanitarianism? not at all. If we seek man in man alone, we lose him; if we seek the divine in man as at variance with man, we lose it; but if we seek the life of Christ in the Soul of man, we find both. These two elements we can indeed separate by abstraction, but the Christian life as it actually exists is not a two-fold but one life. The Spirit of God in us does not depend for its unfolding upon driving out the human, upon suppressing every feeling generic to man, but upon renewing the human, cleansing it from sin, and imparting to it a richer quality. These are mutually conditioning and conditioned. Why should it seem derogatory to religion to hold that for its full power in the soul it is dependent on the progress of humanity, the increase of human capacities through education? The work of God is orderly, and is performed upon the material given: and the natural and spiritual in man are organically connected, flowing together in one current of life. Neither can exist without its influence on the other. Shall we say, then, that Education and Religion are in all respects equal and co-ordinate factors in the development of man? or shall we assign to Religion a less important place than to Education? In some respects a more important place. Religion is itself educational as introducing new elements into human life; while education is dependent for its vital power upon religion. It is chiefly to religion that the soul is indebted for its desire for personal perfection, which is a stronger force than the love of knowledge; and hence religion communicates those impulses to human progress which are fundamental and steady. Without religion, in consequence of the lower tone assumed by human life, education would decline and lose itself at length in mere sensuous culture. The error of those who think that the perfection of man is to be secured by intellectual and æsthetic culture, is two-fold; they forget that religion is one of the elements of the ideal completeness of man, and that it is also the grand quickener of all the faculties of the soul. But their truth is in holding fast to the idea of the complete development of all the powers of humanity. And for this religion alone is as insufficient as education alone. They are mutual helpers, and either will fall to an inferior place without the other. Religion is conditioned in every stage of its progress by knowledge, and must, therefore, ally itself with every educational force in society. This is to-day the great problem of religion, how to enter into all the life of the world, how to appropriate this universal empire of life as its own. How shall Christianity breathe its spirit into the literature, the philosophy, the art, the politics, the science of our times? This cannot be done until, laying off all its unnatural phases, so as to embrace the whole sphere of life, it becomes truly natural; until it takes up all intelligence into its idea. If Christianity ever possesses the world, it must be by assimilating to itself all that is good in human life and human society; all that is true in science and beautiful in art. Over every field on which anything useful to man, anything good, anything pleasant, springs up, it must extend the arms of its benediction. Human nature itself must be made to speak with a Christian voice. For it is certain that human nature will never be driven out of man, and if Christianity cannot make human nature its ally, it can never control the world. Its object is not simply to bring the soul to Christ and get it safe out of the world;—all that is in that soul must be brought into Christ. More of his life is yet to descend into the lives of men and the whole of men's lives is yet to enter into Christ. The first stage of religion is conversion; the next is appropriation. But how shall this object be accomplished? Shall religion attempt to suppress all those manifestations of human nature and social life, out of which have sprung the various forms of literature, philosophy and art; to exclude from the thinking and feeling of men whatever is not contained in its teachings? Shall the church get the work of education into her own hands? But human nature in no one of its legitimate developments will ever be suppressed, and knowledge cannot be monopolized; and hence if Christianity cannot embrace all culture and hold in itself the law of every human interest, it must either empty humanity of all its depths and richness or hold a divided empire and a subordinate place. But is Christianity capable of admitting into itself all the new elements of progress? Is it too an evolution? Upon its human side it certainly is. It does not cease to be divine or become any the less divine by being a development, while only thus does it become humanly intelligible. Out of Christianity as embodied in the New Testament has flowed the Church, which is hence a revelation of the inner nature of Christianity; just as the course of history is a manifestation of the essence of humanity. As no one becomes a fit interpreter of the human spirit by studying himself alone out of connection with the whole mental development of the race, so the true interpreter of Christianity must stand in the life of the Church. The Church is the body of Christ which his Spirit has organized to himself, and thus becomes his fulness, the historical revelation of himself. It is true that, as a body of revealed truth associated with the Spirit of Christ, religion is already complete and does not change; but in its human applications it is an expansive power, taking up into itself every growth of humanity. As the life of man, through the increase of knowledge and experience, becomes ever wider and deeper, it should be expected, under the blessing of Christ, to take on ever new and brighter forms of Christian excellence. He will be the truest exponent of divine things who holds them purely in the largest humanity. And thus all God's means for the education of the race work together; the Spirit of Christ is an intelligent Spirit.

> Nature, crescent, does not grow alone
> In thews and bulk. But, as her temple waxes,
> The inward service of the mind and soul
> Grows wide withal.

Thus far I have taken education in its true sense as the development of humanity, and have found that it cannot properly exclude religion. For a completed life the moral sentiments must be developed evenly with every growth of the mind. From the more common point of view, education is regarded as the cultivation of the intellect. But this is an abstraction. It separates the intellect in thought from the other powers, though no such separation actually exists. There is no such thing as a mere intellectual culture. The effort to learn is a discipline of the will, and its tendency is so far moral. If the education of the mind is pursued in a truly natural and human manner, if it is not *made* abnormal, it will directly influence the whole nature and issue in general elevation of character. But it may be useful for a moment to look at our subject abstractly, that is, from the educational side simply, and show the value of intelligence in itself as related to all the other interests of man and of society.

I begin with the axiom of Aristotle, that in the formation of the mind "the individual is to be led from the sensible, which is the earlier for us, to the intellectual, which is the first in itself, so that what is first in itself may come to have the predominance over what is first for us." The intellect is the universal in man. It is not an idiosyncrasy of our race, it is not peculiar to any order of intelligent being, but is identical in all. The intellectual realm is one. Intelligence constitutes citizenship in the rational universe. We have not even ground to affirm that human reason is essentially finite.* As the off-

*"It is not easy to understand in what sense our minds are said to be 'finite.' Of the essence of our mind we know nothing, except so far as we have observed its workings and can thence infer its powers. To enable us, then, to pronounce that the mind is limited, it would be necessary for us to have reached those limits. Whether or not such an operation would require an intelligence superior to that of man, it is enough here to say that such a complete and final mensuration of the faculties of the human mind, as should authorize us to pronounce that it is bounded on every side by a limit, has not yet been made. We are not therefore at present warranted in affirming that the human mind is finite."—Lowndes' Philosophy of Primary Beliefs.

spring and image of the infinite God, it cannot be shut up to the finite; it is the faculty of universal principles and of unlimited appropriation. "All things are yours." Intelligence is the bond of union among all rational beings and constitutes the universe a community; it is the medium of introduction into that empire of truth where God alone is king. Hence it must be the condition of all progress alike for the individual and the race. It is the only directing agency. Indeed, I may say that among things pertaining to this life, it is the highest interest of mankind. Knowledge is power, and educated mind, all else being equal, will control all things in this world. Out of intelligence comes leadership, comes the direction of energies, comes mastery. The well trained mind everywhere maintains its supremacy. It is the master of kings and stronger than all material forces. The Soul is the mightiest power on this Earth, laughing at the feebleness of the elements and rising unhurt above the ruins of time. The Soul, it is true, is not all intellectual; but its feelings and its will are nothing save as they are rational, save as the illumination of reason has entered into them. "Nations," it is said, "are moved by their sensibilities,—their passions sway them more than their ideas; but their ideas shape their destiny in the end." Feeling is transitory and soon falls back into the empty void unless it is fastened to some rational principle. But an idea once introduced into the mind, abides there forever, and becomes a seed which will germinate and grow. It lives and reigns there until the strongest and most reluctant will is subjected to its power. Hence the abiding influence of an intelligent ministry, which holds men by convincing them. A ministry which terminates in moving the feelings without kindling also a great light of truth in the mind, passes over the face of society as the wind over the waters, leaving no permanent results. Such a ministry may be a blessing during its time, but it does not build, it does not organize, it lays not the foundations of many generations. A vigorous life of faith which lays hold of God's promises, will soon become a life of intelligence seeking communion with God's thoughts. A religion that has vitality in it, will spring up in institutions of learning as well as works of practical benevolence.

But education is also "the supplement and support of all evangelization." The Christian life must be organized into all the living forces of the soul and of society. It seeks this in the expansiveness of its very nature. Christianity has been in all its history the patron of sound learning. It has gone teaching all nations. The light of knowledge has followed it around the world as the light of day the sun. It can hold men only by going before them; and the narrowest policy of missions ever conceived was that Christianity can employ preaching but not the school. When a people become Christian they next call for Education, and they will fall to those who furnish it for them. Without education religion itself runs out.

Thus we reach our conclusion, which must stand without further enforcement, that education is due in its highest practicable form to the whole body of mankind, into whatever classes they may be distributed.

Dr. CUTTING: I hope that in the discussion which is to follow the reading of the paper to which we have just listened, there will be brought

---

Of course the statement above did not have reference to attainments, which are always finite, but to the faculty.

out distinctly for practical consideration the relations of education to missions—whether to Foreign missions or to Home Missions – the relations of education to the growth, development and usefulness of any Church or denomination of Christians; and that it will be brought out likewise, in this discussion, that education is not a thing for the clergy alone, not for the laity alone, but for the development of the human being, the making of the most of the Christian man and the Christian woman, so that each and all in his or her sphere, shall be able to accomplish most for Christ's glory, most for the progress and redemption of the race. It has been my hope that these practical questions would come up, that education might be strengthened in connection with our missions, that education might be strengthened in connection with the work of every Pastor, so that we should go from this place better friends of education and better friends of educational work.

Dr. J. WHEATON SMITH: I heard the closing remark in the very able paper which has been presented, with very great pleasure, the allusion to schools in their relation to missions. Perhaps it is not entirely an accident that on this very day, the 28th of May, the Rangoon college opens with three Professors and twenty-five students. I most heartily believe that missions to be successful must be supplemented with Christian schools, and that we took not one step backward, but many steps backward when in this city some years ago we closed our [mission] schools and locked up our printing presses. I was but a boy then, felt more assurance of being right than I do now, and yet in the light of so able a paper as this which has been read in our hearing I am more inclined than ever to the old opinion, not simply in its relation to missions but in its relation to every department of Christian life and influence. Religion, simple experimental religion, underlies all culture, and touches and suffuses all culture, becoming a constituent part, entering into its life, making it a sort of incarnation of religion.

I remember one evening after a stormy day, when I had been waiting, seemingly in vain, for a clear sunset on the Rhigi, I wandered out quite despondingly towards the edge of the evening, just at the time when the mist broke away and showed me a forest of peaks and crags bristling around me, and at that very moment the sun broke through the clouds and tinged with its golden hue, every minaret and peak, giving them all its own heavenly beauty. It is but a faint illustration of what religion does for culture. It is looking at it only from one point of view when you choose an illustration such as that. It underlies all culture, did I say? That is only a part of it. It is the beginning of all culture. Till with the hopes and purposes and forces of the regenerated soul we approach intellectual development and advancement, we have not got the clue through this labyrinth of education. Till the soul acknowledges its allegiance to another world than this; till it feels out of its own emptiness the needs of a diviner knowledge and a power better than its own, and which comes down from heaven, it is not fit for culture.

Pardon me, gentlemen, if I take the time that belongs to you. I did it that I might be the sacrifice and that you might follow with fuller and more matured thoughts.

Principal SHEPARDSON: For some twenty years I have been looking at this matter of education, and for four or five at the question of woman's education. And it seems to me that we are coming up very rapidly out of Heathenism. We are coming up rapidly to the question of giving to a woman the education that she deserves. We all know her power; we all know what constitutes a home: we all know that the wife and the mother are the life of the home; that when we have intelligent wives and mothers—I mean to say when we shall employ education as it lies in our power to employ it, to elevate this portion of the human race, all our Sunday-schools, our Churches will be gradually elevated. The question whether our young women shall be educated in our colleges with our young men, as was said to-day in a very able paper, is an open question, but is it an open question whether they are to be educated at all above mere primary education? We have discussed the question of the education of our ministry in all our Conventions and Associations. We are alive to the question of educating our young men. But, do we form societies for the education of our young women? It is true that in the State of Ohio less than two years ago, we formed the "Ohio Baptist Women's Education Society," the object of which was to do something for women, as we are accustomed to do for men. But, should we stop here?

It seems to me that what Dr. ANDERSON, President of Rochester University, said in Chicago, a few years ago, "We all know that woman is the God-appointed educator of the race," demands our thought, demands our money, demands our combined effort. Nor shall we ever execute the commission of the Son of God, "Go, teach all nations," until we make more ample provision for the education of our more talented women. We must educate the educator. Nine out of ten of the educators in our Public Schools are women. Our children receive some of the strongest impressions of their lives from their mothers before they are ten years old. They go from their homes to be taught by women. All our Ministers, Physicians, Merchants, Statesmen, all our men, and all our women too, receive their moulding influences from woman, and we must wake up to this question in some form adequate to the necessities of the case. We must educate the educator.

Dr. TURNBULL: I listened to the address this evening with the greatest interest, and more especially from the fact that it enunciated certain principles which lie at the foundation of all our thinking, of all our religion, and of all our education,—principles too, which I do not think, are universally received among us. I should be very glad to be informed that they are generally received. My impression is that they are not so received,—that they are held only by a few individuals among us. To illustrate what I say, I have only to refer you to the well-known work of Dr. MANSEL on the Limitations of Religious Thought, received, so far as my recollection goes, by our journals with universal approbation. I have never seen a line in any of our religious papers of any sort, no not even in our quarterly review opposing the philosophical principles of that book, which are fundamentally the same as those advocated by Mr. HERBERT SPENCER in the present day, and which make all certainty in religious knowledge impossible. Assuming the same ground as Dr. MANSEL, that writer clearly defends the doctrine of Nihilism with reference to all higher knowledge. His postulate is, that neither in science nor in religion can we transcend the phenomenal and formal. The moment we attempt to do so, we pass into the unknown and unknowable; that God therefore cannot be known, in the deeper sense of that word, by the human mind. He holds that all we can really know are phenomena and their relations, so that the knowledge of the soul itself, as a spiritual, immortal essence is impossible. Now such a view destroys all ground of belief in the Bible, in inspiration, in regeneration and immortality. It makes the proof of the reality or the continuance of the soul actually impossible. On the other hand the principles enunciated in the paper read to-night cut up all skepticism of that sort by the roots, and make it possible for us, under God, to know God and immortality, and base all our education upon that grand postulate. We are taught that we are made in the image of God. I am apprehensive that it is not generally understood what is meant when we say that we are made in the image of God, and have a faculty by which we can know God, and know him with certainty. I therefore desire this evening to endorse the principles of that paper. I hope they will be thoroughly discussed. If any body doesn't believe them I hope he will controvert them on the spot, and let us know where we stand in regard to the possibility of being born from above, and knowing God directly, and not merely in the way of symbol and form. If we are created in the image of God, we know that our inspiration is from him, and this must constitute the basis of all higher education. Then are we capable of true knowledge and religion, of holding communion with God as his dear children, and though fallen, of being restored by his Son, our blessed Saviour, Jesus Christ, who is to us the true God and eternal life, and who, being "formed in us," becomes the root of all that is beautiful, great and glorious in the present and eternal destiny of man.

Pres. HOVEY: It seems to me an almost self-evident truth that every power of the human mind, and every natural susceptibility of the human mind, must be improved by exercise. Believing in God, believing that all his works as well as his Word, teach lessons in respect to him, I cannot doubt that it is our duty to study the works of God, and to exercise all the true and right powers and susceptibilities of our nature as fully as practicable, in seeking to know more thoroughly what God has taught us in his Word, and to comprehend more fully his works as leading us, step by step, to our Maker. And as to the direct communion between the soul of man and God, I have no more doubt of it than any of my brethren, though it does not seem to me to come naturally into the subject before us.

It is a beautiful subject, the connection between true education and true religion. However much education has been misdirected and perverted, I cannot doubt even for an instant that true religion and true education belong together, and that the soul of man permeated by love to God will be elevated and developed most rapidly and most beautifully.

Now in regard to our missions. Are we doing nothing in the foreign field for education? It is said that a check was put upon this part of our missionary labors some years ago.—Being a *young* man, my memory does not go back very distinctly to that period, though I have some recollection of it. And I have a conviction that there was more reason for some caution in that direction than is perhaps readily acknowledged at the present time. We had a limited force, we have always had a limited force. But God has most wonderfully blessed the labors that have been bestowed upon the Heathen in a direct way. No efforts in the world I believe have been more highly blessed than ours. And it has been primarily by this religious work; by planting first the seed of divine love in the soul, and then by educating the people in primary schools by teachers from among themselves: by teaching at least in this partial way, and so carrying on the work as rapidly as possible, without a neglect of the preaching of the Gospel.

I believe that we can look abroad over these fields and see that the Divine blessing has rested upon them since that day as richly, at least, as before. But more ought to be done—more is being done. I rejoice that we are taking steps for a more thorough cultivation of the minds of those who have been converted to Christ among the heathen. But I very much question whether all of us know the history of this matter well enough to be sure that any serious mistake was made at the time when some check was put upon this form of labor. Much more has been done than many suppose. The missionaries and the wives of the missionaries have been teaching. They have been teaching young men and young women. There have been schools planted in almost all the churches, and native teachers have been giving instruction. So that education has not been neglected;—perhaps not pressed forward as fast as it ought to have been, and would have been, if we had had more force, if we had had more money to use, and more men there to use it. Give us the money and the men, and we will have the Gospel preached, first and chiefly always; then we will have education as the hand-maid of it, and we will carry forward the education of the people as rapidly as possible. [Applause].

Dr. MURDOCK: I have no disposition to enter into the metaphysical question that has been raised here this evening. I do not know that I am much of a metaphysician, though the old Scotch blood stirs in me sometimes. There is a practical question that has been brought to view, however, upon which I may be permitted to say a word, for it has been somewhat a matter of study with me for a number of years. There are two theories of the evangelization of the heathen. One is the theory of evangelization by means of schools, which was the theory of Dr. DUFF, and which, I believe, there was a tendency among our missionaries to adopt. The other theory is that of evangelization by preaching the gospel, and bringing in schools to supplement the work thus effected. The latter is the theory upon which the American Baptist Missionary Union has acted. There never has been a time when the stations have not had their schools, station schools, and the normal schools, in which young men and women were trained for the work of practical teaching; and as a matter of fact, the teachers who have been most successful, whose labors have been attended with such large success in our missionary schools, in Burmah and different parts of Asia, are the fruits of this humble, unostentatious educational work, which has been for the last twenty or twenty-five years prosecuted with such industry and success in all our mission stations. It is an interesting fact to those who have been close enough to the history of the transaction to observe it, to see how directly the minds of the converted portion of the people tend to the work of education, how kindly and how naturally they take to it. They all feel that the success of evangelical work, that the permanency of it, depends in a large measure upon the general education of the children and of the people; and for the last few years the demand has been coming to us from every quarter, for better schools, larger, broader, more complete educational foundations. The missionaries have been attempting to supply this demand.

Then there was established in Rangoon what was known as the Rangoon Theological Seminary. The school was commenced many years ago, but it was established on its present basis at a more recent date—since the controversies in reference to education to which Dr. SMITH alluded in his remarks. That institution has had under instruction from fifty to one hundred students a year, for the last ten years. It has been sending out to all the missionary stations in Burmah men qualified to act as teachers. It has been sending out native teachers in Bassein, and in the Rangoon district, and establishing churches all over the country. It has been sending out men who have gone to the waste places, visiting the people who have no teachers and bringing them to the knowledge of Christ, and gathering them into the churches. This work has been going on in Rangoon for many years, and now more recently a demand has come for the establishment of a college. We want the children of our missions to reach an equality with the children of more enlightened Christian nations. We are providing means for the higher instruction of young women. A seminary has been commenced, or rather has been reconstituted, in the city of Bassein, for the education of women. Mrs. CROSS is about establishing a seminary for the education of all women who desire a larger and fuller intellectual culture. And now as to this college in Rangoon—a committee during the last year have purchased a site with suitable buildings for the establishment of a college. Last Saturday, Dr. BINNEY, in Rangoon, penned a telegram, sending it to me in Boston, saying: "College opens May 28." That humble institution in the city of Rangoon is destined, as I believe, to grow until its blessed influence shall be felt over all that land. That little institution commences its operations to-day. I regard the coincidence, Mr. President, as auspicious. I regard it as one of the blessed auguries for this time, that while we are here deliberating, we are permitted to announce the great fact that college education is henceforward a fact among those Karens who have received the gospel. They are stretching forth their hands for the means of larger and more complete mental culture; and we may look forward to the time when the light of religion and learning shall spread its blessed beams over all that land, and when the teeming millions gathered from the darkness of heathenism shall rejoice in the brightness of the Saviour's appearing, and in that light which intellectual culture and knowledge impart to the human understanding; and as our evangelical work shall be made secure and permanent through the influence of a larger and sounder culture, we may well congratulate ourselves to-night, and we do congratulate ourselves on this auspicious beginning.

Rev. Mr. CUSHMAN: It strikes me that one of the faults of the paper under discussion is—well, not a fault of the paper at all,—and yet there is a fault, a certain defect that the members of this Convention must hold themselves responsible to remedy. You have heard, I doubt not, of the Scotch minister, who preached a very able and conclusive sermon against Atheism, and that on the way home from church one of the understanding members of the congregation who was in company with a common sort of man inquired of him, how he was pleased with that sermon. Well, the man said he listened with all his ears; he thought the minister talked pretty well, but he believed there was a God after all! Now it would almost seem as if some of our learned brethren here were in that predicament in relation to this paper. It strikes me that the principle underlying and permeating that document needs to be popularized, put home to the people of our denomination and indeed all the denominations everywhere; so that they shall see what it means, understand it, believe it, and then carry it out.

I say then that one of the faults of the paper is not a fault of the paper at all, but of the people, who will not thoroughly appreciate it and understand it. And so its thoughts ought to be put in such a form that they cannot help understanding it.

Take one of those sermons that all denominations preach; however powerful it may seem, if there be no true intelligence and culture in the minds of the people who listen to it, its results will be but temporary and superficial. I could point you to areas of hundreds of miles which we have been accustomed to regard as strongholds of our denominational views, and over which mighty revivals as they were regarded, swept year after year, and yet to-day the churches of those regions are declining, going down. In conversing with an excellent Christian man from one of those sections only a few days ago upon this very topic, the inseparable connection of true culture and solid, substantial, enduring religion, that man said, "Oh, only give us religion enough, we don't so much need the education." My reply was, "You cannot have religion enough without having more education. You cannot find room enough in their minds and hearts for more religion without more culture." Dr. Murdock spoke of supplementing preaching with education. If he means by that that in all cases preaching must go before education, in the order of time I mean, it strikes me that he is mistaken. Each must be the helper or supplement of the other.

Take the principles of this essay home with you, brethren, and put them in such a shape that the people themselves shall be compelled to understand and believe them. For I think they will readily believe them and take hold of them and grapple with them. In short, preach to the people the philosophy of Peter's theology, which was the true philosophy. "Add to your faith, virtue, *knowledge*, temperance, godliness and charity," making the structure of a complete, symmetrical character; as Dr. —— expresses it, "Eight stories high, faith in every story and knowledge at the foundation." [Applause.]

On motion, the following were appointed a Committee on the Publication of Proceedings: Rev. L. Moss, D.D., Rev. C. P. Sheldon, D.D., and Rev. D. B. Cheney, D.D.

Pres. ROBINSON: My friend, Dr. HAGUE, misunderstood me and has left me in a somewhat false position. I made no reference to the doings of the Missionary Union.* Dr. TURNBULL has alluded to a subject which some ten years ago occupied the minds of teachers, thinkers and philosophers in this country and in England. The two men who then opened the discussion are now lying in their graves.

* The previous remarks of Dr. Robinson here referred to are not found in the manuscript of the reporters. The remarks of Dr. Hague are likewise missing.

MANSEL, as good a man as God ever gave to England, a profound thinker, a most thorough scholar and Christian, a man who in his earnest zeal for Christianity, seized a principle capable of the most opposite uses and with it did as good a service of its kind, as was ever given to any man to perform, for Christianity. Professor NEWMAN, FROUDE and others had assumed that out of the human consciousness you can construct a revelation and a religion. NEWMAN had stated that if the Bible and revelation were from God they must first vindicate themselves to our conscience and consciousness, and therefore out of our own moral being we may construct a religion and a "Rational Theology." This was striking at the very foundation of Christianity. MANSEL took the principle he had learned from Sir WM. HAMILTON,—the relativity of Human Knowledge,—and with it set himself to the examination and analysis of the Rational Theology, and he did his work most thoroughly. Then Mr. MAURICE opened upon him with red hot shot: losing his temper and writing a furious book. MANSEL, in return, lost his temper and wrote a personal reply. Within the last few days, MAURICE, a most earnest and industrious Christian man, has gone to his rest. I do not understand that HERBERT SPENCER has followed in the track of MANSEL. HERBERT SPENCER took the Hamiltonian principle of the Relativity of Human Knowledge, assuming that because we know God only relatively and phenomenally, therefore our knowledge is only apparent, and, being only apparent, is therefore untrustworthy and to be set aside from all scientific knowledge. Now I do not understand this to have been the position of MANSEL. MANSEL said we do not comprehend, we do not exhaustively know God. We know him only as he has chosen to reveal himself to us. What man doubts it. On the other hand HERBERT SPENCER says because we do not know him exhaustively, and can know him only relatively, we do not know any thing about him. We repudiate HERBERT SPENCER totally; whether we should equally repudiate MANSEL is another thing. I think we should all agree with the paper which has given rise to this discussion. Like Dr. HOVEY, one or two of the phrases I should not have used. But as to the union of religion and education, can you divide man? Can you separate intellect from conscience? So long as the human conscience speaks, so long God must be recognized. You cannot set him aside; you cannot evade him. Neither on the other hand can we confound the position of the two, Education and Religion. They are united, they are indissoluble. He who educates aright, must educate the conscience. It is to influence the whole being, the whole man; it is to draw out every faculty, and give play to each. So long as man exists, moral science exists; and so long as moral science has to do with moral law, so long God, in his existence, in his attributes, in his relations to us must be recognized. [Applause].

The session closed with prayer by Rev. DR. HISCOX.

WEDNESDAY MORNING SESSION.

The Convention reassembled at 9.30 A. M. Prayer was offered by the Rev. WM. LAMSON, D.D. The minutes of yesterday were read and approved.

On motion, the members of the Philadelphia Committee of Arrangements, not delegates, were invited to seats in the Convention as members thereof.

DR. BOARDMAN read a communication from the Board of Directors of the Union League, inviting the Convention to visit the League House. The Secretary was instructed to acknowledge the invitation, and assure the Board of Directors of the thanks of the Convention.

Dr. CUTTING: I have received letters, expressing regret at being unable to attend this Convention, from NATHAN BISHOP, LL. D., of New York, the Rev. Mr. Gow, of Worcester, Massachusetts, the Rev. Dr. CRANE, of Texas, and the Rev. Dr. PHELPS, of Connecticut. I am very glad to say for the gratification of the Convention, that in the letter of Mr. Gow, he expresses a very confident expectation of being able to raise $100,000 for the endowment of the Academy at Worcester. I know he has at some times felt a little discouraged about it, but he now expresses himself with a measure of confidence which is extremely gratifying.

The Rev. R. C. MILLS, D.D., then read a paper on

HINDRANCES TO THE INCREASE OF THE MINISTERS OF THE GOSPEL.

It was the Lord himself who first told his disciples that the harvest of souls in our world is great and the laborers are few. At no time since has this disproportion ceased to exist. When he for this reason directed his servants to pray the Lord of the harvest to "send forth laborers into his harvest," he did not mean that they should do nothing else. This is essential, but not exclusive. They must in fact do everything which is legitimate to increase the number of laborers for souls; just as they must do everything else that is proper, as well as pray, that souls may be saved.

Among the subjects of Christian care and thought there should come the hindrances to the increase of the number of ministers of Christ. On such occasions as the present, it would therefore be more suitable to apologize for the omission, than for the introduction of this as one of the topics to be considered.

Such hindrances always exist, but they are not always the same. They vary in form and force with changes in the state of the church and of society. The unsecular character and the sacredness of the minister's work, together with the serious responsibility of such a care of God's truth and men's souls as it involves, always cause the proper men for such work to hesitate before they undertake it. But, besides, there are many other obstacles which are felt and must be overcome by all who enter the ministry. Those which exist now and among us demand our attention.

Those which we would consider naturally group themselves into four classes, to which we may give the names of social, ecclesiastical, ministerial, and parental.

By the social hindrances we mean, such as arise from the feelings of a large portion of society at the present time towards ministers of the gospel. There has been a time when a minister had much deference paid him. His position was one of honor; and it had a measure of influence and respect accorded to it, in which no other was its superior and few were its rivals. Now, however, this official consideration and authority have in a great degree passed away. All "benefit of clergy" is in this sense, as well as others, at an end. Men commonly deny that there is any special Divine appointment of the ministry, or call to its work. Some ministers have themselves encouraged, if they did not suggest, this denial. Whatever ministers preach directly from the Word of God bears with it, to many, but little authority derived from its source, but is questioned and challenged as to its truth and authority, just as much as anything else which men utter. To complete weariness have we also heard men insist that the pulpit has lost its place and power, while the printing press and newspaper have seized the position which it once occupied. In a new sense men now ask, "Who is Paul, and who is Apollos?" They admit no "signs of an apostle" except those which their own intuitions or reasonings or feelings furnish them. Ministers are merely public speakers on religious subjects, who may instruct or interest or amuse their hearers, while they may receive or reject what they choose of their preaching.

The knowledge that this state of feeling exists and must be encountered by a minister gives his work difficulties which make it repulsive to many. Under different circumstances, the view of the ministry prevalent in the community aided a person who thought of this as the service which God required of him. But the one now held by many adds so much to the intrinsic difficulties of this work as to deter many from undertaking it.

At the same time, society now demands very thorough preparation for the ministry, if not also much more than fair talents. All men would like to have their own ministers equal to a few famous men whom God has especially qualified for their work. While this cannot be, to acquire the usual preliminary training consumes from seven to ten years. Young men are commonly just ready to begin this at the age at which others are entering on the active pursuits of life. In secular business the old system of long apprenticeships is at an end. Young men receive men's wages at an early age. Many commence business for themselves almost as soon as they close their minority. To their young friends they seem already on the road to success and competence.

Secular business sets all this before Christian young men who are thinking of the duty of preaching the gospel. But, for that, they must endure years of detention from the actual work of life. And these years they must spend in severe study, and also remain through them all dependent on personal friends or others for the means of support.

Such things must be felt. And they are felt with more severity among us than in a different state of society where long apprenticeships must be endured, and then but scanty wages can be earned, and many obstacles hinder a young man from rising above the position in which his active life begins. Even in England "every trade and every profession is over-crowded, and to rise in life is almost an impossibility, owing to the caste that prevails there.*" But among

* Rev. H. M. Dexter, D.D.

us men rise from the mechanic's shop to the Senate, and from a country store to the Cabinet; and the acquisition of millions has become common in every department of business. Worldly success thus imparts a fearful power among us to worldly attractions.

The contrast between this and the ministry furnishes a hindrance to the latter, as strong as the attractions with which it clothes the former. It adds to the force of each that the decision to be a minister of Christ involves the immediate and final banishment of all those plans of worldly gain and advancement which have so many natural attractions to all men that none of us relinquish them except by compulsion.

But these social hindrances which bear against the acceptance of the work of the ministry do not stand alone. Others come from the churches. These, for convenience, we call, distinctively, ecclesiastical.

Ministers, in our days, must not only preach the gospel of Christ, but they must do it with freshness, novelty, variety, and force, that it may be attractive No matter how familiar, or severe, or unwelcome the gospel may be to many hearers, the churches expect ministers to preach it so as to attract, if not to please them. They may instruct, and convince, and save them, if they can, but they must interest them. The fatal defect is, not to be attractive to from one or two hundred to a thousand people at once and in every service. It makes no difference that congregations are of necessity so unlike that they cannot all be pleased with the same topics, nor with the same way of treating topics of general interest. The pressure of this demand shows itself in the shifts to which it drives some preachers. Not really great in intellect, nor honestly capable of meeting the requirements of their churches, they act as if they must fail, unless they seem to meet them by some device, even though it degrades the gospel. One such man accounted to his friends for the reckless course by which he sought popularity, by remarking, that he had noticed that some successful men were in the habit of speaking at random, in disregard of the bearing of what they might say, and therefore he imitated them.

To interest, is essential, but not sufficient. Churches expect ministers to be capable of making themselves welcome and at home with every class of men, and to be ready for every form of labor which Christian benevolence and zeal, or worldly ingenuity has devised for a parish, from a Sabbath-school down to a sewing society, and from a scientific lecture to a reading club down to a pic-nic. Nor must he lack skill to make the prayer-meeting "lively" and "pleasant" in any condition of the church. And he must be careful that he does not make a poor show of the church statistics, when its record is made up for the Association. Not a few churches also make their pastors feel that they expect them to know how to arouse them when cold and inactive, and how to secure the special presence and work of the Holy Spirit, so as to have a religious revival, with almost as much exactness of recurrence as the winter solstice.

And it is by no means a rare thing for churches to desire, not to say to expect, their ministers to make the support of public worship a burden that is not heavy and a yoke that is not irksome. They wink at and bear many things which do no good, but even result in much harm, because the size of the congregation is satisfactory; while they treat many rare excellences as worthless, because they fail to draw a crowd, which would flock together to hear things which neither honor Christ, nor help men's souls, but entertain thoughtless people, and by filling the house with them lighten the burden of expense to those on whom the support of the church devolves.

It so happens that young men who are called to the ministry are members of the churches, and they know how their pastors, not only have their sermons criticized, but their entire work canvassed. They thus learn what a minister must endure, and is expected to be and to do. They can do no otherwise than think of this, when they are deciding the question of their own duty. And in what they observe they must find discouragements which will much sooner attract their attention, than any of the ordinary encouragements of the work to which God may be calling them.

Much has been said of the insufficient means of support given to our ministers. Some would give a measure of prominence to this as a hindrance to the increase of their number. Although a hardship, we question much whether it has ever been more than one of the minor hindrances, or kept out of the ministry any excepting such as were well kept out. But we now have less occasion to consider this than formerly. Our churches are making the ministry more like other professions, so as to furnish all grades of support up to an easy or ample one, according as they find pastors who suit their taste or meet their demands.

It seems more necessary that the treatment which mature age, and large experience, and broad acquirements, and ripe character oftentimes receive should have our consideration. When these are seen to be frequently set aside in favor of youth and inexperience, some must dread placing themselves where such a fate may await them in the course of a few years. Elsewhere, but not here, ripe age ordinarily, brings with it, when deserved, both less of the burden of securing a support, and more of the influence and honor which have been fairly earned. In the ministry there is to most only the prospect of hard work, frequent changes of residence, a limited support until middle life, and then an undeserved and humiliating dependence, merely because they have lived long enough and labored well enough to acquire maturity of character, judgment and experience in their sacred work. More frequently than it does would this deter some from giving themselves to the ministry, if their decision were not called for and made at a period of life when it is hard for them to realize that they will ever cease to be young men. But yet some do see the prospect. The experience of a revered pastor or parent may put it out of their power to overlook it. They cannot therefore avoid shrinking from a closer acquaintance with such an experience.

The activity of laymen in religious work, which is so pleasant a feature of Christian life in the present day, may be abused, so as to become a hindrance to the increase of ministers. Laymen are now much more active than formerly in ordinary religious meetings. They give a larger scope to their work in the Sabbath-School. They undertake much work which is peculiar to our Christian Associations. Not a few are actually lay-preachers. They hold religious meetings and speak on religious subjects, just as they speak on temperance at temperance meetings. This is all well. We are thankful for the good they do. Aaron and Joshua need no more be afraid of it now than of old, when Moses instead of checking Eldad and Medad, declared that he wished all the Lord's servants were prophets.

But we have said that this good thing may be perverted. It may in this way. A young man may feel the impulse to the work of a minister. It is, however, a long and hard course by which it is to be reached. He is already in business, or has a youth's impatience to be in it. He sees that men of business are active in the church, superintend Sabbath-schools, establish and conduct mission-schools, visit the sick, hold religious meetings and deliver religious addresses, with, as well as without, a text of Scripture. It is not strange if he thinks that he can do the same; nor if he thinks this comes very near to being a minister. In this way he too thinks he can be active in labors to save men without excluding himself from worldly business, and being dependent, first for an education, and then in prosecuting his work in the service of Christ. It seems as if he may do good, and yet be actively engaged in business, and thus take care of himself, and perhaps attain wealth, with which he can aid worthy students for the ministry, and even, at last, devote himself "at his own charges" to religious work. In the absence of this form of labor, some might devote themselves to the ministry, who now content themselves with this convenient and pleasant approximation to it.

It is also a serious question whether our churches give care for the future ministry sufficient consideration. We are very apt to neglect anything which does not press itself on our attention by our own experience of its necessity. And it is very comfortable to think that anything good or needful to society or the church will take care of itself. Many treat the future ministry as if they might thus leave it. They feel that it is very well, and quite natural, if some young man among them, left to himself, is stirred in his soul to give himself to this work, and gets into it, after running the gauntlet of all he sometimes must endure to discourage him, and turn him aside to some worldly business.

We have reason to suppose that Christians in other times thought and cared more about this than they now do. They felt the need of men more than we do. This led them to look for the evidence of gifts for the ministry in young men, and they were more ready to suggest their duty to them, or to encourage them to divulge their feelings and convictions in regard to this matter. There can be no question that they acted as they should. Christians always should pray and speak and act so that young men must consider whether it is their own duty to preach, and so that none of them can find any rest in neglect of duty.

From what we know, it is not an unnecessary fear that our churches, with their ministers, have so neglected to care, and so failed to express care, about the future ministers of the churches, that some young Christians have never felt that there is any pressing demands for recruits to fill the ranks of the ministry, or any danger that all who may be needed will not be secured.

It is not strange if we then find that there has also been neglect to pray to the Lord of the harvest for laborers. And without such prayer for them as he has enjoined on us, we cannot expect them. True ministers are called by God to their work. To pray for them, is the one direction Christ gave his servants in order to secure them. When himself pained at the sight of the fewness of the number who are laboring for the welfare and salvation of men, this is the one thing, and the only one, which he instructed his disciples to do in order to increase their number. When we resort to it, we take the course our Lord enjoined on us; when we neglect to do so, we have no promise that a supply will come to us in some other way.

It will make us confident that there has been neglect of this, if we endeavor to recall the number of times at which we have heard this prayer in social meetings, or even in the pulpit, except at an ordination. No sense of the importance of this matter seems to urge Christians to bring it in earnestness to the throne of God. We may well fear then, that the Lord withholds from his churches many whom he would bestow on them for ministers, if they asked him for them.

Ministers themselves have contributed something in the direction of hindering the increase of their number. This makes up the class of ministerial hindrances.

Many complaints have come from them respecting their ill-treatment by the churches. The world has heard much concerning the great demands made on them, and their meagre support; and their endurance of many inconveniences and many indignities. It is not pleasant to work very hard and be constantly shut up within narrow limits, even in respect to the ordinary comforts of life. Yet very many ministers have this to bear. The kind of care which this gives, and of carefulness which it cultivates, is not ennobling, nor elevating, nor spiritual. It aggravates all this, for a minister to know how precarious is his hold on the pastorate in which he is attempting to serve his Master amid all these embarrassments. A few persons in most of our churches or congregations have the power to render it uncomfortable, if not impossible for their pastor to retain his place, when they for any reason desire him to retire from it.

The facts are serious enough, but it is unfortunate that they have sometimes been published and dwelt on in such a fashion, by ministers themselves, as to make it a reflection on the manliness of any one that he should consent to seek, or accept, or even retain such a position To endure such things, and "provide things honorable in the sight of all men," seems impossible.

Any profession, when all its members and work are considered, can be presented on a side which is very humiliating and repulsive. It would not be fair to use a few of the most favored of our ministers to furnish a picture of the ordinary and average minister's life. It is just as unfair to use some of the least favored, whose experience has been the hardest, for the same purpose. Neither represents what is usual, and makes up the experience of the great body of faithful ministers. We object when a few extreme cases of domestic tyranny and abuse are employed, by the enemies of the family and domestic purity, to represent the ordinary lot of wives and mothers. We should be careful to avoid a similar misrepresentation, when we would attempt to secure for ministers a fairer appreciation and better treatment.

These complaints of the hard experience of ministers of course come under the notice of our young men and their friends. The obligation and capacity to accept such a trying position must be considered by any one who is settling the question of being a minister. It is represented as the lot of so many, that every one must count it among the probabilities, and not merely the possibilities, of his experience. This must hinder many from consenting to devote themselves to such work. It has, quite probably, stopped not a few.

But this is not all. Besides, it is common to encounter such statements of the grade of talents and the amount of requirements necessary for the ministry as make it a great assumption for any one in his senses to intimate that he even fears that it may be his duty to give himself to this work. Such statements are made in newspaper articles, in sermons, and in addresses on ministerial education, on the work of the preacher, and on the relation of the pulpit to the world or the age. A specimen of what is meant may be found in "The Sword and the Garment." This is a volume on preparation for the ministry which one of the professors in the Boston Theological Seminary recently published. It quotes Mr. Weiss, the biographer of Theodore Parker, as "happily expressing the truth," in a late essay, by saying, "Unless a man is born a great religious genius, who can learn instinctively, by contact with men and women, all that the present epoch needs, and can subsidize, as he walks, all the knowledge that divine truth claims for its support and recommendation, let him throw himself on the town's poor tax, sooner than become another kind of burden on the parish. How many such men are there? No man has fingers few enough to count them." This teacher of candidates for the Methodist ministry strangely commends this transcendental nonsense by adding, that "If Mr. Weiss were as correct in his interpretation of religion as of these matters, the world would have reason to rejoice." Perhaps "the world" would; but we are sure that neither the church nor any person who loves the welfare of men would do so.

The service of the Gospel indeed needs, and should have, the highest powers with which God ever endows men. But, that is quite another thing than saying, that it is a shame and an imposition, for any one of inferior capacity to undertake such work. When Christians, into whose souls the Holy Spirit has put the call to the ministry, in the form of fair talents, connected with ardent desire to save men from perdition, read or hear such things, they must either have strength to reject them, or else turn their minds away from their duty and God's call.

Again, the same error is committed by speaking as some do, about the studies and attainments necessary for a minister. What is very valuable, what every one should secure who can, what is the normal course in any proper system of intellectual training for the ministry, needs so much attention from those who have the welfare of the churches at heart, that we sometimes speak as if no one without all this were fit to enter a pulpit; and if he should force himself in must be frowned on until he retires from it in shame. This is so far from true, that some men have shown us, that one may avail himself of every help, to preparation for the ministry within reach on both sides of the ocean, and still be very inefficient; while not a few of the very leaders of all branches of the church in usefulness and power, have had only a small share of a full or even proper course of training. It is wrong then, because it is hurtful, not to put in the strongest lines, the distinction between what is desirable, and what is indispensable, what it were well if every one could enjoy, and what is sufficient to give a man whom God calls to be his minister, promise of usefulness. The space is wide enough between complete preparation for the pulpit and exclusion from it, to condemn any confusion of the two.

But many have heard such things on this subject, as have made them think that thorough preparation and exclusion touch each other, and there is no middle ground between them. They had not the one, and their age and circumstances precluded them from securing it. They therefore considered themselves pushed over to the other, as the only place left for them.

In some cases, the pride remaining in the converted man, may have hastened and fixed this decision. Those churches do the most, and the best work for

Christ and men, which engage all the best talents and highest qualifications, they can command in their service, and yet have a place, and encouragement, and work, and respect for all grades of capacity, and qualification which they can secure and employ.

We must also give place here, to the influence of the large number of ministers who are without employment. These make the impression that the number is already too large, or that only unusual endowments adapt a man to the ministry, and thus exaggerate the probability of failure, on the part of any one who undertakes this work. It is not strange if the difficulty of explaining why so many are not at work, after they have actually entered the vineyard of the Master, should present to many a hindrance to following them, if not an excuse for not incurring the danger of a similar experience.

These hindrances to the increase of the number of ministers of Christ, add their weight to the social and ecclesiastical ones. But there are also some others which we must charge to Christian parents. The biographies of ministers, teach us how large a place parents have in the decision of young men to preach the gospel. The call of many, in this world, began in the hearts of their parents; in not a few cases, even before their birth. The feeling has sometimes been a common one among the pious, that in every family of sons, there must, as in the family of Jacob, be one Levi. And this was not felt as a duty merely, but as a privilege. It was desired as an honor.

Such a feeling seems more rare now. There appear to be fewer Samuels who have been asked of the Lord, to be given back to him for his service. Perhaps this is traceable in part to the fact, that the need of ministers is not pressed on the notice of Christians, by prevailing alarm at an evident scarcity. But we may fear that it must in the main, be charged to the unfavorable social influences which now affect the pulpit, the severe demands and criticisms endured from the churches, the hard fare, which ministers of no more than average abilities frequently suffer, and the attractive and facile openings and promises, which secular business furnishes. Above all, the prevalent worldliness affects the piety of parents, so that they do not esteem it a good thing for a son, and a privilege for themselves, that he should serve God in the ministry of his Son, instead of competing for the prizes of this world, in the fields of business and honor.

Even ministers have spoken in such a way of their own sons, in this relation, that we may suspect that not a few Christians have checked, instead of welcoming and fostering, the Spirit's call of their children to this work. They must then have submitted to it when it came, instead of rejoicing in it; and they must have feared its coming, rather than prayed earnestly to secure it.

If this has been the case, we must reckon this parental influence among the forces existing in the churches themselves to repel young men from the ministry. Of course this makes it necessary that the impulse of the love of souls, and of the gospel, and the conviction of duty, should be very strong, far stronger than would be necessary in the absence of these unfavorable influences.

All these things weaken the things which need strengthening in this great business of providing our churches with ministers; and at the same time strengthen those which need to have their natural force abated. They make this work seem to young Christians more arduous and less important than it really is, and less worthy of the exclusive employment of a man's life. At the same time, they give to business and wealth and honor and power and display and luxury a false glare and a factitious importance, which render it all the harder to turn one's back on them.

A call to the ministry of Christ does sometimes come to men in our days with almost the distinctness with which theirs came to Isaiah or Paul. But this is not usual. It is more commonly like the quiet summons of the disciples to leave all, and go to men and preach the gospel. It is a deliberate sense of duty, gained by the leading of the Holy Spirit in connection with a man's situation and characteristics. It must, therefore, feel the influence of circumstances. And just as surely as some have entered the ministry uncalled, others have been called, but have yielded to the hindrances in their way and refused to go. It would be strange if many young men did not see with too little clearness and feel with too little force the claims of Christ and souls on them under such circumstances as those claims now come to them. Any conviction of theirs about preaching, or any impulse to it, finds itself surrounded by obstacles, repelling in one direction, and alluring in the other, but hindering in both, their decision to perform what they suspect to be, and what in fact is their duty.

We cannot, in view of all this, be sufficiently thankful that there are yet so many who, in the face of every obstacle, are drawn into the ministry. Statistics recently furnished by our Publication Society, show that we have been saved from any greatly increased disproportion between the number of our ministers and that of our churches and members amid the large increase of our denomination during the last twenty years. We should be thankful that, while we need many more, we are so much better furnished than we could expect to be.

We have but little room to refer to what we may do in weakening and diminishing these hindrances to the increase of our ministers. The mere statement and enumeration of the hindrances should be sufficient to bring into existence counteracting influences. But on all Christians one duty certainly devolves. That is, to secure a piety which will cause them to feel that all which pertains to this world is as inferior to the soul in importance and excellence, as they know it in truth is; and that all which relates to the soul is really as grand and precious as they profess to regard it. Then they will be less worldly. Then they will more truly value and honor work which is devoted to the saving and training of men for eternity and heaven. Then they will treat the work of the minister of their Lord in such a way, that the young men of the church will not dread it. They will be aided to consider their own duty in respect to it with more candor, and less obstacles to a right decision. Christians should not regard the ministry with any superstitious reverence, but they should show that they understand and appreciate its work, and expect only what is reasonable in its performance. No more than this is needed to remove many things which are the most serious obstructions to the increase of ministers now existing either in our churches, or in the world amid which we live, and to which we must carry the word of reconciliation and salvation, or leave it to perish in its sins forever.

Dr. LAMSON: I want to express in the first place my appreciation of the importance of the subject before us,—and my appreciation too of the excellence and thoroughness of the essay to which we have just listened. I am called out on a committee, but there is a single point in the essay to which I wish to direct attention,—our brother's reference to Mr. WEISS in the biography of THEODORE PARKER. To be sure, if none but religious geniuses are to be put into the ministry a good many of us ought to go out at once. But at the same time it is true that a large number of men have been pushed through the preparatory course for the ministry, and have entered into the ministry, who are now unemployed. In the State of Massachusetts, although there is a large number of churches without pastors, there is almost an equal number of pastors or ministers without churches; and a young man in Massachusetts who is contemplating the question whether he shall enter the ministry or not, if he attends one of our Conventions, and hears the number of churches without pastors, if it ended there might think there was a great demand for ministers and rush into the ministry; but if he waits and hears how many ministers are without churches, and how many ministers have gone into secular occupation, he will feel there is already a superfluity of ministers in the State of Massachusetts. Now the question occurs, why is this? I think we are to look back in the first place to the churches who have recommended these young men to seek a preparation for the ministry. A young man has been converted, and in the fervor of his Christian experience has some disposition to exhort in the prayer meeting. Good brethren and sisters of the country churches feel that there is talent there that ought to be occupied in the ministry. Some one mentions it to him and he thinks so too. In a few weeks he is recommended to apply to the Education Society, the Board of which meets in Boston, to be made a beneficiary, to prepare for the ministry. These churches are not always capable of judging whether a young man is by natural gifts and by qualifications fitted for the work of the ministry, They have a love for him and his Christian zeal. They recommend him, and in due time he comes before the Board in Boston. There there are certain influences perhaps that are inclining us to accept the young man. There are a few young men about whom we have hesitated in years that are past, who have been accepted and have proved useful. Therefore when one or two such instances come up to our recollection, we say, such a young man we hesitated about, but we accepted him and he has gone through his preparation and has been eminently successful in the ministry. Influenced by such examples we too often put forward cases which are doubtful, and thus a large number of men have been pushed through their preparatory course by beneficiary aid. If I may be permitted to name a little incident—I had an associate in my early studies who thought he ought to enter the ministry. He came from Vermont to prepare. He was a vigorous, athletic young man when he came to the academy. He came with an impulse in his heart that it was his duty to preach the Gospel.

He was my companion through my preparatory course, and then entered college with me, and was my companion through college. He was eminently a Christian man. We separated after our college course. He went through Newton. I did not till afterwards. Some ten or twelve years later I was in a neighboring state attending a convention. At the close of the morning services this brother said to me, I want to speak to you. We walked out into the woods and sat down on a log, and he looked up to me with an expression of countenance I shall never forget. He said, my brother, I should thank God for any providence that would render it right for myself and wife to go to the almshouse and spend our days there. I looked up to him in astonishment. Said I, what do you mean? He said, I will tell you. You know when I came from Vermont, I was a strong, vigorous man. The course of study has ruined my health. I am not able to get my living. You know too, that my early education was such I am not fit to be a teacher, and there is not a church that wants to employ me. Can you tell me what I shall do to support myself and wife and children? I turned away and told him I did not know. Now, if that young man had been told by his church or education society when he presented himself to become a beneficiary, that he had better serve God and his race in some other line than the Christian ministry, it would have been a mercy to him and to the Church of Christ. While, therefore, I fully accord with what brother MILLS has said, and enjoy it exceedingly, I think there is danger on the other side.—That one of the reasons why young men, fit for the ministry, are not pressing into the work, is that there is such a large number in all, as in the New England States, that have gone through the preparatory studies and are without employment.

Dr. ROBINSON: I am unable to keep my seat, although it was not my intention to make any remarks in this connection. Twenty years' experience in teaching in a theological seminary has made me acquainted with some facts, and awakened my mind to some considerations which have taken strong hold upon me. I suppose there is no more perplexing question at this hour among the several denominations, than to know what to do with a large class of unemployed ministers. It is one of the most perplexing questions of the General Assembly of the Presbyterian Church of North America. They have proposed to organize a bureau, and I believe they have adopted some kind of measure by which to bring the unemployed ministers into relationship with the unsupplied churches. One of their most prominent men said to me a few weeks since: "With us the question is not how to get more men, but what to do with our unemployed men; it is not an increase of numbers, but of kind; it is not quantity, but quality." Now, is the deficiency in the men themselves? I suppose there is no greater deficiency of talent in the ministry than in other professions. On the whole, I am well satisfied that the general culture, breadth of understanding, amount of acquisition and discipline in the ministry to-day, is fifty per cent. superior to that of the profession of law or of medicine. [Applause]. I speak advisedly upon this subject. And yet you may say, "Preachers, preachers everywhere, and not a man they want." The churches say, "We desire a man equal to our position." "Well, there is Rev. Mr. So-and-So." "Yes, we have heard him. He does not meet our wants." What is the solution of this? There are men who have worked laboriously, men of capacity, acquisition, honesty, zeal, self-sacrifice, and yet by some sort of mystery they fail to meet the demand which is made upon them. There was a remark of great significance dropped by Dr. SEARS yesterday morning, that the young preacher who, for the first ten or fifteen years, is very popular, and is received with great applause, finds that at forty his popularity begins to decline, and at fifty nobody wants him. Now, why should not a man at fifty years of age be as much stronger, more effective, more sought for than at thirty as he is more mature? At fifty years of age, a man with an unbroken constitution should be an abler man, a wiser man, a man of profounder sympathies, a man of more tender susceptibilities than he was at thirty. He will be, if he is a true man. He is more competent as a spiritual adviser. Why, then, should he not be a man better fitted for the work of the ministry? Is there not a fault somewhere? Haven't we got an idea lurking among us that we are a caste? Suppose instead of assuming that we are to have this, that and the other, because we are ministers, suppose we take off our coats and say, "In God's name, is there work to be done here?" [Applause]. I occupy a sort of midway position between the clergy and the laity. I have never yet seen a Christian church anywhere that opened its eyes to a man earnest, self-forgetful, honest, intent on doing his duty day by day, and doing it earnestly—and to do it earnestly is to do it successfully—I have never yet seen a church that did not lay hold of him and say, "Brother, you must live and die with us." Is it not true anywhere? Take the business man, take the clerk. A man who has grown up with the business and knows what it is, will not be sent adrift. No, they increase his salary and hold on to him. Why should it not be so with the ministry? Now, while saying that I am not unaware that there is another side to this subject. There is another side of this great truth; when a man has worked long, laboriously cultivated the vineyard, he becomes aware sometimes that somebody is suggesting, "Would not a change be advisable?" and before long he is turned adrift. People do not sympathize with him. How shall that side of the subject be disposed of? Brethren, I am better acquainted with that side than I am with the method of disposing of it. What are the inducements now offered to young men to enter the Christian ministry? They are actually bought up and paid for entering into the Christian ministry. I have known young men to say, "I have given myself to the ministry, and I expect now to be provided for."

They start out with that idea. When a young man says, "I propose to give myself to the law," he has no common treasury to which to resort. He works on laboriously, and expects to live a laborious, self-denying life for ten, twelve, fifteen or twenty years. What right has a young man who is called to the ministry, to demand that he be supported and cared for simply because he has obeyed his conscience? What right has he to expect it any more than a mechanic who says, "God has laid upon my shoulders a bed-ridden mother, and I must care for her." Suppose he should stand up and say, "Gentlemen, it is a great hardship. I have a sick and suffering mother. I want the church to take care of me." What is the difference? When God laid it upon my conscience to go into the ministry, I struggled and resisted desperately, but I did not know that I had the slightest right to ask anybody to give me a cent—and, thank God, nobody ever did. [Laughter]. I have known young men who received from an education society in one State a certain amount for their support, to go from that State to another, and receive the same amount from another education society. I have known young men to receive aid in this manner from three distinct sources, and leave school with a better library than many a man has after five years' experience. I have known letters to be written to the theological seminaries to know the amount they furnished to beneficiaries. I have known young men to enter into minute calculations as to the expense in the several seminaries, and, after striking a balance, say, "I go to the place where I am best paid." Brethren, there is something in this to be thought of and to be talked of. This is the place to talk of it, perhaps, if anywhere. I don't know that it ought to be talked of anywhere, but I have been pained sometimes as I have looked young men in the face and said, "What will come of it?" This is something that ought to be thought of. There ought to be an understanding on this subject. No worthy young man ought to be allowed to suffer. I don't believe in encouraging the kind of thing that the stories refer to, nor do I believe the stories, about young men living on oatmeal gruel and corn cakes. I don't believe there is a place in our land where young men are trying to live on corn meal and molasses. This is a land of plenty. Wherever you can find a young man who has genius or a calling, or an earnest, nameless something that carries him irresistibly over all obstacles —when you meet such a man stretch out your hand. I am happy to say that I have known for years past a class of business men in New York who say, "Every young man that needs aid, if you will put your name to his endorsement, we will aid and carry him through."

Dr BOSWORTH: This latter part of the gentleman's remarks I hope will be remembered when the subject comes up at a future part of our session. There are many points to be considered, and I may, if permitted, speak a word on that point then, and, withal, refresh the memory of my brother, as I am able to do, on one point correcting him. But there is one point which has been alluded to, to which I beg permission to call attention now, as having been impressed with great weight on my own mind. I would say, as expressing my own thought at this moment, two things bearing in the direction of "hindrances." The one is that it becomes ministers to have true ideas of the character, the importance, and the dignity that belongs to their calling. It seems to me that proper views in this direction would have something to do towards controlling the hindrances so fairly presented. But without dwelling on this there is another point, around which I think cluster most solemn responsibilities, where I think we are at fault; and I speak of the ministry as a body. There are several gate-ways to the ministry, through which every aspirant to that office must pass before he enters the temple and takes up the sacred vessels. One was alluded to by my friend, Dr. LAMSON—the church that sends a young man to the Education Society. Another of these gateways is the Boards of Education Societies, and of the Theological Institutions. The examinations of these candidates are very nearly the same. Every one of these candidates must be subjected to these examinations, and be let through the gate-way. Now, of course there are some difficulties in forming a judgment in a church. They are hopeful for a young man. There is need of a large increase in the ministry; and if there is any promise of talent in the young man, they are likely to see it, and if there is any hope they are likely to feel it, and so are willing in the judgment of charity to send the young man along, hoping that if he is subjected to trial, and should be found incompetent, he may be checked farther on in the course. But the last gate-way is found at his ordination; and from my observation, I am seriously convinced that it is at the last gate way that many pass in, on whose heads the hands of the bishops should never be laid. It seems to me that this last and highest responsibility lies with the ministry, and they ought to exercise it in the fear of our Ascended Christ, and with a most profound regard for the interests of his church and of the world. Let me give you one simple illustration. A young man was sent to me, as Secretary of the Education Society, in the hope that he might be aided. The policy of the society is not to render pecuniary aid to any young man until he has entered college. He had been to an academy and had left it for an unsatisfactory reason. I advised with him, and in endeavoring to aid him, sent him to one of our more promising preparatory schools, with a letter of introduction to the principal of that school, commending him to his care and scrutiny. He gave him both care and scrutiny. After a few weeks I heard from him that he had got more light on the subject of communion. I am not quite sure he did not join the Congregational Church. After playing about in this fashion for a while, I was informed by a friend that a certain church in New Hampshire, up in the hills, had recently received a new pastor.

What is his name? Mr. So-and-so. "What were his initials, his Christian name?" Could not remember. I inquired a little, what sort of a man he was, and I was satisfied it was the same young man. Pursuing the inquiry, I found it was; and a few weeks after I met one of the ordaining council, a minister of excellent training and excellent character, in whose judgment I should, in nine cases out of ten, confide. I addressed him in a very familiar way and said, "What on earth did you lay hands on this young man for?" He said, "I did not wish to, but the council did not want to refuse him." I said, "You yielded. If you had stood up like a man and followed the convictions you uttered to me, you might have saved the church from disaster." That man has made a wreck of everything. Now that is, I know, rather an extraordinary case, but it is one of too many of similar character. It does seem to me that while the ministry is suffering from that large class to whom reference has been made, we may charge to our own account somewhat of this difficulty.

Dr. TURNBULL: First of all, I heartily endorse the essay which has been read. I also endorse in the fullest way the remarks made by Dr. ROBINSON. My soul was stirred by them, and I, like him, could not keep my seat. Indeed, what is the chaff to the wheat? where you have good wheat you have much chaff. And you must let the chaff go. I do not make so much account of the refuse. A great many must leave the duties of the ministry on account of ill health, on account of failure as to body, failure as to mind, failure as to circumstances, the condition of their families, and so on. A great question presses upon us, and every one feels it. Every young minister feels it, every old minister especially feels it; every teacher in our theological schools feels it; and I believe almost every church member feels it in some degree, but a great many do not quite understand it. There is failure on both sides. Although I admit the deficiencies on both sides, upon the whole I admire my brethren of the Christian ministry, and can say all sorts of good things of those who hold on and do their duty as best they can in the work of their Master; and, upon the whole, I can say many good things of our churches, especially those churches with which I have been connected, and above all of that good old church in Hartford, Connecticut, of which I was pastor for about twenty-four years. For my part I am surprised that they treated me so well from the beginning to the end. But since I ceased to become their pastor in name, I have learned a great many things, and some things about this matter. I will call attention to one or two points only, as my time is short. In the first place, a minister, to be a true minister, must be called of God. That is an old doctrine, I know, but we must emphasize it over and over again. And that man, therefore, by the call is proved to have a genius for the Christian ministry, for he is a man called of God. Jesus Christ is in him, and he must speak, if he speaks at all, by the inspiration of the Almighty, not as an orator, but as a man of God. He must speak as a sort of prophetic man. That is to say, a man that speaks from God; for that is the old idea of a prophet—a man that speaks from God and for God. If he so speaks, he will be heard everywhere. But the temptation now-a-days is to speak of something else.

And now, in reference to the churches. Is it so, that our churches want to keep a man until he dies? I do not believe the churches want the ministers to live and die with them. I wish I had more time to discuss this subject. I have left it very bare; but my time is exhausted.

The President stated that there would be opportunity for further discussion of substantially the same subject, after the reading of the paper on the Methods and Limits of Beneficiary Aid.

Dr. BAILEY: Reference has been made here this morning, to a large number of ministers who are not employed now by churches, as if there were some great fault in reference to this, as if some great mistake had been made to bring about this state of things. But I well recollect when I went as missionary to the capital of the state of Illinois twenty-six years ago, there was a district of country around me as large as the entire State of Massachusetts, with not another Baptist minister in the whole field who was devoted entirely to the work of the ministry. What if occasionally a farmer preached a sermon, did we not rejoice to have such co-laborers then? What if we occasionally ordained a man to the ministry who had not received a college education? Such men were indeed in the field, and such men have done a grand work in the fields of the West; although they were not wholly given to the work of the ministry. In the progress of the settlement of the country and advancement of intelligence, many of these ministers who were thus ordained to meet an absolute necessity, are not now employed. They are doing a little work occasionally here and there; they are men of God. They are not prepared to occupy prominent fields and churches there now; but let us not speak of them as if they were outcasts. Let us not speak of them as if they were men who never ought to have been ordained to the ministry. We honor their memory. We look back upon their services with thanksgiving to God that he raised up such men. We will not overlook their noble and self-sacrificing services. Reference has been here made to the Seminary through which young men are introduced to the ministry. It has been said here that they were bought up, and that those who give the largest premium will get the young men; and it has been remarked here that young men sometimes receive competent support from three different sources. Coming from one city they receive aid from that Board, and then from the Institution to which they come.

Dr. ROBINSON: (Addressing Dr. BAILEY.) You have used the word "competent" which I did not use. I did not say "competent support." I simply said they had three strings to their bow.

Dr. BAILEY: Let me remark that we are not in the habit of doing things that way out West; and it seems to me that any Board of Education rightly doing its work would diligently inquire into the means of support that a young man has. A Board of Education should never furnish aid to a young man without diligent inquiry as to his means of support and other sources of help. Let me say still farther that there are many young men whose hearts are burning to enter the work of the ministry, who can perhaps manage to get along with a course of study occupying ten or fifteen years by working half their time for their support if they choose to do so, or can, perhaps, borrow the money and come out of the institution a thousand dollars in debt to be burdened with that debt for the next ten years. But is that the best way to do this thing? If our young men have afforded them while prosecuting their studies an amount of aid which is absolutely necessary, after they are using all due diligence to help themselves, it seems to me that this beneficiary aid is a very important matter. You can call to mind some of the noblest men that the land has ever had that have been beneficiaries, and have needed that assistance. Some are on this floor to-day, men whom the churches honor, men who have made their mark in the world. I can rejoice in saying with Dr. ROBINSON I never received one cent from beneficiary aid while prosecuting my studies, but there are men in the ministry much better than I, who have been aided in the prosecution of their studies.

Dr. CUTTING: Though the hour is far past, there are a few things which I should be glad to say upon this subject—a subject in which I have been for a long time profoundly interested, from the conviction that there is an apathy in the Baptist denomination, and in other Christian denominations, in reference to the future ministry of the Christian Church, which is perilous to the interests of Christianity. Nor is it a thing of our own country alone. It is a difficulty of other countries as well. One of the greatest perils of the Established Church of England to-day, has reference to the future ministry of that church. The great body of the young men going into the ministry of the Established Church of England to-day, are not well educated men. They are not graduates of Oxford or of Cambridge. I suppose at least eighty per cent. of those now entering the ministry of the Church of England go through the short course of the Diocesan Colleges, and not through the University. I met, at a dinner at Brighton, in England, a clergyman of the Church of England, to whom I spoke upon this subject, and he said to me that the great body of the graduates of the universities could not be induced to enter the ministry of the Church of England for love or money; that the civil service law of England, opening to the competition of the young scholars civil promotion, and taking them at that period, when, graduating from the universities, they were too young to enter the ministry, drew those young men at once to examination for civil positions, and they took civil positions, abandoning the ministry, while formerly they were accustomed in such large numbers from those universities to enter it. I met at Liverpool two clergymen of the Church of England, who were of this class of men, who had gone through the Diocesan Colleges by short courses to the ministry, and they expressed to me the profoundest regret and even alarm at the tendency of things in England in respect to this matter; that while rationalism was so fortifying itself at Oxford, and sending forth so many of its emissaries, Christianity was finding so few there who were to be the ministers of its churches. Now we are experiencing similar difficulties in this country. There is a hesitation on the part of young men of energy and force and enterprise to go into the Christian ministry. There is a reluctance on the part of parents who are well to do, to train up their sons with the idea of going into the ministry, if it shall please God to call them to that service. I do not believe that every man goes into the ministry whose duty it is to go into the ministry. A call to the ministry is a call which may be declined, as may any other call of duty be declined. Young men in families well to do and rich, receiving the blessings of the gospel, are under the same obligations to the ministry of the Christian Church, as the sons of the poor. [Applause]. We are all one in Christ Jesus, and I fear any plan of filling the ministry of our churches, which depends, on principle, upon training the sons of the poor only for the ministry. It is the duty of the poor to contribute their portion, and the duty of the rich to help them. I believe in education societies and the beneficiary system, but I do not believe that the sons of the rich have the right to decline the ministry of Christ any more than the sons of the poor have the right to decline it. [Applause]. I want to see a new sentiment in the Baptist denomination, and a new sentiment in American churches generally, on this subject. For the ministry is so important to the progress of Christianity, that unless the best minds are willing to enter, and do enter, joyfully upon the ministry, the cause of Christ must be so far retarded through the unfaithfulness of the people of God.

Hon. Mr. DOOLITTLE: I had no intention of speaking on this subject; I came as a listener simply. There has been, however, one point which has impressed itself on my mind, which I have not yet heard discussed, to-wit, that education in its greatest and broadest sense means the education of the whole man. We have heard his mental, moral and religious education discussed with great ability, but there is one species of education which, in America, I think is neglected in most of our schools, and that which I believe lies at the foundation—that is physical education, the education of the body; this Temple of the Holy Ghost; this body which gives all the vital force to the mind; this body upon which the brain must rely for its power, if it would move man morally, intellectually or in religious matters. I believe one of the greatest defects of our religious training, both of males and females, is the fact that the brain is constantly educated—is overtasked very often, and our educated young men and young women come home from seminaries of learning educated almost to death; come home too frequently to die; come home without the power which is necessary to give them force and strength in any department of life. I think one of the reasons why our educated men sometimes are not more successful in leading public opinion, is the fact that they have exhausted their vital powers, and that they have ceased to have that kind of relation with the common mass of men which has its power or influence, a sort of physical or animal magnetism, if you please, which impresses them. Now, I think our theological schools and others that have young men in their control, should aim to develop not only mind but body; to make them perfect, strong men, capable of enduring the hardships and the rough and tumble of life. Such a young man in every society, Christian society and everywhere, will have a power and an influence and popularity which he could not have if he did not retain his physical power, as well as mental and intellectual power. It may be said with truth, that all this applies also to our American young women. To one that looks over our country, with an eye to things as they are, as we see the decay, so to speak, of the American men and women, it is a source of great sorrow, especially to those who look to the future of our country. We know very well that the supplies coming from abroad, and the children of foreign-born parents, are largely taking possession of this country. We ought, it seems to me, to use our influence everywhere, our pastors, our schools, to build up our American women, intellectually, morally and religiously, and not the least, to adorn the beautiful temple where dwells the Holy Spirit.

At the request of the President, the Hon. Mr. DOOLITTLE, Vice President, took the chair.

Hon. Mr. WAYLAND: I had no intention of saying anything when this discussion commenced. But it seems to me that some remarks should be made especially pertaining to the exact subject of the essay from the point of view of a layman. What I say, I say with unaffected diffidence because I have not that experience which entitles me to consideration from such gentlemen as I see before me. But I want to make a few simple suggestions really in the form of questions. Now, to consider the matter practically, let us take the case of a new religious society of our denomination. In the present day every society in the city—I have no experience with any other society—wishes to erect what will be a handsome church, an edifice that will compare favorably with those of other denominations. Now, we suppose them beginning like sensible men, only as they can pay. They erect a chapel. On what basis shall they select a pastor? I may venture to suggest that this is really the business of the church and not of the society. But, practically, the society, paying the money, regulate this matter. Now, they look first and foremost as a society for the best and most attractive talent. They say, "We must have a man who will fill the pews; although we are a chapel, we shall be a church. Those who hear the man in the chapel suppose that he will be in the church, and we must get such a man as will enable us to build such a church as we want." I don't say whether it is right or wrong. I don't know that I am competent to judge. But that is the fact. Man after man comes before them. Honest, worthy, able, if you please. But there may be some slight defect in his manner which prevents his being quite acceptable. There may be two or three rich men in the parish who for one reason or another say, "If that gentleman is called we shall decline to subscribe." Man after man is tried and rejected until by and by they find somebody, and very often not the right one. Every man who is rejected suffers from that rejection. He goes before the public as a rejected candidate. It is not his fault. I don't know how far it is the fault of the society. It certainly is not his fault. Then what is the test by which this society judges of the ability, the popularity, the possible or probable success of the candidate. They judge of the man by the standard of a lecturer—a most erroneous and unfair standard to be sure, but that is the fact. A brilliant man prepares with much care one or two lectures. He delivers those lectures everywhere. Those members of the society who don't go to the theatre, the circus or the opera, go to the lecture. And those members go on Sunday to the church. If their candidate does not come pretty near the standard of the most popular lecturers in the field they say, "He won't draw and we don't want him." Then again it is easy for a few discontented men in any society to unsettle any minister if they have sufficient perseverance. [Applause.] An able, honest, worthy and most faithful clergyman can in six months be ejected from his church and turned adrift upon the world without a dollar in his pocket and with a family to support, for no other reason than the enmity of two or three men. [Applause.] I have seen it over and over again. I never knew it tried thoroughly where it failed. Now, this certainly is not the fault of the clergyman. Then again societies after about twenty years get tired of these clergymen. If he does not exchange sometimes they certainly get tired of him. If he does exchange they compare him with the younger, more brilliant and certainly fresher men that they hear from time to time, and the comparison is to his disadvantage practically Then again, they do not appreciate, it seems to me, the intellectual labor—to say nothing of the moral responsibility and pressure upon their minister—the intellectual labor of the clergyman. Not one of the society is called upon to write two sermons a week or to do any sort of work that compares with it. The labor of the lawyer is compared with it to the disadvantage of the clergyman. But the labor of the lawyer and the labor of the clergyman are two things, and different as light and darkness. The lawyer has constant excitement, change and variety, with the impending prospect of a large and increasing fee. It makes a difference so great that the comparison is absolutely good for nothing.

One other point. Nobody seems willing that the pastor should save money. Well, why in the name of common sense should he not? If he pays a sufficient amount of money annually for his life insurance the daily comforts of his family are abridged. With very few and exceptional cases in large cities no pastor can pay a premium on a thousand dollar policy and give proper comforts to his family. But the very moment a clergyman ventures, in a small way, to lay aside something he is called penurious and mean, and suffers discredit from that moment. With this additional account in the bill of indictment I have against *somebody*, I close what I have to say. [Laughter and applause].

The PRESIDENT: (resuming the chair). It does not come with very good grace from the one who made the last speech to say that the discussion must be closed, but really the time is long past. [Laughter].

The following communication was received and read:

PHILADELPHIA, May 29th, 1872.

To the Baptist National Educational Convention:

In behalf of Mr. William Bucknell, of this city, we hereby extend to the members of the Convention a cordial invitation to partake of a Breakfast in the pavilion at Fairmount Park, on Friday morning at 9½ o'clock.

H. G JONES,
W. R. BUCKNELL,
W. W. KEEN, } *Committee.*

On motion of Rev. C. H. WINSTON, the thanks of the Convention were tendered for the invitation, which was unanimously accepted.

Prof. GEORGE D. B. PEPPER, D.D., of Crozer Theological Seminary, read a paper on

WHAT IS A THEOLOGICAL EDUCATION?

To this question, we demand as Christian educators a Christian answer, and as practical workers a practical answer. The prescribed brevity of this paper excludes fulness of discussion, and admits an attempt at suggestion only. The course of thought is naturally determined by the statement of the theme, for as the word "education" designates a process, the word "Theological" designates the sphere of the process. Reversing this order, we consider the sphere first and then the process.

I. *What is Theology?* We are here in the interest of our schools. We would know what properly belongs in them, and into what they are to introduce their pupils. The subject now in hand, therefore, should be treated with direct reference to the theological school. The term theology, in order to this, will be used not in its merely etymological, or its historical sense, but rather as designating the body of study properly constituting a theological seminary's course.

The proper business of a theological school, as of any other institution, is to be determined by the end for which it exists. If then we know what is the true end of theological seminaries, we shall be in a fair way to understand what is properly comprised in their course of study. But they obviously exist, in general, for the development of Christian life in the world, and in particular for the immediate preparation of the religious teacher requisite for this development. The history of the different seminaries shows that they have been originated and sustained to serve this purpose, to meet this one want, and that unless they continue to meet it, they must be cast off as incumbrances. The church will not maintain them when they cease to be demanded for the general good.

Now the religious teaching, needed for the life of the church, is manifestly that which pertains to life and which nourishes it. The seminary, therefore, has to do with the doctrine of the Christian life. It has so to teach its students this doctrine that they in turn can become its teachers in the various spheres demanding their labor. But this Christian life is nothing else than God's kingly rule, freely accepted and obeyed; loving loyalty to his divine government, and the doctrine of the Christian life is the doctrine of this government as administered on earth. If we call this the Kingdom of God, we shall have as the definition of the Theology which constitutes the legitimate seminary course, "The doctrine, or science of the Kingdom of God." Like Medicine and Jurisprudence, it is a practical science, cultivated, not for any theoretic purpose, but to unite God and man in holy love, for the healing of the soul and for the advancement of moral government. And well has an able German writer remarked, that "he who is not inclined to serve the church as the Kingdom of God with his attainments and scientific activity by exhibiting the unity of the divine and human as it was actually realized in Christ, and by aiding to give this union increasing realization, among men, has not in him a single theological vein."

If we ask for the central principle, the common bond of theological studies, it will be found in the central fact of the Kingdom of God. But the central fact of government universally is law. The word government is a term of relationship. It implies two parties, the ruling and the ruled, the Sovereign and the Subject, and law is the bond of relationship. It makes of the parties ruler and ruled, sovereign and subject. In this respect God's government over man is no exception. The moral law, God's preceptive will, is the centre in which converge all the facts of the divine kingdom, the pivot on which all turns. Man's will accepting God's will—this is the very essence of religious life. It would have been so if redemption had never been needed. It is so under the redemption provided. So too all irreligion is rejection of the divine will by the human will. "Sin is the transgression of the law." The single fact of moral law gives to human existence all its sublime and awful import. This alone has made possible sin, redemption, holiness; a religion, a revelation, a church; a heaven and a hell,—eternal life and eternal death—the majestic harmony, the terrific discord. This it is, then, that both gives to us our Theological studies, and determines their nature, range and relations.

"The theology of the schools," having such aim and principle, stands opposed first of all to those baseless speculations of the understanding, which falsely claiming to be scientific attempt in defiance of the first law of science, not to learn from existing evidence what is, but to determine *a priori* what must be. Though such speculation usurp the name theology, it still remains a mischievous perversion of thought, and is no better than intellectual suicide. Thinking to construct from the timbers of his own imagination the universe including God, the dreamer only builds the perishable monument of his own folly, and while he calls upon us to see the eternal reality, he exhibits a vanishing phantasy. Our nature's quenchless thirst for truth, theology at least attempts to gratify, never mocks. It will not consent that an idle dream or baseless speculation, much less a deliberate lie, shall take the place of truth.

If in this it is not alone, but at one with all genuine science, it yet has in this a far deeper interest, an interest quite inapproachable and all its own, and hence sets itself to the accomplishment of its work with a quite matchless energy.

Again, "the theology of the schools," as eminently practical in aim, stands in favorable contrast with studies which are mainly or wholly theoretical, remotely, if at all, connected with human life and development. Knowledge, for its own sake, is worth seeking, and there is no truth accessible to mortals that may not also minister in some measure to the general good. Still the whole man is greater and nobler than a single power of man, and that knowledge has the greater value which immediately and predominantly serves the sensibility and the will, nourishes the whole system so as to give symmetry and strength, and thus comes out to view in the fuller and purer life. True utilitarianism is to be, not scouted and shunned, but lauded and cherished. Theology has indeed been sometimes branded as unpractical, and on this ground condemned and abused. How false is this charge, if urged against the genuine theology, has already been shown. This does indeed present to the speculative reason many profound and even insoluble problems, and does not forbid the attempt to solve and settle them, but the unsolved and insoluble problems are not theology, and he is no true theologian who finds his entire calling in wrestling as an athlete. The seminary is not intended for circle squarers or inventors of perpetual motion. Speculation is there subject, not king, for theology culminates not in thought but in life.

The "theology of the schools," yet again, by virtue of its aim as moral or spiritual, stands to all other departments of truth in the contrast of kingly pre-eminence. Even Darwin regards conscience as the last and most perfect development from the prolonged and prolific struggle for existence. Consciousness, human history, and God's Word, with a single voice and a startling emphasis, assure us that in our moral-religious nature centres our infinite worth, that if this be ruined, nothing is saved, while if this be saved, nothing is, nothing can be, ruined. Down from heaven, up from hell, out from the great deep of our own being, along through all the generations past, with solemn and sublime authority sounds the clear testimony: "FIRST THE KINGDOM OF GOD." At this testimony an able and well-nigh dominant school of philosophy contemptuously sneer, and stigmatize it as "other-worldness." Sedulously with elaborate reasoning and persuasive diction they inculcate and insinuate the opposite doctrine of *this worldness*—a doctrine not original with them, but first promulgated in Eden by their spiritual father, and faithfully transmitted through generations of the crawling fraternity. But this crew are not to gain command of the sea of God, for as its wrath-lashed waves have swept over many another pirate ship as noble as their own, so too shall theirs and they be engulfed. So then, not more by the difficulty of its problems and the vastness of its objects of thought, than by the supreme transcendence of its practical aim, is fixed the rank of theology as queen of all human sciences. This imports that the contrast is not that of antagonism, but of pre-eminence. Theology can no more be unfriendly to other departments of truth, than can the conscience to the eye, or the eye to the hand. As queen of all, she must needs both cherish and use her subjects.

From the aim of Theology as determined, we may also ascertain its extension;

from its centre explore the area of the circle. Since law is the central fact in moral government we have as the central question in theology: What is law? And since law is a fact of relationship we can know it only as we know at once its author and its subject. Thus does theology, the science of the Kingdom of God, embrace two great departments. The first, the doctrine of God as man's Moral Governor, the second, the doctrine of mankind as God's moral subjects. Here is given that organizing principle of theological study which determines at once the order and range of inquiry. Whatever studies reveal God in his regal character belong in the first department,—whatever reveal man in his subject character belong in the second. The precedence to be given to studies in either department is determined by their relative adaptation to accomplish the design of either. Many lie so remote from the central object of inquiry or cast so little light upon it that they could not be embraced in any but an extended course, while others are so necessary to the most moderate understanding of that object that they could not be omitted from any course.

Taking this principle of distribution we may briefly outline its application. But we must first stop to notice a denial of the possibility of its application. The principle pre-supposes that there is a doctrine of God. But there is no doctrine of God unless God is knowable. If as a prominent philosophy teaches, the terms God and the unknowable are synonyms, if we cannot know God as truly as we know either matter or our own minds, then there can be neither a theology nor a religion. The ultimate answer to all religious inquiry then is that inquiry is vain, and the only true religion is the renunciation of all religion. Thus are revelation, Christian experience, human aspirations, and the very make of the soul, branded with falsehood. That such a doctrine can have currency only shows that error has not yet laid down the sceptre.

In general the moral law is known as both will and one. We have thus to learn of God, as both person and one, one person. Thus as against Atheism and Pantheism and Polytheism, Monotheism has to establish itself.

But in particular, the law in its true conception, carries these three ideas, a nature as the absolutely holy, an authority as the absolutely supreme, and a sanction as the absolutely inviolable. By the first we are led to the study of the moral perfections of God, and brought face to face with the problems pertaining to the nature and ground of right. Here at once we are in a sphere which combines the extremes of the speculative and the practical, where the liability to mistake and the peril of mistake are both at their maximum. The second bids us determine what that is in God which, with his holiness, gives to him his sovereignty as the Supreme Legislator, and thus it leads us to study all the non-moral, or so called natural perfections of his being. The third specially demands that we learn and state the true doctrine of God's executive control over the universe. Man is so a part of the universe and so linked with other parts that his control manifestly involves the control of all known forces whether material or immaterial. Hence if any man bid Theology keep clear of the physical world as that belongs to natural science, he shows either ignorance or impudence. There is no solid foundation for a genuine religion, and hence for a genuine theology, save that laid by the first sentence of revelation. The position of that sentence is as philosophical as its import is majestic, and the junction of the material with the moral economy is to the end of Scripture not once forgotten, nor must it ever be by the theologian.

Again, if God as the author of law must be known, so must man as its subject. How can man be under God's law? Why must he be? Here is met at once the doctrine of his moral nature, what it is and how it stands related to the other factors of his being. With this must also go the true doctrine as to the governmental economy or economies in which man has been or is to be placed. What have been the developments of the past and what are to be the issues of the future? Here lie those great departments of truth known as Anthropology, Soteriology, Ecclesiology and Eschatology. Here gather problems as difficult as they are practical. The demand for their solution is urgent. They must be answered—not indeed fully, but truly. Mankind must have a guiding faith safe and clear. Hence to these vast problems Theology must give answer, not ambiguously and hesitatingly, but with clearness and authority. This must Theology do, or be driven from the world in disgrace.

We come thus to ask where the answer to such questions can be found? Is true and safe answer anywhere given? This question is vital. Christian Theology answers it affirmatively. She finds her answers in both a person and a book—the person Jesus Christ, the book the Bible. She maintains and at the peril of her life must prove that the Bible not only contains but is God's Word. Doing this she brings at once within her sphere whatever studies are needful for the right interpretation of Scripture. These studies, whether in language, history, geography, or whatever else, are her indispensable instruments. It is by them that she interprets Scripture, and is so put in position by Scripture to interpret human life and destiny. There is indeed a voice of God in the life and literature of men outside the Scripture. There is a science of comparative religion which brings its contribution to the knowledge of the Kingdom of God. But whether within or without the church, in Christendom or heathendom, all to be understood must be tested. The Comparative Theology which co-ordinates the Bible with any other source of doctrine, is neither a factor nor a friend of Christian Theology, but its opposite, and its foe.

The Rhetorical Department belongs in Theology, for the seminary has to show its students how to teach not less than what to teach. If the former work be not well done, the latter becomes in large measure fruitless. He cannot be a teacher of others who does not know how to communicate. It avails but little that the graduates of our seminaries are sound in the faith, and well furnished with divine truth, if they are incompetent to minister truth to the faith of others. The Rhetorical Professor thus holds the keys of the whole system of the Schools. His work gives worth to all the other work, binds the seminary to the church, and makes it minister to the Kingdom of God.

Abstaining from further suggestions as to the question what is Theology, we shall proceed to notice,

II. *The Educational Process.* As we have begun so we continue the discussion with special reference to the Theological Seminary. But the seminary course stands between two developments. To both alike it is vitally related, and we may therefore fitly pause to give a hasty glance at the mutual relation of the three.

As we live though not biologists, and think though not psychologists, so to be Christians we need not become theologians. Yet Christian life is never without Christian light. By the word of truth the soul is begotten of God, and by the same word sanctified. This Divine truth is the same as that which forms the true body of Divinity. Still, as known to the mass of Christians, it does not make of them theologians. Here, as in other spheres, there is implied a distinction between common and scientific knowledge. But as Dr. Porter has well remarked, to suppose, as many do, that there are two kinds of knowledge, is an error none the less serious because superficial. With the true philosopher and the uncultured, the process employed, and the principles of procedure are the same. "Both define and divide, and in one sense do little else. The one defines with greater exactness, and divides with greater care, than the other." This then is mainly a distinction of degree. The close affinity of the two kinds of knowledge, and of the two processes of attaining it, are thus indicated.

There is, however, another broad distinction which respects the ends of attainment, and still leaves intact the affinity. The general process is predominantly, though not exclusively, for the learner's own spiritual development, that he may appropriate the truth. The scientific process is predominantly, though by no means solely, to make of the learner a teacher and helper of others, that he may communicate the truth. The scientific exists for the general. Here emerges the great Christian law that the greatest is least, that the chief is servant. At the same time there is indicated the nature of that third stage of activity which follows the seminary course. The great majority of graduates will be pastors of churches, and preachers to the masses. They will minister truth to men with a view to its immediate personal appropriation, and thus aid in carrying forward the general process just noticed. Yet many of the graduates will enter other spheres of labor not less legitimate for the theological graduate, and essential to the welfare of the church. The progress of Christianity has made the forms of ministerial labor not less, but more, numerous than at first. Not now, indeed, is there need of inspired apostles and prophets, but there are departments of work in this day which to the early church were unknown. Hence is required a corresponding division of labor. Aside from preaching, with its many diverse requirements, there is the press. And how various the demands made upon the religious instructor by the possible forms of literature. Nor are we to forget that theological seminaries, and in part colleges and other literary institutions, should be manned with teachers whose theological training has been thorough and extended. And when we consider the relation of Divine to human law, of the gospel to every phase of philanthropy, we shall see the need, if not the practicability, that the actors in government and social reform should have thorough grounding in at least some branches of theology.

To lay securely and broadly the foundation of these varied activities is the work of the theological seminary. But however different the destinations of the students, the body of truth with which the theological education deals is one. Yet this word education is only relative. There is no complete education. And for men destined for spheres so varied, there should be not only allowed, but required, a wise discrimination in their training. Not all are to be taken over the same curriculum. There is a considerable class of men of deep piety, of strong, sound minds, of admirable practical tact, in no position to study the ancient languages, yet able to gain command of their own, and to employ it successfully, some of them eloquently, who, as splendid examples, living and dead, in our own and other denominations, triumphantly prove, can become able, even mighty ministers of God's gospel, but who, for their best success, need wise instruction and skillful training. Shall these men called of God be rejected by the Church? It must not be. Shall they be driven into their work unaided? That is mingled folly and cruelty. Shall they be thrust into a course wholly unsuited for them? Absurd. Let them be taught to interpret God's Word as best they may from the English text, with English helps. Such is the nature of Divine revelation, that all the inaccuracies of our grand old version, not to mention other versions, are but as the spots on the sun. And when all shall have been done for these men that can be, it will be alike unjust and unphilosophical to call them uneducated. He rather is uneducated who has been forced along a course totally unsuited to his tastes, abilities, and conditions, because of the contemptible theory that the only legitimate entrance into the ministry is over one and the same iron track. Such a theory is a curse and disgrace to any denomination that holds and practices it, and may the day never come when Baptists shall copy the criminal folly.

And yet such men, even the best of them, and much rather the rest, must be, as they themselves would be the first to confess, comparatively uneducated. The theological seminary is a professional school, and presupposes in its students long and thorough preparatory discipline. To serve the Church and the world efficiently it must adjust itself mainly to this class, and this class it must have. It cannot do its proper work without it. This is manifest. No man can become an exegete without a knowledge of at least the Greek and Hebrew languages. He will need other languages also as he advances. Now to know the Greek language so as to make use of it in interpretation, is to know language, and this involves long and thorough training. It is not enough to be able to make out the meaning of the words by a lexicon, one must have caught the spirit of the language, and become familiar with its genius. That work must be done before coming to the seminary. There is no time for it there. It must not then be attempted. Unless it has been done the Professor of Greek exegesis must largely fail in starting his student on that line which will lead him to future eminence, to the best success in his department. The same holds of the Hebrew. There seems to be but just one reason why this language is excluded from the college course, and that is because its ancient and sublime classics are not of heathen but of Divine origin. This shameful exclusion cripples the energies of the theological seminary, and compels it to spend time in elementary drill in language which is all too short for instruction in the principles, method, and exercise of interpretation. Is it strange that students sell their Hebrew Bibles and lexicons at graduation, and the church has so few Hebrew scholars?

But not less essential to a tolerable success in Systematic Theology is thorough discipline of mind, and with this a systematic training in both physical and mental science. The very first question of Theology, the question whether there is a God, introduces the student into regions of thought which are to him darkness, without such preparation. And as study in this department begins, so to the end it continues to move amid those problems which tax to the utmost the mental powers. Without the previous discipline one will indeed get the statement of doctrine and the main arguments for its support, but he will not, cannot, so enter into the spirit of the study, and understand its connection with the varied phases of human thought and delineations of human science, as to become a recognized power in the department, an authority inspiring confidence and commanding assent.

So too in Sacred History little can be done in the seminary unless much has been done before. It is a rare and very high attainment to gain the historic spirit. It is of little avail that one gathers facts whether as to the doctrines or the life of the Church, if he does not know what to do with them. But much as one must have previously learned in order to become an independent gatherer of facts, far more must have been done in the way of philosophic discipline, in order not alone to find the interpretation of the facts, but even to comprehend it when pointed out.

And since the Rhetorical department presupposes the accomplishment of the work of the other departments, whatever previous training they require, it requires. It is plainly in no position to lower the demands for preparation. Its business is not to put pumps into empty wells, or to lay pipes from dry cisterns.

We now reach the important conclusion that for thoroughness of theological education the seminary requires a long previous process of more general mental discipline, and that this process is so vitally connected with its own as to be virtually taken up into it, incorporated as a constituent.

With this point gained we see more clearly what the seminary should undertake. We can assume that the principle which should guide in one department should guide in all. Hence as we speak only of principles the departments will not be viewed separately. We regard the course in its completeness as a whole. The application of the principles can the better be left unnoticed since it will necessarily vary according to the character of the instructor or the condition of the class.

A theological seminary is to do for its students three things, to accomplish three ends, and these give us our three great guiding principles. It has first to enkindle in the student the theological spirit; second to confirm the student in the theological method; and third, to impart to the student the theological outline.

Our first principle, then, stated as a law, is, that the theological training must enkindle the theological spirit, or stated as a general truth, that the theological spirit is one chief factor of a theological education. In the theological spirit we find two constituents. The first is that love of truth which comes from love of Christ, and is common to all Christians. It is in general the Christian spirit. The second is that love of truth which comes from an appreciation of its harmonies, and is common to all men of science. It is in general the scientific spirit. The former roots itself rather in the heart, the latter in the head.

We thus at the start recognize the great truth which lies in Augustine's often repeated aphorism, "*Pectus theologum facit,*" and at the same time indicate that it is but a half truth. There can never be a profound theologian, in the true sense, where there is not a profound piety. Though *a* knowledge precedes faith, *the* knowledge follows faith. The best German theologians have recognized the vital relation of the Christian consciousness to theological knowledge, though in some instances this consciousness has been perversely put in the place of God's word. It is not our rule of faith, but without it we can never interpret that rule of faith. It is as true now as in Paul's time, that spiritual things are spiritually discerned. It is as true in the lecture-room of the theological seminary as in the meeting-house. That seminary which does not aim to deepen and develop in its students holy love, may succeed in something, but not in its proper business. If its graduates turn upside down anything, it will be not the world, but the church. It needs either burial or resurrection, for if it find any place for the Holy Ghost, it is in a dead theory, and not in living hearts.

With this Christian spirit must be developed the scientific enthusiasm. The possibility of this presupposes that theology is a science, that there is system and symmetry. The various departments of study are interdependent and naturally correlated, while order characterizes all that comes within each department. Religious truth would be unfitted for man's soul, were it in reality but a jumble, or could it be seen only as a confusion. If the bosom of God is the home of law, human reason cannot be at home with the lawless. For any one, and most of all for the religious teacher, a perception of the harmonies of gospel truths and of Christian activities, is not simply a pleasure, it is a necessity. Only thus will the reason keep its grasp on single truths, and push on to higher attainments. Only thus, indeed, can the gospel itself be known or taught, for the highest and grandest of gospel truths are the rhythmical harmonies of its truth. There can be no genuine theologian, there ought to be no religious teacher, whose soul is not aglow with admiring love of the unities of Theology. So there ought to be no Seminary where the teaching does not at once spring from scientific enthusiasm, and so by its manifestation enkindle it.

Again, the graduate must have acquired the theological method. Whatever else he be, or do, he is not to be a mere pedlar, only selling what he has bought. He is not to hawk about the country the products of other minds, the fruits of others' thinking. The man whose mind is only a receiver, can never be educated. Education presupposes not only capacity, but capability. The student must be trained to think, and so to become a producer. It is not enough to fill his bucket for him, he must be taught himself to draw water, both for his own wants and for mankind. Until he can do this he must needs remain strictly uneducated. But productive thought has its laws, and depends for efficiency upon their observance. Not a whit less true is this in Theology than elsewhere, and hence method here is all important. The whole drill of a young man should be such that he will be unconsciously brought into this method, so that when he leaves the living teacher the habit already formed will need only to be strengthened. Unless he has been moulded to this, in whatever sphere he works he is doomed to a waste of energies, and a failure in action. He cannot organize the materials that he may acquire, or even know how to acquire materials with reference to organization. There is here no time even to suggest what is the true method, enough to assert its existence, and its place.

But the graduate if he is to be called educated, must also have the theological outline. By this is meant that his course must have done for him in each department two things; it must have laid open to his eyes, mapped out for him in a distinct and definite yet only in a general and comprehensive outline, the contents of the department, the territory embraced in it. It must also have succeeded in carrying his thorough hearty assent to those great truths and principles which go to make up the outline. It is not enough that one know that there are laws of interpretation, he must know what they are; not enough that he know that there are true doctrines which constitute an outline of systematic Theology, he must know the doctrines. The same holds of History and of Practical Theology. To send men into the world without grounding them in the sum of divine knowledge, is to create for leaders a fraternity of skeptics, and so to curse the church and the world. Acquisition alone is not education, but there is no true education without acquisition; and especially is this true where as in religion the teacher must stand as a witness and speak with authority as heaven's ambassador. The gospel is a body of dogmatic faith, and must make and hold its way by assertion. But this assertion must be born of assurance.

The hour having arrived for the reading of the report of the Committee on Organization, it was moved and seconded that that report be now read, and that discussion upon the paper of Prof. PEPPER be deferred. Carried. Report read.

Dr. CUTTING moved that the report of the Committee on Organization be made the order of the day for this afternoon at 4.50, and that in the meantime it be printed for the use of the members. Carried.

Dr. CUTTING: I have observed with pleasure the presence in our assemblings of an illustrious scholar, long an educator, and always interested in the work of education, though not now connected with our institutions of learning. I move, therefore, that the Rev. THOMAS J. CONANT, D. D., be invited to sit with us as a member of this Convention.

The motion was carried unanimously.

Adjourned to 2.30 P. M.

THURSDAY AFTERNOON SESSION.

The Convention was called to order at half past two o'clock, and was opened with prayer by the Rev. Dr. HOWARD MALCOM.

Prof. N. L. ANDREWS, of Madison University, read a paper on

THE MORAL ELEMENTS OF THE TEACHER'S ART.

To gather and transmit the accumulating knowledge of the ages, and to communicate those moral forces, principles and sentiments necessary to human progress, to carry onward the torch of truth, undimmed and still more luminous, and to perpetuate all influences that elevate and ennoble character—this is the province of the world's teachers. To stand in this grand line, to fulfil this lofty mission is a distinction that may well be coveted. Such a contemplation of the teacher's work redeems it from monotony and routine, excludes all sense of annoyances, glorifies all its sacrifices.

Teaching has justly been called an art. It is entitled to this designation, by its directness and practical relations to life; by its combination of means to ends; by the constant study of adaptations; by its need of tact and skill, fertility of expedients, and fullness of resources. Like all high art, it is in part the gift of nature, the product of organization. But art is more than inspiration. The development of original capacities comes only from their exercise. Natural aptitude must become artistic adaptation. No mechanic ever had need of such persistent application in the execution of material designs, for while he deals with inert matter, mechanical laws, and physical forces, and works to a model comparatively fixed and imitable, the teacher is to wield moral and spiritual forces, that he may impress and fashion human character. As with the artist, the loftiness of his ideal transcends any perfect realization. He aims at more than conformity to a model. Rules and methods are but his instruments. His ideal attracts toward heights continually more exalted. He who has fully realized his conceptions, be he sculptor, painter, or teacher, is no true artist. If the ideal has been attained, and there remains no conscious drawing upward, there may be work, but, in its best sense, there is no more art.

To consider all those qualifications which should constitute the representative teacher would involve a discussion too wide in its range, too extensive in its details. An attempt to treat of the moral elements demanded by his calling is enough to impress us with its difficulty and its dignity, to inspire humility, and yet to awaken exalted aspirations. He who is to impart knowledge must of course possess it. Some power of acquisition, a tolerable store of learning, at least in his own department, and a certain facility of intellectual communication are presumed. Shall he thus only be furnished for his work? Nay, to be content with this is crime against the student. Such men may have marvellous power of acquisition. Let them find their use as book-worms. They may accumulate vast learning by laborious investigations. Let us thankfully use the results. They may give scholarly reputation to an Institution, but unless they have personal power, unless they be able to impart themselves, they are unfit for the higher work of the teacher. By moral elements, then, we mean those that we derive from one's personality, and we affirm that the possession of such sources of power is far more important than mere intellectual discipline and equipment, and immeasurably transcends all questions of external facilities and appliances.

I. As a primal and indispensable requisite we name MANHOOD. The qualities which make up the ideal man are essential to the ideal teacher. We instance a few only that bear upon his personal relations.

There must be *freedom from all affectation*, whether of thought, as manifested in effort after originality for originality's sake, of feeling, as illustrated in a false and unhealthful sentimentalism, or of manner, as betrayed by any assumption in bearing, or by striving for sensational effects. Not what a man takes on, but what he expresses of his own proper nature, affords genuine power. If thorough naturalness, and perfect simplicity be wanting, the healthful spirit of youth will quickly detect the deficiency.

The teacher must illustrate also *high moral instincts*. Whatever his department of instruction, he will often be called to pronounce his ethical judgments. If the very grain of his nature be not loyal to the great principles of right, the flaw will be manifest. In all the relations of discipline, especially, his integrity must be transparent. He must be strictly just. All moral subterfuge, indirection, and Machiavellianism are sure to recoil, and their success would be more deplorable than any evils they might be employed to remedy. He must be a man of honor. In manifold ways, amid the intimate personal relations which he will hold to the student, this more delicate sense of justice will be demanded. The scrupulous honor of Arnold, the exact justice of Wayland, were buttresses of strength. To fail here is to have the supports of moral influence fatally sapped. Let students make up their mind that a teacher is "mean"—a quality more easily and certainly detected than defined—and his hold upon them, for all the higher ends of teaching, is gone. Not only in his relations to his pupils, but to the community at large, his integrity must command respect and confidence, or he must give way before a current that he cannot stem.

The crown of ideal manhood is *unselfishness*. In this, as in many other things, the teacher and the preacher are at one. In resolute mastery of self-indulgence, in uncomplaining endurance of vexations, in cheerful subordination of personal tastes, in the subjection of private aims to his supreme devotion to the student's good, he has abundant opportunities to cultivate an unselfish spirit. Like the Great Teacher, he must be able to say, "I came not to be ministered unto, but to minister." He will find his highest recompense, not in emoluments and distinctions, but in watching the growth of worthy sentiments, and the increasing power of high ideals in his pupils, as illustrated by successful careers and noble living.

The manhood of the teacher is to the student the standard of that conscious or unconscious assimilation which is more or less inevitable. His whole tone and spirit ought to be every way healthful. No less important, however, is the consideration that high character is the source of all true *authority* in the teacher. It was truly said long ago, "There is no culture from him who does not please." Popularity, indeed, often attends what is superficial and spurious. Catering to the lower impulses of the student may for a time secure approval, but sooner or later all worthy popularity comes to him who deserves it. It is but another name for authority. Without this, the effort to impart knowledge will meet but a listless reception, and any attempt to influence character will be repelled. Fear is not incompatible with this authority, nor does it always imply affection, but it is grounded in respect. Mere attainments will not secure it, nor is there any necessary loss of authority in the confession of mistakes and ignorance. He who lacks authority of character will suffer disparagement in his learning and in his capacity. The ordeal that tests him is no trifling one. The student must believe in him. If it is true that the child has instincts, which, by subtle drawings and antipathies, serve as moral indices, it would seem that young men and young women have preserved more of such intuitive power than we who have grown further away from the susceptibilities of childhood. Nowhere sooner than in such a community does a sham utterly fail. Untoward influences may give rise to perverse and malicious currents of sentiment, but the general judgment of a student community, for any length of time, unfavorable to an instructor, is probably right. True authority implies weight of character. In our own land and time it has characterized none more remarkably than Wayland, and Taylor of Andover. Nothing so strongly enforces discipline or commends truth. No weight of scholarship, no official parade, no "little brief authority" of a factitious nature can be a substitute. It is this personal authority which identifies the school and the teacher. Rugby was Arnold, and Arnold was Rugby, while Union College, for half a century, was synonymous with the name of Eliphalet Nott. The success of such an instructor rests not on a mere *ipse dixit*. It is not a moral compulsion that aims to break down the student's convictions. It creates, however, a presumption in the teacher's favor; it engenders a proper and healthful reverence, without which there is no true culture. We do not insist on respect for the office. We mean that a man's character is more than his position. It is scarcely necessary to add that only the religious man can fully illustrate the authority of manhood. By a broad and healthy character, by his moral depth and tone, by the sense of responsibility and dependence upon God, he must, in the totality of his influence, be worthy of his office. Only a man can fashion men.

II. High success demands also ENTHUSIASM. This implies inward propulsion, fervor of spirit, and ardor of manner. It is an exaltation of aim and feeling above the common moods of men. Here, too, nature, in one's temperament, decides much beforehand; but enthusiasm is not incapable of increase. It grows by what it feeds on. There must be genuine *thirst for truth.* It revealed loftier conceptions when the teacher began to call himself no longer "the wise man," but the "lover of wisdom." To dole out facts from an unreplenished store is not teaching. Private study and personal investigation must renew and augment the supply. To meet all demands is not enough. Unless the mind be kept active by fresh accumulations, not even old truths can be so presented as to vivify and expand the student. Earnest pursuit of truth is his only safeguard against routine.

Enthusiasm involves an *exalted estimate of the teacher's work.* It is more than a business. Much less is it a resource for the impecunious. Until salaries at least rate higher, only the lower grade of talent and character will be drawn by sordid motives. Let it never degenerate to a mere shift of employment. Don't elect men to professorships simply because they have failed in the ministry, and you think they must have been made for something. One's attitude toward his work is of vital importance. He who feels that his powers might be more nobly engaged is unfit for it. Arnold might have shone in statesmanship, but he placed teaching higher, and indignantly resented the sneer that he was "cutting blocks with a razor." This high estimate of the teacher's art is necessary to enthusiasm. Energy may be exerted upon what is below one. Even earnestness may attend poor and inadequate conceptions. Enthusiasm is a quality livelier and more exalted. It is the artist's secret. It proceeds from the attraction of an ideal that is never reached. Ambition is a sorry substitute if it goes not further than position and emolument.

Enthusiasm must largely spring also from a *sense of vocation.* The notion of a calling belongs not to the ministry alone. If the teacher is, in great part, born, not made, we may expect his call to appear in his consciousness. He will at least find that delight in his work which will confirm his capacity and his vocation. If one deem himself "called to teach," when none are called to learn, experience will correct his self-delusion. The teacher cannot be eminent unless the drift and under-current of his nature are in the channel of his chosen profession. He who has not known the joy of teaching, whose imagination does not kindle as his work opens up before him, is to be commiserated. What else can reconcile him to his vexations, or content him with his appropriate rewards, without envy of those who in other spheres are amassing wealth, or winning applause? This enjoyment of teaching which accompanies the sense of vocation tends to secure permanence in the relation, and so supports it by that moral capital which only permanence supplies.

Enthusiasm in the teacher will be fed, moreover, by a *central devotion to his work.* I say "central," for one's life must have scope and play. He must not fail in breadth of interest. He is preparing men for the world. If for no other reason, he must be abreast with its movements. Dr. NOTT was largely identified with legislation and all public progress, but not a whit the less was his proper work supreme. One's paramount interest must be in teaching. Outside reputation is desirable, but loss of power at home is too great a price. So far as learning is tributary to teaching, the more the better, but not so with learning for mere learning's sake. If possible, let all our Institutions be both seats of learning, and schools of intellectual and moral training. Bnt if the two cannot be united, let us not hesitate between the merely learned professor and the enthusiastic, devoted teacher. Let us have men who, like Arnold, "could hardly live without teaching." Enthusiasm belongs not alone to poetic or imaginative natures, nor to dazzling genius. It marks the man wholly given to his work.

Institutions are not for themselves. They are not to be conducted as corporations. They do not exist for their Faculties. They have more to do than to maintain traditional reputation. They are for the students who attend them. However learned their professors, untiring in investigation, and successful in discovery, the student has paramount claims—a right to demand that all shall be subsidiary to his interests, that private study, general reputation, profound discovery, or brilliant authorship, shall not diminish, but rather add enthusiasm in teaching.

III. Both the investigation and communication of truth will, in the true teacher, be marked by CATHOLICITY OF FEELING. Otherwise, enthusiasm will often be fanaticism in himself, and dogmatism towards others. Catholicity primarily implies honesty. He should be neither a slave of prejudice, nor a bundle of prepossessions. He is not called to bolster up theories, nor to advocate systems. If he understands this, he will not seek to shape facts into prescribed moulds, nor to adjust the truth to predetermined measurements. He will have his theories and his system, but they will be his not by legacy and tradition merely, but will be the products of facts apprehended, classified, and correlated by independent thought. Nor even when by his own processes he has reached such a system, ought he to be narrowly intensive in its maintenance. Let him feel that truth is broader than any theory, more comprehensive than any system. This is but to say that the finite cannot compass the limitless. It is to accept the lesson of history.

The processes of the world's thought have been, in great measure, *tentative.* How has philosophic speculation rested now on this phase of truth, now on that touched here one problem, and there another, often reverting by cycles upon itself, and again soaring toward the empyrean. Science has made its successive generalizations, and these have in turn given way before wider induction and more exact classification. Its path is strown with exploded theories, and problems still obscure await their oft-sought solution. The truths of theology have been interpreted and formulated by successive thinkers. Now this doctrine has received emphasis, and now that has assumed the foreground. Statement has followed statement, each colored by the individuality of the framer, or adapted to the real or supposed spiritual needs of the age. And in every period, how lamentable has been the mistake in theology, science, or philosophy, to assume in one's thinking or teaching that truth has been attained and compassed, grasped and confined, in its totality, within some accepted creed, theory, or system! Has nature unbarred all her recesses? Has she unlocked all her secrets? Have the great problems of philosophic speculation found complete solution? Or in theology, has reverent inquiry reached its *ultima thule?* Are the treasures of the Divine Word fully laid open? Are the mysteries of God's nature and God's dealings with man fathomed to their depths? Not till we can answer these questions affirmatively, may we write "infallible" upon system, theory, or creed, and dogmatize *ex cathedra*, with anathemas upon "him that followeth not us."

True catholicity is entirely *compatible with earnest conviction and decided assertion.* The ideal teacher is not a man whose mind is in suspense on all leading questions. In all that is central, he must have opinions, and must teach what he believes. Otherwise, how shall the student have faith in the reality of truth, or be encouraged to seek it? Shall he succeed where his teacher has failed? No wonder that the Sophists engendered skepticism. Yet Socrates, though the champion of objective truth, asserting the duty and possibility of its attainment, cherishing convictions on all fundamental questions no less positive because concealed by his unique method, was thoroughly catholic in his loyalty to the guidance of sound reason, wherever it might lead.

Catholicity mainly concerns *the circumference of one's thinking.* One ought to hold some views so central and well considered that he need not re-examine them at the challenge of every comer. As years go by, the speculations and theories that have floated on the circumference will one by one flit away, or become a part of the fixed guiding-lights of his thought. But if enthusiasm for truth continues, the outer limits of his thinking will still be undefined, and that spirit of inquiry which still leads him forth in unappeasable aspirations, will impart catholicity to the affirmation even of what he most certainly holds.

We cannot accede to the view (urged in a recent inaugural) that the teacher ought not to inculcate positive opinions upon mooted questions. The issues involved are often too vast. Besides, to suspend judgment discourages even inquiry. To conceal convictions is as unmanly, as it is impossible. Rather let beliefs be expressed with ingenuousness, opinions urged with fearlessness and candor, with inquisitive mind, but conscientious heart.

It is needful to feel sufficiently the force of objections. Difficulties are met in every line of inquiry. The domain of axiomatic truth is limited. Mathematical demonstration covers but a portion of the realm of truth. For the rest, difficulties must be weighed, and probabilities balanced. He who underrates an objection, even in the interests of truth, is at best guilty of "pious fraud." He has done worse, for he has robbed his pupil of his probation and his discipline. Intelligent assent is worth far more than blind submission. Moreover, a difficulty unfairly set aside may return to overpower one. Previous concealment may prepossess him in its favor.

In fine, the genuine teacher will recognize truth wherever found. He will seek out its elements everywhere, with a loyalty that shall hail even its partial aspects. Half-truths will not be confounded with sheer errors. Truth does not gain, but loses, if we refuse to see that it is partial truth which gives vitality to many a system on the whole erroneous.

We must concede the honesty of other thinkers, and appreciate their position. The intolerance of the human will is the secret of dogmatism, as it has been of persecution. How often is an opponent's position unfairly or weakly stated! The "man of straw" held up in the lecture-room is easily demolished, but the flesh-and-blood antagonist of real life does not "down" at mere bidding. Men do not thank their instructors for such concealments, and condone the mistake only as they ascribe it to narrowness or timidity. If we could thus transfer ourselves to the position of others, and take into account their temperament, their training, and their surroundings, we should not necessarily lose hold of our convictions; but we should learn much of that charity which prompts at times the inquiry: "Who art thou that judgest another man's servant? To his own master he standeth or falleth."

He who would guide young men wisely and safely must be catholic. Youth will not slavishly bow to authority. Only the weary, disappointed thinker of advanced years makes this his refuge. If the student is to be an independent thinker, he must approach the great problems of thought as to open questions. So, under wise guidance, truth will come to him with all the freshness and power of a new discovery. Safety demands candor. Better give up what cannot be maintained than attempt to repress inquiry. Honesty will commend the truth; unfairness will foster falsehood. From one who is broad and appreciative men freely accept what, from any other, they are prone to reject. Of course, the teacher must be loyal to truth, must pay proper deference to the past, and yield due authority to that general concurrence of thought which constitutes so strong a presumption. He will not, therefore, be rash, but in candor and catholicity he will appreciate opposing views, and welcome truth from any and every quarter.

IV. As another grand requisite, we name SYMPATHY WITH THE STUDENT. Some, indeed, affirm, that the relation of teacher to student is merely professional. It is assumed, that both are interested in the particular branch of study, that the student looks to the instructor for the advantage of his superior attainments, and that this is all. Instances may perhaps be cited of men who have won reputation and had brilliant success with but limited personal connection or influence. Rare stores of learning and peculiar brilliancy of genius may in part have compensated for the defect; but such cases are quite exceptional. We believe, on the contrary, that the teacher should be identified with the student, and have a hold upon his confidence and love.

He must, first, take *interest* in him. Not that general sort which exhausts itself in common-place, goodish platitudes about the "rising generation," but individual and genuine. Woe betide the teacher who feigns what he does not feel. Let him never regard the student's improvement and good-will merely as helps to his own reputation and advantage.

Now, it is easy to be interested in the talented and the brilliant, the well-disposed and the amiable. No temptation is more subtle and agreeable than to work disproportionately for these. All higher instruction is especially appreciated only by the few whom it most profits. One may properly cherish peculiar satisfaction in choice intellects. But we do insist that no such admiration shall detract from ample justice to the variety of inferior gifts. Let the dullest feel that his instructor believes in him, and has faith in his future. The assurance of this will be his chief inspiration. Scholastic training may do little for such; but they may absorb much from the common life of the school which will repay sympathetic interest. Unless he be at least capable of this, countenance no man in the life of a student. Let the teacher have sufficient discernment to discover the strong point, the hopeful element, the feature of promise, in every student. It may be different from his own bent; but it should no less elicit his interest. He must appreciate his pupil's purposes, profession or calling, and know how to hold up the highest ideals for every vocation. It is criminal to be so interested in any single calling as to undervalue any honorable employment of the student's powers. In this qualification Arnold and Nott were conspicuous. Their sympathy with all worthy pursuits not only evinced a wholeness and healthiness of manhood, but fitted them the better to instruct and to win young men.

The teacher should concern himself in the student's necessities and trials. Here is noble opportunity to cement personal regard. Doubtless many whom I address gratefully remember the timely aid of some early instructor in their sore straits. Never devolve upon the official machinery of an Education Society all responsibility for the student's condition.

Sympathy signifies *power to enter into the student's feelings.* The first question to every candidate for teaching ought to be "Do you remember how you felt when you were a student?" It is not enough to insist on acquaintance with human nature. . Such knowledge is quite too general. He must understand student-nature, which is *sui-generis.* It is much to be in sympathy with young men; but young men engaged in study, linked in class relations, and sharing a community of life, present additional elements greatly complicating the problem of their management. Student-life has its peculiar tendencies, customs and spirit, its distinctive sentiments, its diverse and apparently unaccountable currents. Caprices, freaks, nay epidemics, often attend it. To these the teacher must be habituated. He must be able to enter into the feelings that underlie them, and, in some sense, appreciate them. The currents of his own life should be fresh. Somewhat of the buoyancy and exuberance of the boy-spirit is desirable to promote mutual understanding. Do not seek out teachers among those who continually remind us that "the former times were better than these." To enter into the student's feelings will foster patience and good temper, and that forbearance which comes from distinguishing the thoughtlessness of sport from depravity and malevolence. Even the wayward and perverse may not rightly be shut out from that personal interest which might keep them from ruin. The moral standard of student-life is indeed often deplorably low; but it occasionally demands toleration. To inculcate lofty principles is better than to impose stern restrictions; and if sympathy be not lacking, high character in the teacher will be far more effective than petty repression. It was the policy of the Roman Agricola, no less appropriate to a teacher than to a general, "omnia scire, non omnia exsequi."

If it be feared that sympathy will tend to indulgence, let it not be forgotten that the student's feelings are not all upon the surface. Beneath his floating sentiments are his profounder convictions; behind his passions and his inclinations is his manhood. He who knows these deeper moods will often cross the surface-currents, calmly conscious of his hold upon the student's interior sympathies.

Above all, true sympathy *takes in another's case,* and enters not into his feelings only, but into his condition. It recognizes the student's possibilities, and engenders the sense of responsibility. "No parochial ministry," said Arnold, "can be more a cure of souls." "My comfort depends more and more upon their good and bad conduct." "My work has all the interest of a great game of chess, with living creatures for pawns, and the adversary, the Devil." The teacher will sometimes be content to part with present good-will, confident of future approbation. A just sympathy will not occasion weak compliance with the transient freaks of wilfulness and passion. So will faith in the student become fidelity to the student.

The maintenance of this sympathy, in all its breadth of meaning, is no slight self-sacrifice. It is an expenditure of life's best forces, but its recompense is ample. Happy is he who can replenish his spent energies from its tender and enduring friendships, from its endearing and delightful memories.

V. It remains to notice the crowning qualification for the teacher's art, and the crucial test of his success — I mean THE POWER OF INSPIRATION. This is in great part the resultant of all the other elements and forces of his nature.

It must be felt, first of all, in *holding the student to his work.* We may assume that the teacher's personal enthusiasm has overcome in himself all sense of irksomeness, but he should have such abounding interest, and such ability to impart it, as shall do the same for his pupils. Fortunate is the student when the teacher's magic touch has power to illumine and lend attraction to every task.

A *love of learning* will be thus awakened. It is a sorry comment on much of our teaching that the graduate often drops so soon all scholarly pursuits. The practical exigencies of some calling or business which fully engages attention have much to do with this, but it should be the instructor's constant aim to develop scholarly tendencies and cultivated tastes, and in very many the inspiration of the teacher will determine the pursuit of knowledge as the work of a life-time.

More important still is its *power to stir and quicken thought.* Let the student forget what he may, if he come out of the teacher's care a thinker. The instructor must himself be a thinker, not a mechanical hearer of recitations, hampered by methods, and tied to forms. Not upon subjects of instruction alone, but upon every topic which personal intercourse with his pupils will suggest, let him stimulate mental activity. Who does not recall with kindling of spirit times in his student-life when the lesson of the day suggested, perhaps remotely, some interesting point which the mechanical teacher would have ruled out, as not belonging to his department, but which furnished to the more apt instructor the text for some grand, inspiring talk, under whose spell time passed unheeded, the lesson but half recited, and the bell dismissed the class all enkindled and alive with some great truth or lofty motive. Such a power of talk, not the mere effervescence of verbosity, or flow of sentimental twaddle, but the real kindling of sacred fire, is of inexpressible value. Many a student who has little aptitude for formal, scholarly attainments can thus be lifted, according to his measure, toward higher levels of thought and aspiration.

The true teacher, moreover, will afford *impulsion to noble living and elevated character.* He will not only make work inspiring, but life earnest and hopeful. In a variety of ways, he will inevitably reveal and impress himself. "To come under Taylor's influence," says a graduate of Philips Academy, "was to move into a new system of gravitation." In him inspiration was not incompatible with rigid discipline. This personal power should be exerted to produce not scholars alone, not thinkers alone, but high-toned Christian men.

To constitute this power of inspiration, all other moral elements combine.

Manhood and personal authority conduce to it; sympathy prepares the way; while enthusiasm, catholicity, and earnest conviction are vital constituents. Dogmatism may inspire, but only catholicity can healthfully inspire. There is no inspiration, however, without conviction. Even a physical element enters in. That product of organization and of temperament which we call personal magnetism is a part of what the born teacher brings with him. It is more than the energy which in every walk of life promotes success. It is the power to draw men, which to a few in all departments of activity lends wondrous, mysterious power. Such teachers appeal to the student's imagination, and are what the student's nature craves—something to boast of.

Without inspiration, few teachers have been eminently successful. With it, men destitute of facilities have done work of superlative excellence. Humble men, unlearned men, have often accomplished what men of sounding reputation have failed to do. Of this large or pretentious Universities have no monopoly. It is not unknown to our smaller colleges, our academies, and our common schools. Buildings, apparatus, libraries, text-books add efficiency, but do not constitute power. From Socrates and Plato down to the present, the world's teachers have been those who have ministered inspiration, and given impulse to thought and life.

If such are the elements that constitute the teacher, let us understand that more than additional institutions, more than so-called educational facilities, we need men who shall fulfil their calling. Let pastors seek out "teaching gifts," as well as "preaching gifts," nor be over-much grieved if a supposed "call to preach" turn out a call to teach.

Happy will it be for our Institutions, if whatever else they be noted for, they are distinguished by good teaching. And nobler ambition no one of us could cherish than that after a life of self-forgetting devotion to our work, it might be inscribed on our tombstones, and more sacredly enshrined in the hearts of our pupils, "He was a true teacher."

The PRESIDENT: The time allotted to this theme and its discussion has more than expired, but I dare say the Convention would like to hear one or two brief speeches upon it. I take the liberty of calling upon Professor Lincoln of Brown University.

Prof. LINCOLN: I have but a few words to say. I have listened to the paper which has just been read with profound interest. It has seemed to me a most hopeful and auspicious indication of the good to be wrought by this Convention, and also for the future of our educational interests as a denomination, that we should have to-day, in this paper, such wise and true sentiments, so wisely and truly expressed by one of the youngest of the teachers in this present company. [Applause]. It made my heart leap for joy that a young man should stand here before us, and teach us so well what are the moral elements of the teacher's art. [Applause.] I agree heartily, sir, with every word of the paper, and I am glad you have given me an opportunity to say so. For I believe—and I hope I am not alone in this company of teachers and friends of education in the belief—I believe that the heart out of which, as we have from the highest authority, are the issues of life, the heart is more than the head, and character is more than knowledge. It is of far greater importance what a man is and what he is becoming, than what he knows. And so I say that the moral elements of the teacher's art have a correspondingly higher rank than the intellectual, as the moral elements of the teacher's being, and of the being of the pupil are also far higher than the intellectual.

I have heard so many things in this paper that I should like to speak to, that I hardly know to which, in seven minutes, to try to speak to at all. But the paper, I noticed, incidentally cited Socrates in illustration of one of the elements of the teacher's art. I thought directly of Socrates as an illustration on a still larger canvas of the same great thing. Yesterday, you know, sir, we had in the essay of Dr. Kendrick, set forth and illustrated before us, the noble and ever enduring influence of classical studies. And I thought of that paper, and the influence of these classical studies in the promotion of all true culture. Then I thought of Socrates again, and of what he wrought, and then came to me one signal illustration of the moral culture to which classical studies and ancient literature minister. May I recall, as it comes to me again, one word among many others, a most truthful word too, I think it is, that has come down to us from those treasures of Grecian letters which it was the dutiful design of yesterday's paper—and most dutifully executed—to set forth and illustrate. It was from one of those dialogues of Plato, which, you know, contain so much moral wisdom and truth, embodied in a diction of such surpassing clearness, force and grace. It is in the dialogue of Protagoras, the great sophist, who had just come to Athens, bringing with him a world-wide fame as a man of learning and wisdom, and a most accomplished speaker. A young Athenian, Hippocrates by name, all aglow with zeal to avail himself of this new intellectual resource that had just opened to the youth of Athens, posts away to the house of Socrates long before day-break, gets the philosopher up, and begs him to go straightway with him to the house where Protagoras is, and introduce him to the philosopher. As we may well believe, Socrates thought it a very early hour to visit a stranger in Athens. Meanwhile he took a turn with his young friend up and down the court of his house, and there put some of those sharp, incisive questions which nobody but he ever could put, in regard to what this youth was going to do; and he said, "My young friend, who is he, pray, and what sort of a man is he whose knowledge you covet so much? What sort of a man is he going to make of you, what kind of a character to form in you, I pray?" The young man was scarcely prepared for this. He only said "I want wisdom; I want knowledge; I want the whole of it if I can get it." "Ah, indeed, my young friend, you are making a mistake. Here you are, going to that house to get this knowledge, and you don't know from whom you are to get it, and what sort of a man he is going to make of you. My question is, is he going to make you a better man, being a good man himself? Here you are committing your soul, on whose well-being or ill-being your all depends, to the keeping of this stranger; not knowing whether you are committing that soul of yours to good or to evil." He believed, sir, in this supreme importance to be attached to the moral elements of a teacher's art. And that, I submit, is a tolerably good lesson for us Christians to learn and to apply. A tolerably good lesson to come down to us from those ancient writings, which—unlike, to be sure, the Hebrew Scriptures are, as we were reminded yesterday, of heathen and not of Divine origin. I submit, sir, even from such a source we should take it, and make the most of it; and I should be glad if, as teachers, we make as good use of it as the heathen Socrates. I am getting on beyond my seven minutes, but I do not want to sit down yet.

VOICES: Go on.

Prof. LINCOLN: I am full of this subject, and I rejoice that the subject comes before us here, the friends of teachers and of education in our denomination. I could refer to special points that were made so well in this paper. I was very glad especially that the writer of the paper spoke of the need of the teacher's entering with sympathy and personal interest into all that concerned his pupil. Oh, sir, I believe in that with all my heart, and I wouldn't give much for any teacher who was incapable of that. Well did Prof. Andrews say that we must all know how to remember that we were boys ourselves once. Not only must we remember it, sir, but we must have the feelings still that we had when we were boys, and a conscious knowledge of all that we went through then, the evil as well as the good—the foibles, follies and weaknesses, as well as the aspirations which throbbed our hearts in those early days. I think if the teacher could only remember this, he would have more of that charity that hopeth all things, endureth all things, and never faileth. And if there should chance to be occasionally in his pupils, the appearance of a bit of vanity and conceit coming to the surface, it would be well for such a teacher to remember that there was a time when he, too, was accustomed to think of himself a little more highly than he ought to think. [Laughter and applause].

But, sir, I must pause. I have only to say, to sum up the whole matter, that I look upon it as essential to the teacher's success that he live in these moral elements of his art as in an atmosphere, and breathe it all the while. And I am sure that unless he lives in such a world as that, and has such a light as that about him, every new morning that he is to go to his work, and such an atmosphere in which he is to live and evermore to breathe, he will be unable to accomplish the noble purposes which are given him to attempt—and, with God's blessing, to accomplish too—as a teacher of youth. [Applause].

Pres. DODGE: I am quite sure that I can add nothing to the testimony given, but yet I am a witness in the case, and I wish to appear at the bar and give my testimony. I am so much impressed with the fact that the man himself determines his principles, his methods, his governing ideas and his regnant sentiment, that when you have a man and a soul, if you have that man and that soul before you, you can always determine beforehand the methods that are to govern him, the principles that are to guide him, and the ideas that are regnant in his character. It is those methods, those principles and those governing ideas which make him a teacher, and from the nature of the case the moral and spiritual elements must be the thread that runs through them all, must be the one thing over and above all others that puts him in a right sympathetic relation, and helps him to do the work. The greatest curse, sir, that can fall to a young man is an incompetent teacher. [Applause]. And every teacher is incompetent who is not held aloft by his own ideas, who has not so incorporated those ideas in his own being that he can impart not only his ideas, but something of his very self. Oh, sir, it is a great thing to save youth: it is a greater thing perhaps to lift them up to a higher plane of thinking and feeling. But neither you nor I, whatever be our profession as teachers, neither you nor I can do it, except as we be inspired by the spirit of the Great Teacher himself. And why was he a Great Teacher, except that he was a great man and child of the race, as well as the Son of God; the flowering out and culmination, of all that is great and true and real in humanity, and not as we all are, fractional in our characters and natures? By the fact that he could bear out his own experience, the supernatural and the natural; the experience with God and in sympathy with him; the experience with man and in sympathy with him. It was this great fact or these great facts that made Jesus the Foremost Teacher, as he was the soul's Redeemer. So I say the moral elements must enter in to help us to do our work. The most painful thing that the teacher ever experiences, it seems to me, is that, in spite perhaps of all his efforts, here and there a young man makes a life failure. The teacher can bear the want of facilities, can bear the struggles that are incident to the building up a great institution, and having it embody the spirit of the denomination that has founded it, he can bear all this, but the one loss that he cannot bear is the loss of a noble youth.

Dr. MALCOM: One point which has not yet been named at all, sir, I think is of eminent importance—and I speak from experience. I would be inclined to place it as the very first and foremost qualification of the instructor, that he should *love* the boys. That he should instead of playing President or Professor, play *father* to them; take them in his heart, go to bed with them, get up with them, and go about with them in his heart all day. And it is only that sort of a teacher that I think will ever accomplish much with his boys. Let them feel that he loves them, and then he will not have to be jerking the bits in their mouths, and making himself apparently a very great stickler for order. There will not be very much disorder—none at all, I think—if the boys love their teachers. Because students are not brought up before the faculty constantly, it is sometimes supposed that there is no order. Once a trustee spoke to me about the college. He thought there was no order because the boys were not brought up before the faculty. I heard him very patiently, and when he got through I said, "Sir, how often have you thought about your liver to-day?" "Why," said he, "I haven't thought about it at all." Said I, "If it had been diseased wouldn't you have thought about it? The reason you think there is no government is because there is no disorder." That is the way to stop it, sir—to love the young men and to feel that God has put us over them for great use, and that we are responsible in the day of judgment.

Prof. H. H. HARRIS, read a paper on

METHODS AND LIMITS OF BENEFICIARY AID.

Educational facilities are furnished at less than cost. Public Free Schools, increasing endowments and rivalries between competing institutions, are co-operating to reduce still further the price of tuition. The time is possibly not distant when students will be admitted gratuitously to schools of all grades. Yet even then, there shall be many, who will need pecuniary aid to fit themselves, without great loss of time and energy, for the stations of honor and usefulness to which they have a right to aspire. "The poor ye have always with you," and a wise Providence has ordered, that as wealth increases, the opportunities of using it for good are correspondingly multiplied. All professions and occupations would be benefited by some well-devised system of beneficiary aid, but for obvious reasons, this discussion will be confined to that branch in which most has been done and most is still needed—the aiding of candidates for the Christian ministry. The topic as thus limited, is eminently practical. Some questions will arise to which no answer, that shall be always and everywhere applicable, can be given. In such cases we cannot do more than fix the guiding principles, to which all good rules must conform.

The writer has had correspondence with a good many Secretaries of Baptist Education Societies and has freely availed himself of facts and suggestions communicated by them. He proposes first to submit some general remarks on the nature, the dangers, and the necessity of organizations for beneficiary aid, then to take up more specifically the persons who should be aided, and the amount of aid in each case, and conclude with some hints on the method in which our purposes can best be accomplished.

I. THE NATURE OF THE WORK.

The work of an Education Society is three-fold—first to disseminate such facts and appeals as will incite Christians to pray and labor for an increase of ministers; but chiefly, to aid worthy young men in acquiring such an education as will increase their usefulness in preaching the gospel, and incidentally to use this most favorable time for winnowing chaff from among the wheat—in a word, the aim is to multiply the number of preachers and to elevate the standard of ministerial attainments and character.

In this age, it is needless to argue the superiority of an organized system of benefactions over spasmodic aid by scattered individuals. The influence of conscious power resulting from combined forces, is a felt necessity in social, political, financial and ecclesiastical as well as educational movements. It is even more obviously needful in this work, since those who are to be aided are numerous, and though widely scattered must be congregated in schools. But there are undoubtedly grave objections to any system of beneficiary aid. Some urge that support by a Society, supplants in the young preacher a feeling of dependence on God and a spirit of proper self-reliance. Perhaps it may sometimes, but the evil deprecated is clearly an unnecessary abuse of privileges. Even the gospel proves to many a savor of death, but we must nevertheless give and work for its support. The possibility of the evils suggested may well lead those who manage Education Societies to see the dangers and guard carefully against them.

It is again objected that the Lord of the Harvest chooses his own laborers—often the foolish and weak to confound the wise and mighty,—that he says to them not "prepare" but "go, work"—that not many are impressed with the duty of preaching, till the most favorable time for acquiring an education has passed, and that this is an indication of Providence that such men should not seek the training of the schools but be content to fill the places which we think to be less honorable but *He* sees to be necessary. These objections do not apply with force to young men in those studies, which are technical, professional-theological, nor to those whose age, talents and previous preparation fit them for pursuing a liberal course. Whatever validity they may have lies only against an effort to bring all candidates for the ministry up to one standard. The proper conclusion would be that our energies and means should be devoted not merely to declared candidates for the ministry, but also to the culture of as many as possible, and that we should look for a supply of profoundly learned ministers, not so much to those who set out to acquire an education with the ministry in view, as to those who, under the guidings of an ever-watchful Providence, are educated before they are called. Moses was learned in all the wisdom of Egypt before he was publicly sent as the leader of Israel. Saul, at the feet of Gamaliel, thought he was preparing to be a Rabbi, but really he was in training for the apostleship of the Gentiles. As God wrought in times past, so may we expect him to work now.

Occasionally it is suggested that a young man really meritorious will always receive the requisite help from those who know him most intimately. If in the immediate circle of his acquaintance aid is withheld, it is *prima facie* proof that he lacks one of the scriptural requirements for a Bishop. Waiving the unwarranted assumption of the ability and willingness of the particular community to render the required assistance, it is conceded that just here is a danger that needs to be watched. Æneas sailed once only between Scylla and Charybdis, but, in our days, the path of duty and safety lies often between fatal extremes. Would that it were sounded in the ears of all our churches and pastors, that those, who see the daily walk of a man, who know his mode of life and influence at home, who are cognizant of his spirit, his type of piety and special ministerial aptitudes or inaptitudes, have the best opportunity and the real responsibility for deciding upon the probabilities of his usefulness. It is moral cowardice for churches to shift an unpleasant duty upon those who have less aptitude for its performance. An Education Society is rather designed as a central agency for arousing and directing public opinion, distributing information, collecting the benefactions of the churches and disbursing them in the most judicious and economical manner. System and combination are not intended to obviate but to quicken and secure the success of individual exertions.

There is a growing demand for trained ministers. The schools which combine the crystallized wisdom of many centuries with the vital energies of the active present, afford the cheapest and best facilities for acquiring well-rounded education. The existence of such opportunities for improvement is a plain indication of Providence to which no pious young man can guiltlessly shut his eyes.

Many, perhaps a majority, of those who seem called to preach and give promise of usefulness, are not able to meet the expenses incident to several years' residence at a College or Seminary. For these a well-managed organization is almost a necessity. It certainly has great advantages over sporadic efforts for cultivating among Christians a spirit of prayerful exertion for an increase of laborers, for judging without personal bias of the character of candidates, and so for elevating the standard while increasing the numbers of the ministry. The organizations now existing can point with humble pride and profound gratitude to the fact that not more than five per cent. of those aided have proven unworthy, while the remainder constitute nearly half—many of them the ablest and most influential of our ministers. Societies for this purpose took shape among the Baptists of America about sixty years ago. The work has grown till now there are in 13 States (representing, however, more than half of the Baptist strength,) 453 beneficiaries, supported at an annual cost of about $50,000. This estimate does not include 300 or more freedmen, preparing for ministerial labors in the useful Institutes of the Home Mission Society, at a cost of $50 per annum. These figures increased by 50 per cent. would, perhaps, fairly show what the Baptists of the United States are doing in this direction. To approximate what we ought to be doing, they should be more than doubled.

Now it is not claimed that these 1,500 young men would not, without some such aid, become good preachers. Genius and grace can make a man under the most unfavorable circumstances; but it is claimed that these men will rise more rapidly to positions of usefulness, and fill them more satisfactorily than if their noble ambition were chilled by unaided penury, and their moral and intellectual growth dwarfed by struggling in early life with burdens too great for undeveloped powers.

II. THE PERSONS TO BE AIDED.

The most difficult and delicate of all duties in this work devolves on those who decide upon applications for aid. The difficulty is not to determine what class of men shall be aided, but to decide whether or not this brother belongs to that class. The delicacy is not in requiring certain professions of purpose and other overt qualifications, but in the necessity of going behind these professions, and trying to probe the inmost soul. It will not do to rely on talents and morality singly or combined, nor on the esteem and fondly cherished desires of friends,—the man of God must have infinitely more than all these. It will not do when favors are to be distributed to rely on mere professions. Constantine did irreparable harm when he offered a holiday robe and ten pieces of gold to every convert from heathenism. It is to extreme liberality in benefactions that Dr. Jacobus in the N. Y. Observer attributes the troublesome surplus of ministers in the General Assembly. To be more explicit, devoting however least space to what is most important, and therefore most obvious, an Education Society must require of every recipient of aid,

1. Essential *moral* qualifications. These are all embraced in what constitutes a divine call to the ministry, of which the best proofs to others are *a*) the approval of those brethren who have best known one's private life; *b*) a simple and intelligent account of his conversion and call; *c*) an humble yet independent and determined profession of purpose to devote his life to preaching, and *d*) clear, sound, though not logically developed or minutely exact views, on the cardinal points of Christian doctrine and duty. To these tests might well be added another—early training in the principles and habits of morality—by pious parents, Sunday-school teachers, or other such agency. Without this there is little or no guarantee of stability. Chiefly the poor are called to the ministry, but they are the honest and industrious, not the shiftless and vicious.

2. Necessary *mental* qualities, which are capacity to learn and aptness to teach, as evinced by the extent and character of previous acquirements and the success of actual trial—not that any man should ever be required to undertake that self-contradictory something called preaching a trial-sermon, but that when occasions to speak publicly for Christ are so frequent, various, and urgent, no one should be aided by an Education Society, who has not felt, like Elihu, constrained by the spirit within him, to open his lips and answer, even in the presence of older men. Woe to him who is called of God, if he preaches not the gospel, but that does not imply that his brethren are bound to send him to college. There are more gradations in the Christian ministry than in the Romish hierarchy. There has been and will be constant need for some *uneducated*, or partially educated ministers. Our benefactions must be bestowed only on those who have time and talent to profit by them.

3. Suitable *external* conditions as to health, age, and pecuniary circumstances. Freedom from serious organic disease must be required—it were worse than useless to keep in a sedentary, scholastic life, one who, if he lives to graduate, will soon pine away with consumption or destroy his usefulness by dyspeptic misanthropy. We still need men who can endure hardness as good soldiers. One seeking education for a life-work should be old enough to have fixed resolutions and steady purposes of his own—not built on the sands heaped together by partial relatives and personal friends, but based on a careful and prayerful consideration of the nature and demands of the work—old enough therefore both in years and in Christian experience to count the cost, and yet young enough to be docile, pliable, and acquisitive. The limits cannot be accurately fixed, but if we should say not under *eighteen* nor over *twenty-five* years, there ought to be very few exceptions. According to the Apostle's rule in the somewhat parallel case of widows, only those who are really dependent and not provided for by any of their own house, should ask support from the

church. Great will be the error and grievous the consequences if young men are led directly or indirectly to think that because they devote themselves to a calling which requires self-sacrifice they are thereby entitled to all sorts of gratuities and clerical courtesies. Religion among the masses must suffer if the clergy, unlike Him who ate with publicans and sinners, separate themselves from the people into a privileged caste. Education societies then must help all, and not only those, who have all other qualifications, but for want of money cannot complete a liberal course of study in any reasonable time. These are not few; they constitute in numbers and in strength nearly half of our rising ministry.

III. THE AMOUNT OF AID.

Self-reliance is essential to success. It is better to transplant into your garden a stunted oak from the hillside than a luxuriant palm from the hothouse. The churches do not need elaborately wrought pulpit ornaments to be borne on the palms of their hands, but sturdy leaders in every good word and work. We must not relieve those who are in the full vigor of youth from the necessity of close economy and strenuous exertion, but render just so much assistance as will encourage their own efforts. There is, however, no well-defined mean between the chill of penury and the stimulation of necessity, between that aid which develops and that which weakens self-respect. The average amount to each beneficiary in the Middle States is from $125 to $150; in New England and the West about $100, and in Ohio and the South less than $100 per annum. But instead of naming any fixed sum it would be better, if practicable, to decide in each case according to its circumstances,—to offer more help than one really needs is superfluous if he declines, injurious if he accepts it. The maximum should cover only tuition and board during the scholastic year. If a young man in this country cannot secure from other sources the means of paying for books, clothing, and incidentals, it is very doubtful whether he has energy enough to get or use an education. Much may be done if those favorably situated will use their influence to get for needy students suitable and remunerative employment for vacations and other leisure hours. This deserves the constant attention of brethren connected with or living near all our institutions of learning, and if carried out will enable almost any young man to meet his incidental expenses. Tuition in most colleges, founded as they generally were, primarily for the education of the ministry, is gratuitous to ministerial students. So that Education Societies usually need to provide only for the board of those under their patronage. The cost of this in several Colleges and Seminaries has been considerably reduced by adopting a modification of the old Spartan *Syssitia*. Experience has shown that when rightly managed it satisfies the students, diminishes the cost of living, and facilitates the collection of means, by allowing contributions in kind as well as in money.

The proper amount of aid will also vary according to the grade of the school itself. From the time that one has mastered the rudiments of practical education, the advantages of liberal culture increase in geometrical ratio. Every acquisition expands the soul to receive the next with more ease and in fuller measure. Every upward step not only enlarges the horizon, but brings out more clearly the relations between different parts of the landscape. Regarded simply as an investment, $200 a year in the higher walks of literature and science pays better than half that sum in preparatory studies. Two days on the serene summit of Parnassus were worth a whole year amid the thorny jungles at its base. Besides this increase in the value of education there is another important point—as the recipient of aid advances there is ever less and less likelihood that he will prove unworthy, either by casting away his professions, honestly changing his purpose, or proving unequal to the task of acquiring a good education. When an army moves, many faint-hearted or foot-sore fall out in the earlier stages, but long days of marching and fighting make those who remain trusty veterans. So an Education Society, however careful in accepting beneficiaries, must drop not a few beginners, but rarely one who is well-advanced in study. It would for these reasons seem to be legitimate and just to beckon the faithful and successful student ever onward by allowing increasing appropriations as he advances from the Academy through College to the Seminary. And if at any time through multitude of applicants and scarcity of funds some must be rejected, economy requires that it be rather those who are just beginning than those who are about completing their course. These ideas may be, I might say have been, realized by determining to give no aid until students are well-prepared for the Academy—to help them there only in extreme cases, and to a comparatively small extent—say one-third or one-half their necessary expenses—to help them at College more liberally both as to persons and amount—keeping however within the limits above laid down—then to help at Theological Seminaries all approved students who need it, and to the full extent of their necessary expenses. Beyond this we may not go; for however desirable it is that a few at least of our ministers should enjoy the benefits of a fellowship, or of a residence at some American or European University, the bestowal of such privileges is clearly beyond the sphere of a society organized for educating preachers, and must be remitted to other organizations or to individual effort.

IV. THE WAYS AND MEANS.

In what method an Education Society can best accomplish its objects, is a question on which opinions are much divided. It is deemed best to state in this paper, regardless of seeming egotism, simply the writer's own views, and trust that, where wrong, they will be corrected in the discussion that is to follow.

1. An Education Society should have an Executive Board of not less than five, nor more than fifteen, located near each institution at which it proposes to help young men. When a society represents a large area, let there be one central and several auxiliary Boards. Let each Board consist partly of instructors, who will know how every beneficiary stands in the class-room, partly of brethren not connected with the institution, for they on many subjects have better judgment and less prejudice than professional teachers. Let each Board have at least one officer, President or Secretary, who can and will devote a good deal of time to correspondence and other such work. When practicable to have a salaried Secretary, it promotes system and really saves money.

2. The funds needed should be raised by direct contributions from the churches, and if possible from all the churches. This may be partially done by employing agents to visit the most accessible and liberal, but much better by mailing circulars and contributing brief articles to the religious press. It is

the universal testimony that when pastors are interested and bring the matter properly before their churches, there is no lack of means. This cause lies near the hearts of the people, and they will not knowingly allow it to suffer. The accumulation of endowments either by bequests, large gifts, or investments, should be by all means discouraged. This for several reasons. The recipient of aid from such a fund receives it as of right, not as of favor, and so his sense of obligation is much weakened. And what is of more importance, a fund makes the society comparatively independent of the churches, and so far weakens the connection so necessary to the vitality of both. The bonds of warm Christian love and zeal are safer than Government five-twenties, and yield a better income than Pacific 8's. An endowed church tends to become petrified, much more an endowed Board. It is equally dangerous to the prosperity and piety of Christians to relieve them of the necessity of frequent contributions. Ministerial education is a wand with which even stones may be smitten, and caused thenceforth to send out refreshing streams into both home and foreign mission fields. Therefore let brethren, who of their abundance wish to promote education, be urged to the greatest liberality, and advised not to entail benefits on a favored few, but to found or enlarge the endowment of some institution at which not only these few but many others may be benefited.

3. Each applicant for aid must forward a letter of endorsation from his church, after which, if practicable, let the Secretary correspond privately with his pastor or other discreet brother, for it is a sad truth that one sealed letter is more reliable than many open recommendations. When duly recommended, he should be carefully, though with as little formality as possible, examined by a Committee of the Board, on all the points heretofore indicated. Passing this satisfactorily, let him be advised with due regard to his own wishes and circumstances, as to his studies, whether to attempt a complete liberal and special course, or to omit partially or wholly the one or the other. No sculptor can carve an Apollo from a block of granite, no engineer would bridge the Mississippi on piers of Parian marble. We need men differing in their education as well as in native talent. But after arranging his course let him be held steadily to it, unless good and evident cause to the contrary should arise. "A double-minded man is unstable in all his ways."

4. Every recipient of aid must be held accountable to the Board for general deportment and for advancement in study, yet in such way as to avoid anything like a system of espionage. Perhaps no better plan can be devised than to have quarterly or monthly reports by his instructors of class-standing, and by the student himself of how each Lord's day is spent. It is not unfrequently necessary to drop from the list, after trial, some who have been accepted. This should be done with a gentle kindness that will not needlessly wound the sensibilities, nor chill the better feelings, but also with a frank firmness that will not for sentiment or seeming expediency swerve from the right. Want of faithfulness here, whatever of temporary advantage it may promise, will very soon sap the confidence of those who contribute the means and lower among their fellows the standing of all beneficiaries.

5. Every student aided should be required to give in due form an indemnifying bond of sufficient amount to cover all sums advanced to him with interest, but so conditioned that if he enters actively on the duties of the gospel ministry, or if he is prevented from so doing by death or disease, then his ob-

ligation to become null and void. Some societies take informal bonds for the repayment of advances without interest, whenever the signer becomes able. These, like multiplied oaths, serve only to hamper and harass the sensitively conscientious, while they are easily evaded or ruthlessly trampled under foot by the less scrupulous. A faithful pastor, in freely inciting his flock both by precept and example, will do more for this or any other cause than if his obligation were measured by a money standard. The Christian's free-will offering is better than the Jewish tithe. Other societies give freely without any refunding bond—the great objection to which is that those who get a gratuitous education for a specific purpose, and then pervert it to some other, should be required in common honesty to make full restitution. The course first suggested, though not free from objections, seems to be a mean between the other two, and to secure as nearly as can be the desirable aim, to *give* aid to those who deserve it, and to secure repayment from any to whom it has been improperly loaned.

Finally, let it never be forgotten that whatever plan may be adopted, its effectiveness will depend on the skill, fidelity, and zeal with which it is carried out. No machinery invented by human wit can run itself. Those who manage the affairs of Education Societies have rare opportunities of accomplishing great good—their responsibilities are correspondingly weighty. They must be awake to the ever-varying needs of churches and of individuals and be ready, without departing from the ancient landmarks which the fathers set, to adapt their plans to circumstances. The duties and difficulties in the way can be met only if one is inspired with a proper enthusiasm, and this will not fail to be awakened when we think of the multitude of pastorless churches, the thousands in our own land who never hear the Gospel, the myriads of perishing heathen, the blessings in time and in eternity which flow from a faithful presentation of the pure Gospel, and the countless evils inflicted by those who handle the word of God deceitfully or ignorantly.

Dr. SHEPARDSON: It has been said that in the Presbyterian Church there are 1603 pastors, and 1609 ministers that are not employed, either as pastors or as stated supplies, and that assisting beneficiaries produces weak men, that it has caused young men to rely upon others for help, until they are unfit for the profession. It is a very difficult matter for us to estimate the exact value of figures, and when it is stated that we have many young men who by being assisted have failed to have self-reliance it would seem to be a very great evil, but there are men, and men in this house, and some who have read papers before this Convention, who have supported themselves, sir, upon "indian meal and molasses," week after week and month after month. There may not be such cases now, there ought not to be. Our brethren are becoming wealthy, and there are men in every strong church who will assist those young men who really need assistance. A young man comes forward to study for the ministry. He feels like the Apostle, "Woe is me if I preach not the Gospel." He has seven or eight or ten years that he must devote to the work of preparation for which he receives nothing. It looks formidable to him. A business man of this city said to me to-day; young men of talent go into business rather than the ministry because they have not this apprenticeship to undergo. They can go to their work at once. Let us take the young men who have power, and let us test them, and suppose we contribute $100 a year for ten years; it is but $1000; which one of these young men if in business life would earn in six months. Suppose one of these young men should not prove worthy; is the loss so great as to frighten us from contributing to those who are worthy? I ask if the endowments of our colleges are not in the nature of gifts for beneficiary purposes? A gentleman lately contributed $6000 to Vassar College to help some worthy young women. There are men now that will contribute by the thousands, Christian men who are willing to give. I think we can afford to be generous. We have entered upon a great career. We have a very great work before us, and there is no amount of ministers to be spared. We ought to be careful how we receive these young men, of course, but let us take the worthy and encourage them on; let us be noble and pour out our thousands and cheer these young men into life, and if one or two fail a good lawyer or physician or farmer, may be made, and made a better man. I think we are in the right way, only let us urge the thing on to success.

Pres. HOVEY: I was very much inclined in the course of the discussion a while since on another paper, to rise and say a word to about the same effect with what has been said by my friend on the left. (DR. SHEPARDSON). I certainly felt at the time that there were men here who have known what it is to receive aid, and who have yet known what it is to respect themselves; to labor diligently, and even to break in upon their course of study, and who have been thereby detained for several years from the work for which they were preparing. That was the case with myself. When I commenced my studies I was old enough certainly—17 years of age—to press through without any break from beginning to end, and I longed to do so. But I was utterly without means except such as I could procure from month to month, or during the vacations, and it was practically impossible for me, without the assistance of friends, to pursue an uninterrupted course of study. I speak of this case because I know it better than I know any other. [Laughter]. I am sorry to say that I was compelled sometimes to live even in the manner in which my friend on the left (DR. SHEPARDSON) says he has known persons to live, and I wonder now that I am so well to do in flesh as I am. [Laughter].

No young man should ever be permitted with the knowledge of the churches, to endure such hardship. That is certain. No father here who has a father's heart, would allow his own son to endure such hardships if he could avoid it; and no man who understands what human character is, I think, would unnecessarily put one to such straits. There are young men now willing to do it. I doubt not there are as brave men, as heroic men, men who are making practically the same kind of sacrifices which we made twenty-five or thirty years ago. It costs much more now to live than it did then. I don't know that a man could live on indian meal and milk or molasses, as I did at that time for a quarter of a dollar a week. I think he would fare poorly in these days. These things must be taken into account. The whole style of living is different. The board bill is almost three times as much now in most places, and in the place where I live it is six times as much as I used to have to pay when I was in college. And were our students not able to manage the matter wisely, the cost would be insupportable with what aid they now receive. My own belief is that though there are sometimes mistakes made, yet a very large proportion of our best and worthiest men have received aid in some such way, and indeed, as has been said, all our institutions are, in part, beneficiary institutions, and those who never think of becoming ministers are receiving a larger amount of aid than is commonly supposed to be given to those who are studying for the ministry. It is only a small pittance in addition that the churches are urged to give and ought to give for the assistance of men who need such aid. I don't care how careful the scrutiny is, but I do ask that we should love them as brethren, sympathize with them as persons of flesh and blood, as persons liable to be discouraged. For not every man who has genius and heart has the physical constitution and the indomitable will that can carry him through every thing. There are two sides to the question undoubtedly. But while it is very desirable that we should weigh carefully and adjust our assistance to the needs of the recipients, it is important that we should aid those who really need the aid and not cast them upon the churches as pastors, with a crushing debt upon them. I like to see a student who looks as if he had one good coat and one respectable hat to wear, who looks as if he had one good meal a day and who greets me with as much cheerfulness as I greet him. I want to feel that he is my brother and my equal, and I do feel so in regard to most of the students, and desire that they should, in every proper way, receive the assistance needed. I believe they must have it, or many of them be stopped in their way, and not accomplish the purpose they have in view as rapidly as they ought to accomplish it. A man who is twenty-six years old—and that is the average age of our students when they enter the Theological Seminary—ought not to spend two or three years in earning his bread before he completes his course. He will be more than thirty when he goes into the ministry. Let them go into the ministry early, in the very flower of their lives, ready to do good and effective service. The churches love young men and vigorous men as well as old men. I wish they loved the old men more. I wish the old men were younger in feeling and in spirit, and then, perhaps, they would be loved just as much as the young men. In fact I cannot realize myself, as I think of it, that I am more than twenty-five years old. [Laughter.] I suppose I am, on looking over the almanac, but still it doesn't seem so. It doesn't seem to me that Dr. Sears is more than thirty-five. [Laughter.] I never could make it out that he was an old man, and I think that any good teacher or good minister needs to feel that he is young and needs to go heart to heart in full sympathy with the young men who have such great burdens before them, and who, if they know what they are coming to—and they do, most of them—know that they need all the help, and all the vigor, and all the heart, and all the soul that a man can have in this stirring age to do well his work. [Applause.]

Dr. BOSWORTH: I must confess, sir, that I somewhat regretted some remarks that were brought out this morning. In some respects I was glad to hear them, inasmuch as all such expressions tend to the thorough examination of our means. But I fear that the effect may be to diminish the sympathy in the direction of a good cause. I would beg leave to suggest that this whole subject needs to be reviewed, and carefully and searchingly examined; for if there be a better method of meeting these necessities, by all means let it be devised and developed and brought forward. Take, for example, this simple fact. In the Institution presided over by our excellent brother who has just taken his seat, there are sixty students; of those fifty-three are recipients of the aid of churches distributed through the Education Society of that commonwealth: fifty-three out of sixty. I think I have looked each one of these young men in the face. I have heard, I think, the religious experience of each one. I have taken in hand and examined the credentials given by the church from which he came. By that church he is approved of God, in their judgment, as called to the ministry, and worthy of the office; also that he is poor, that he needs the aid of the society. This in addition to the personal examination to which he is subjected and to the various inquiries made concerning him, has been deemed by the Board sufficient as a test of his fitness to receive that aid. I take it for granted, and I am assured of the justice of this assumption, by the personal conduct of these young men, that they came to the society only as a last resort. They have no personal friends. There are other young men that have been put through their course of training by the aid of individual friends. Those are the recipients of benefactions, and there is no material difference. Now this is the question before my mind. If there be any other method more free from objection, by all means let us have it. I have known of individual cases where students anticipated aid themselves in their courses of study, who have been taken up by friends and put through. Ordinarily these benefactions are much more liberal, and one who has been engaged in this work confessed to me last Sabbath day, that he feared they erred in bestowing their aid too freely. It has come to my knowledge too, that some institutions have given larger aid than others. I am sure the Boards have been candid and careful and generous. It would give them joy if there were any other method to reach the wants, the absolute necessities of these young men, than the ones that have been so long sustained. My only regret is, that these methods of some sort are not more liberally sustained; for it is within my own personal knowledge that a great many of these young men must stop in their courses if they cannot receive enough to pay their board at least during term time; and that is all which in our society we have attempted to meet.

Mr. COLGATE: I wish to say a word only on this subject. It is with extreme diffidence that I rise to speak to this body. But I think this subject of aid to beneficiaries is a very important one, and should claim the attention of this Convention to a large extent. The remark was made by the reader of the last paper that there might be a difference of opinion in regard to endowments for beneficiaries. I believe in endowments for Colleges and for Seminaries, as far as the support of the institution is concerned, to pay the professors and all the expenses of tuition, but I have always been opposed to endowments given to colleges for the education of our young men without a direct appeal to the churches. I believe that the churches should be kept in perfect sympathy with the education of those whom God has called to preach. And I think that the true way to support our beneficiaries is to teach our churches that the responsibility rests upon that church in which God places a young man who feels that he should be educated for the ministry. I know there are many churches in which there are young men who feel that they ought to preach the Gospel that think they are too poor to support those young men during their course of study. It is the duty of such a church to go to the next church. If it requires $100, $150 or $200 a year, and the churches can only pay $50 it is the duty of that church to go to its neighbor and say: "In the providence of God a young man has been raised up who wishes to study for the Gospel ministry, and we can only pay $50 towards his education; can you help us with $30 or $50?" And then go to another until the whole amount is raised. And let that church from which that young man goes become an education society that shall prepare him for the ministry. I believe that this doctrine should be taught to the churches. And if every church would assume this responsibility, we should have no further need of the Education Society at all. Each church is an education society. And then we will send the young men to our academies, colleges and theological seminaries, which we trust will be properly endowed. This is a vital subject. I do believe that there are now in our denomination hundreds of young men who feel inclined to study for the ministry and would do so if it were not for the uncertainty of support. And there is a shrinking and a withholding from going away from the churches to which they belong to a foreign institution or society to which they are strangers. Therefore they go into secular employments. But if the church would only take the young men in hand and say, "We will see that you shall receive the education you require,"—if this were done I believe our academies, colleges and seminaries would be crowded with young men engaged in studying for the ministry.

Prof. MARSH: I stand here as the Secretary of the Ohio Baptist Education Society, and I wish to say a word or two on this subject. I only want to speak on one point. I am glad to hear brethren say—I don't mean I'm glad to hear them say it; I am glad they *can* say "I thank God I never needed any beneficiary aid." I can thank God that I was able to work for three years and a half after getting out from my college course, and that, so doing, I then entered into the ministry, having paid off my debts. But, brethren, let us be careful how we compel our brothers who are laying themselves on the altar of Christ and the church, and men with the spirit of that work in their hearts, to falter and stop at the beginning of their course. Let us be careful how we degrade their consecration, and how we make it impossible that that spirit of consecration should be devoted to the spread of Christ in the world. They say it degrades a young man to be a beneficiary; brethren, did you ever know it degrade any body but a beneficiary of an education society, to have his education given to him? Did you ever see a son degraded because his education cost him nothing? I have, in twenty-five years of work, seen many a young man ruined because his father kept his pockets filled with money. I have seen many a father make mistakes with his money, a greater mistake with his money than he made when he put it into the treasury of the Education Society, or when he put it into the hands of his church treasurer with instructions to give it to noble, consecrated young men. I said to a man the other day, to whom I appealed for help for a young man, there is no better investment you can make of your money in God's world than to invest it in educating a consecrated, Christian young man; you cannot do better with it. We, none of us, undertake to carry young men in the lap of luxury; none of our education societies propose to support young men; we dare not do it; but we do propose, by the help of God to show to young men that we will make it possible for them, by the help of their own exertions, to prosecute their studies. There are one or two other points in the paper I would be glad to speak of; I will only say we need to look at this question all around. There are more points in it than one or two. But I do specially ask you, do not go home with the impression, with a feeling or desire to make any young brother who comes to ask aid of you or your church or Education Society, feel that he is degrading himself or the cause of Christ or the work of the ministry by so doing.

Pres. ROBINSON: I am sorry that the few words spoken by me this morning should have been misunderstood. I have labored too long and too earnestly to help young men for me, at this day, to be misunderstood by my *young* brother who followed me this morning [Dr. BOSWORTH,] and whom I remember as a somewhat noted preacher when I was just entering the Theological Seminary to find out how to preach. Perhaps I might say that I have made as many appeals, public and private, for money to help beneficiaries as any man on this floor. And I have done more than that,—I have seen the time when three-fourths of the students of the Theological Seminary with which I am connected must be helped or quit their studies immediately. Never a man of them, before God, can say that I did not hold out my hand of sympathy to help and lift him into courage and strengthen him with all the strength I had. There are some here to-day who know what I mean when I say this.

The question before us on the paper was on the increase of the ministry. Dr. LAMSON spoke of the great number of men unemployed. Now say what we will about it, brethren, there is a connection between that and the matter of help. I don't know what the connection may be, but there is, somehow, a connection. The thought flashed on me when our lay brother (Mr. COLGATE) alluded to the fact that the churches should send up their young men. They do send them up. And dare we in any mistaken case send them back? That is the question. They are sent up with direct orders. I have now in mind more than one such instance. "Why, who are these professors that they question our wisdom? We have settled that question. We have licensed them! We have sent them there to study! It is not for them to say whether they shall continue their studies." There is one source of difficulty. Now some one should have the courage to say to the young man who is likely to occupy a place in the ministry without filling it, "You had better not continue your studies." There are dangers sometimes when young men start from the churches. I have in mind now the case of a young man who was a clerk and was receiving a salary of $1000 per year. He thought he had a call to the ministry. The church of which he was a member said: "You go to college and we will see you through." They furnished him money—no matter how much. Now what is the prospect after that young man gets through and is invited, after nine years of study, to go to a church that will give him $500 a year or $300 and a parsonage? The question is to be thought of, gentlemen.

The Convention, at five o'clock, proceeded to take up the report of the Committee on Organization, which had been made the order for that time.

The following was the report:—

REPORT OF THE COMMITTEE ON ORGANIZATION OF THE EDUCATIONAL WORK OF THE BAPTIST DENOMINATION.

The Committee to whom was referred the subject of the Organization of Educational work, beg leave to present the following report:

Your Committee believe that the permanent endowment of Christian institutions of learning is one of the most effective and economical ways to evangelize the world. To educate Christian men, is to create moral forces which are self-generating and perpetual.

To save time, and concentrate denominational strength upon this object, they would recommend the formation of a National Society, which should be the recognized organ of churches, through which funds could be wisely applied in helping men to help themselves.

While it is always better for institutions to secure endowments upon their own fields, and by their own exertions, so far as practicable, your Committee believe that such an organization could do much in directing effort, and providing temporary support for struggling interests, while they are so engaged; and by advising the churches with reference to the most deserving objects, and the best methods of bestowment, thus inspiring confidence in such enterprises, on the part of those who cannot personally inquire into them.

Your Committee would, therefore, recommend that we proceed to organize a National Society on the basis of the following constitution:

PROPOSED CONSTITUTION.

ARTICLE I. This Association shall be called the American Baptist Educational Commission.

ART. II. This Commission shall have for its object, the promotion of education, and the increase of the ministry in the Baptist denomination. It disclaims any intention to interfere with existing schools or education societies. Its work shall be to collect and diffuse information, and to foster and sustain institutions of learning, by annually contributing to their current expenses, until they may be able to raise permanent endowments upon their own field or elsewhere. It shall not take part in the work of raising endowment funds, except by advising the institutions under its care, when and how to take the field, in order not to interfere with each other, or unduly burden the churches.

It may, however, receive and hold in trust, designated or undesignated funds raised by the agents of any institution, or given by any individual, until such time as needful conditions may be met for their final transfer to special Boards of control.

ART. III. This Commission shall be composed, for the time being, of the subscribers to the original five years' fund of the Commission, and of the members of the present National Baptist Educational Convention, and hereafter, as follows:

1. Of delegates from incorporate institutions of learning, whose Boards of Control are wholly or chiefly of the Baptist denomination. Colleges, or Universities, having undergraduate classes or schools and conferring degrees, Theological Seminaries, and Education Societies of one or more States, may each send two delegates. Academies or Preparatory Schools may each send one delegate.

2. Of delegates from Baptist State Conventions or General Associations, and from Baptist State Pastoral Conferences. Each such Convention, General Association, or Pastoral Conference, may send two delegates.

3. Of persons or associations paying money into the treasury of the Commission, to promote its purposes, as follows: Any person paying twenty-five dollars annually, shall be a member while so paying; any person paying five hundred dollars at one time, shall be a member for life; any educational association formed to aid the purposes of the Commission, paying into its treasury not less than fifty dollars annually, may appoint a delegate.

ART. IV. The officers of this Commission shall consist of a President, two Vice-Presidents, a Recording Secretary, a Treasurer, an Executive Committee of ten, whose seat shall be at New York, and three Advisory Committees of twelve each, whose seats shall be respectively at Boston, Chicago, and Richmond. These officers, when sitting together, shall constitute the Board of Councillors. The Board of Councillors shall appoint a Corresponding Secretary.

ART. V. The Executive Committee, of whom three shall be a quorum (except for the investment of money, or for its disbursement for the maintenance or endowment of institutions of learning, in which case the quorum shall be five), shall appoint such assistants or other agencies as may be necessary to carry out the purposes of the Second Article of this Constitution. It shall be intrusted with the administration of the Commission, it shall fix its own modes of procedure, and shall have power to fill vacancies occasioned by the resignation, removal or death of its members. It shall call annual meetings of the Board of

Councillors, to whom it shall make report in detail of its proceedings. It may also call special meetings of this Board, and all calls of such meetings, whether annual or special, shall be by published notices.

The Executive Committee may refer local questions to the Advisory Committees, and the Corresponding Secretary may call meetings of those Committees for the consideration of such questions. At such meetings four shall constitute a quorum.

ART. VI. The Board of Councillors shall hold annual meetings, as called by the Executive Committee, and shall determine the general policy of the Commission, but the care and disbursement of funds shall be entrusted solely to the Executive Committee. The Board shall have power to fill vacancies, other than those which may occur in the Executive Committee, and shall report triennially to the Commission. At least eleven members shall be required to constitute a quorum.

ART. VII. The Commission shall hold triennial meetings, which shall be called, and for which arrangements shall be made, by the Executive Committee. The officers above named shall be chosen at these meetings, provided that the Executive Committee shall be divided into two classes, five only (except to fill vacancies not filled as herein before named), to be chosen at any triennial meeting.

ART. VIII. Funds for the maintenance and endowment of institutions of learning, shall never be paid from the treasury of this Commission without satisfactory guarantees to secure the purposes of the donors and of this Commission against waste or perversion.

ART. IX. This Constitution may be altered or amended by a vote of two-thirds of the members present at a triennial meeting, provided that no change shall ever be made in reference to the main object of the Commission, and that none shall be at any time made in respect to the election or duties or powers of the Executive Committee, except by a two-thirds vote at two successive triennial meetings.

In behalf of the Committee,

SAMUEL COLGATE, *Chairman.*

Dr. WOODS: I am fully convinced, that a great debt of gratitude is due from the whole Baptist denomination, first, to those liberal-minded brethren who have for several years past sustained by their contributions this Educational Commission: and, in the next place, to the far-seeing Secretary of this Commission, whose wise counsels and indomitable energies, even with imperfect health, have planned and so successfully carried forward the projected work; and especially to Almighty God, whose inspiration, I am persuaded, first prompted and has since guided our brother Secretary in this noble enterprise.

That this work, so auspiciously begun, and so successfully carried forward to its present stage of progress, may result in an organization on a broader basis, embracing within the range of its beneficial influence our whole country, destined by heaven to be one and indivisible, is a consummation devoutly to be wished.

The plan presented to us for such an enlarged organization, appears to me to be, on the whole, wise, practicable, far-reaching, adapted to combine in one grand effort our now scattered energies and to throw wholesome safeguards about the disbursement of the funds. Should a merciful Providence spare the life and health of our worthy Secretary, and enable him to supervise the work in its enlarged developments, I am confident the work will be done faithfully, and, with God's blessing, will be crowned with a glorious success.

As a member of this Convention, I desire to say, that our most hearty thanks are due to the Ex-President of Brown University, (Dr. SEARS,) for his able, masterly address, at the opening of this Convention, on the general interests of education in all its momentous bearings, and especially upon the absolute necessity of our denominational Academies, Colleges and Theological Seminaries.

Mr. PRESIDENT: It has long been a received axiom, that Knowledge is power. A more important motto for us as a religious denomination to inscribe on our banners, is Education is power. What we especially need as a people, is, to draw out, by education, the wealth of undeveloped talent existing among us. Universal education, in all its gradations from the lowest to the highest, and in every branch of learning, is the demand of the hour. Instead of being compelled, as we have been within my remembrance, in order to obtain the best education, to send our sons to Academies, Colleges and Theological Seminaries of other denominations, there is no reason, why we should not make all our own Institutions equal to the very best, both in the amplitude of their endowments and in the skill and varied learning of their professors. By doing this, we should attract to our seats of learning pupils from many a family where there is now a criminal neglect of education.

But to accomplish this, there must be awakened among all our people a higher appreciation of the value and the power of an enlightened Christian education. In every State and Territory of this broad Union, our rallying cry should be, educate, educate, educate. Every man among us should be made to see and to feel, that he has failed essentially in his duty to God, to his country, to his own religious faith, if he has not done what he could, first for the education of his own family, and then for the encouragement and ample endowment of our Academies, Colleges and Theological Seminaries, on which, under God, the prosperity of our denomination so eminently depends. Let this work of faith and labor of love be prosecuted with vigor and untiring perseverance through the whole length and breadth of our land, and the direct amount of good accomplished will be incalculable; and one of its blessed reflex influences will be seen in the union once more of the hearts and hands of all our Baptist brotherhood, North and South, as in days of yore. With this feeling of oneness, oneness of cause and of purpose, pervading the whole million and a half of our widely scattered membership, and with the abiding conviction, that, as a religious denomination, we have God's truth on our side, that we are building on the foundation of the apostles and prophets, Jesus Christ himself being the chief corner-stone, shall we not become strong in the Lord and in the power of his might? Shall we not be stimulated to far higher efforts and more generous sacrifices for Christ and for his cause than any we have yet made?

Dr. J. WHEATON SMITH: I think this is a time when every one, young or old, residing here or elsewhere, owes his contribution of independent thought to a great question. In the judgment of four or five men who have read this paper, it needs re-casting from beginning to end. When you have altered half a dozen minor points like this that you have now before you, there will still be much more to alter. Then the great design itself of creating into a separate corporate life another national body suggests questions of the gravest magnitude. Nothing is to be lost by taking a little time for the consideration of this matter. The honest judgment of one of the youngest, and certainly not the wisest, of this company is, that to the time of the proposed Triennial meeting is not too long for the mature consideration of a paper which might then be wisely adopted.

Dr. BROADUS: I see a number of objections to the proposed plan. The gentleman says, there are objections to everything. There are a number of difficulties in the way of carrying this out. I see many difficulties in the way of our Home Missionary Society; many in the way of our Sunday-schools, and in the way of everything that attempts to combine and concentrate the energies of our independent and extremely free Baptist Churches. There are very great difficulties and quite a number of objections; but I see that it must go over all the difficulties and set aside all the objections. I think it is one of the things that are not made, that grow, and it has been growing through these years. The suggestion of the honored brother who just spoke, that we ought to take time to think about it, was wise enough. We have taken two years. It was proposed at Brooklyn to form such an organization, and then it was stated we had better take time to think of it; and in the call of this Convention, the question of the propriety of making such a permanent organization was made prominent. I was a good deal impressed, Mr. President, with a remark made to me by a layman in Brooklyn. He said one evening, that "gentlemen must give us somebody or other to tell us what are the worthy objects to give to. We are busy men; we have something to give; we are willing to give it; but we have not time to look around and find out what are the most worthy objects, and you must do something for us, or we won't for you. You must find out some means or other of helping me decide the question, or I shall be tired of giving." It seems to me, that that presents an important practical phase of the matter. Unless I can see far greater practical difficulties in the way of carrying out this scheme than have occurred to my mind, I shall be forced to believe that it must be done. No doubt this is a matter about which brethren are as free to differ as in regard to anything else; but, for my own part, I see the thing has been going on so that we are obliged to have it, and the only question is, which is the wisest way of doing it.

Dr. WAYLAND: My honored friend, Dr. Smith, to whom I have often looked for counsel, has observed, that there are objections to this plan. Perhaps I err; but it seems to me that my brethren living at the east, where all matters of education have taken form, are liable not to apprehend the necessity for this thing as much as those who have lived further toward the setting sun, and who have, indeed, as I have, *seen* at least one *setting sun.* [Laughter.] As to the particular details of it, I do not know; but the general object which is contemplated in the proposed society is of the utmost moment. I will speak only for the north-west. The north-west needs, in an educational point of view, help and counsel. I know that the Almighty favors us, because, if he did not, we should have sunk out of sight long ago. We have been going on without anything like system, now and then blundering into success, but for the most part successfully escaping it. [Laughter.] There are two ways in which we can move: one is converging towards a point, and the other is diverging from a point. We have been working on the latter plan; working a little here, getting discouraged, and then working a little there. It seems to me, that our institutions of learning, in the matter of their organization, in the matter of their location, and their way of operation, have demonstrated—if anything is susceptible of demonstration—our need of somebody that shall advise, that shall give unity, that shall impart efficiency. As to the matter of location, why our colleges have been located, for the most part, not for the benefit of the college, but very largely for the benefit of something else; not because the college needed the location, but because the location needed the college. Every now and then, when a village has arrived at the dignity of aspiring to be two or three horse, the people have said: "We must do something: we have tried in vain to have a railroad crossing, a woollen mill, or a distillery; now, we must have a *college!*" [Laughter.] And they have said to some denomination that was ambitious in an educational line: "Here is land that is worth twenty, thirty or fifty thousand dollars (at *our estimate*) that you may have; here is the place for you; and here is a Baptist church; it cannot get along without a college, and you must come here." The nascent College has said: "Here is chance: here is an opening;" and it has gone thither. And the location has been fatal. And the vitality of our institutions is amazing. I agree with Dr. Smith when he says, that societies and institutions of learning are hard to die. They are hard to live; but I believe the time they occupy in dying is unparalleled. [Laughter.]

Dr. TAYLOR: I hope, if there are any serious objections to the organization of this society, we shall hear them; not simply that we do not want a new society; not simply that it is introducing a new organization into the Baptist denomination. If there are men on this floor who have solid reasons why no such organization as this should be introduced into the Baptist denomination, I hope we shall hear those reasons carefully and candidly stated. For my own part I think that what this Commission has already done, has earned it the right and privilege to live and have a place in the Baptist Denomination. I do not believe, sir, that we shall ever accomplish what God has laid upon us as a Baptist Denomination to accomplish in education, without some such organization as this. I believe there is no reason why we should not have had to-day, not simply one or two institutions in the West that are doing a noble work unembarrassed, but ten or fifteen, if there had been a proper organization by which the men from whom we are expecting the money could have looked with confidence, and have been assured their money would not be thrown away. [Applause]. I know there are other men on this floor who know that there have been thousands and tens of thousands withheld, and that are being withheld to-day from colleges and institutions of learning in the West, simply because our men have no confidence whatever in the general proposals and appeals that have been made to them, and that there has been any amount of money, if not squandered, turned into different channels from that for which it was originally contributed, by which confidence has been weakened and, if confidence is to be restored in the minds of these men to whom we must look, it must be done by some such organization as this. Like brother BROADUS I have heard it said, "I have not time to examine," not from one man but from scores of men who have had their thousands to give, and who would be cheerful in giving their thousands if they knew where it would be appropriated wisely, but who have not the time or the opportunity to investigate these general claims and who cannot be expected to do it, but who will look to a board wisely selected, composed of men who will feel their responsibility to investigate carefully every claim. I do not wonder that there may be some objections, on the part of some men who are not willing that the institutions or objects they would present before us for their money should receive earnest and thorough investigation. I believe there are too many of these applications before us where investigation would simply destroy the hopes and prospects of such individuals. We need, therefore, for this purpose, just such an organization, just such a board, just such men as should be wisely selected, to whom shall be intrusted this grave responsibility of saying to our people, you can put your money there safely; and they will give it. We have men of means who understand the importance of this work, who will give their money if they can only be assured they are giving it safely, and if there are serious objections why this organization cannot be formed, I want to hear them.

The PRESIDENT: It is my duty to inform the Convention that the regular hour for adjournment has arrived. I suppose there is not a delegate present who does not feel that we have reached the very question that has brought us together, and that this is the most important question to come before us. It will be for the Convention to decide whether we will go on with the discussion.

It was suggested by a delegate that the discussion upon the Report of the Committee on Organization be resumed in the evening.

The PRESIDENT: The exercise set down in the programme for the evening will occupy about half an hour. If gentlemen are here promptly at the hour announced—7.45,—we can get through the appointed exercises by 8.15, which will give us, if we adjourn at the regular hour, an hour and a quarter to discuss this subject.

Dr. CUTTING: I wish to say in regard to Dr. CASWELL's paper that in the Convention of 1870, so long as the decision remained in my hands, I thought it necessary to make a rule that the writers of papers, alone, should present them. In accordance with that rule, a paper written by a gentleman who had been appointed to write and who could not be present, was retained in his hands. Another paper was sent, and the Convention so far overruled my plan that that paper was read. I understand that the paper written by Dr. CASWELL is in the hands of Prof. LINCOLN, and that the reading of it will consume twenty five minutes. I would therefore propose from our great deference to Dr. CASWELL and from the intrinsic importance of the subject that we listen to that paper, and that 8.20 promptly be the hour for resuming this discussion.

The motion was seconded and carried.

The Convention then adjourned to 7.45.

WEDNESDAY EVENING SESSION.

The Convention assembled at 7.45. Prayer was offered by Rev. G. S. BAILEY, D. D.

The PRESIDENT introduced Prof. LINCOLN, who read a paper prepared by REV. A. CASWELL, D. D., LL.D., President of Brown University.

Prof. LINCOLN: I beg leave to say, in behalf of our honored and beloved President, that he wished me to express to his brethren his very great regret that he should not have the pleasure of meeting them in this Convention and performing in person the task that had been assigned to him. He wished me also to say, that nothing but his own engagements at home in the cause of education would have prevented his being present.

THE RELATIVE CLAIMS OF OUR INSTITUTIONS OF LEARNING ON THE PUBLIC BENEFACTIONS OF OUR CHURCHES.

The subject assigned for this paper is, "The Relative Claims of our Institutions of Learning on the Public Benefactions of our Churches."

The design, as I understand it, is not to invite a discussion of the relative claims of our different Institutions of Learning, compared one with another; but the claims of *these* institutions as compared with other institutions and other objects which receive the patronage of our churches. And in specifying "churches" the appeal, I suppose, is not intended to be made to churches in their organic capacity, but to the Christian men and women, who are members of the churches, or more comprehensively, to all those who acknowledge the obligations of Christian benevolence.

The statement of the question implies that there are some institutions, including educational ones, which have claims upon the benefactions of Christian people. On this point there can be little difference of opinion among those who bow to the teachings of Christ, and believe with the Psalmist, that "the silver, and the gold, and the cattle on a thousand hills, are the Lord's."

There is another point suggested by the language of the proposition, which deserves a passing notice in these preliminary remarks. It is the *propriety*, perhaps, the *necessity* of denominational institutions. There are persons who deprecate all denominational enterprises, and there are other persons who deprecate all but their own. But we think it will appear on examination that denominational action is the necessary consequence of deep and earnest convictions of truth and duty.

Outside of the domain of pure mathematics and experimental physics, we may be sure that independent critical judgments will lead to different conclusions. The most casual glance at the history of opinions on all moral and religious subjects, puts this question beyond a doubt. The nature of the subject, taken in connection with the imperfections, if not the very constitution of the human mind, precludes an entire agreement in logical conclusions. Where the discrepancies of opinion are marked, and where the points at issue are deemed to be of importance to any great interest, there parties will be formed, there denominations will take root. Those who agree upon distinctive vital principles will band together, and adopt such measures as their wisdom and prudence shall direct, to defend and propagate their peculiar views. Hence arises denominational action. This is legitimate. This, indeed, is forced upon conscientious, earnest men, as a solemn duty. And precisely in this earnest contention for the faith once delivered to the saints, rests the hope of the ultimate triumph of the truth. The chaff and refuse must be separated from the wheat by many siftings and many winnowings. But it is obvious that in all critical investigations in the interests of truth, the judgment of the inquirer must be left free and unbiased, ready to follow where the light of evidence leads the way.

The laborers in this field for the elimination of error, and the establishment of truth in its purity, must bring to the task a freedom from prejudice, a fairness and candor, an exemption from the trammels of creeds and theories, which, I fear, in theological controversies are as rare as they are indispensable to any real progress. What valuable service, in a cause like this, will he be likely to render who feels himself bound first of all to defend the creed of his church or his party? With what difficulties must he struggle who foresees that the honest expression of his opinion will put in peril his position, or his professional reputation, or his personal friendships?

But we will not despair. We will cherish the hope that charity and candor are making progress in the world, and that the imperfections of good men will diminish as these prevail. If we would truly serve the sacred cause of truth in our denominational action, we must claim for ourselves, and we must allow to others, the most perfect freedom of opinion.

Educational institutions in this country have grown up under two conditions; either by State patronage, or by the fostering care of some religious denomination. Some few of our colleges have had the benefit of State patronage; the greater part of them have had their origin in the wants of some religious body, and have derived their endowments from private munificence. Most fortunate has it been for the cause of good learning that this policy has been pursued. It has enlisted a much larger and more effective interest in the higher education than could otherwise have been secured. It has been fortunate also that while the control and direction of different institutions have been in the hands of particular religious bodies, the advantages of instruction which they offer have been freely and equally extended to all. No religious test, so far as I know, has ever been introduced into any American College as a condition of admission to its privileges. Denominational action on these principles is not only legitimate, but eminently conducive to the general good.

The Baptist denomination has in former times, as is well known, had special reasons for desiring schools of its own. The period in the history of the country is comparatively recent when in different States members of this persuasion were laboring under severe civil disabilities. They not only had no institutions of learning under their control, but they were not allowed the privilege of holding religious meetings and preaching the Gospel of Christ according to their own convictions of its true intent and meaning. That period has happily passed away; and it only remains for us to rejoice in the progress of religious liberty, and, to the utmost extent of our power, to guarantee to all the inestimable boon of Freedom for which our fathers so nobly contended.

We have now, following the example of others, founded and built up educational institutions of our own, which have done excellent service in advancing the cause of liberal education. And the question now returns, what are the relative claims which they have upon our benefactions?

Christian civilization calls to its aid a variety of institutions. It makes them efficient instruments in the accomplishment of its great work. Without any formal enumeration of them all I may, for the purpose of the present discussion, group the principal ones under three heads: Educational, Missionary, and Charitable.

(1.) Under *Educational* Institutions I include Academies, Colleges, and Theological Schools. Purely Scientific, Medical, and Legal Schools, though Educational, do not call for any distinct consideration here.

(2.) Under *Missionary* Institutions I include Missionary Societies proper, Bible Societies, Tract and Publication Societies, and whatever other organizations may exist, having for their object the spread of the Gospel, or the creation and diffusion of a Christian Literature.

(3). Under *Charitable* Institutions I include Hospitals for the cure of Diseases, for the Insane, for Inebriates; Asylums for the poor and the fallen, and Homes for the orphan and the outcast.

These are all excellent institutions, all worthy of support. They appeal with unequal strength to different individuals. It is, perhaps, an essential element of the constitution of society that men should have different sympathies and susceptibilities, as in artistic tastes, one prefers statuary, another painting, and a third music.

Some persons are keenly alive to the sufferings of their fellow-men, and

9

spontaneous in their proffers of aid. They scarce look at all at consequences, and are content with ministering immediate relief and gratifying their own benevolent feelings. Others with less sympathetic but more reflective natures, consider upon what principle the charity is to be administered, and what will be its practical bearing upon the interests of society. In like manner some are sensitively alive to the wants which are near them, but deaf to the calls of those which are at a distance. It is obvious therefore that the advocates and patrons of these different institutions will be grouped around them by their natural sympathies, and yet none, I presume, will maintain that they all deserve the benefactions of the public equally and to the same extent; nor will the most devoted friend of any one of these institutions, deny the claims of the others to a portion of the public patronage.

To determine the limits, and the just measure of these claims relatively, is evidently a question of great difficulty. Indeed from the nature of the case we cannot expect to define the boundary lines between different claims with any great precision; and yet there must be underlying considerations, which if brought into view, will go, I think, to show us pretty clearly upon what general principles we ought to proceed. They will show us, if we would be wise master builders, upon what foundations we must build.

Now, I think it will appear on a little reflection, that in every prosperous civil society, Educational Institutions are underlying all the rest. They are the outgrowth of society, and they again determine the character and form of society. There is a constant action and re-action between them. A community is just what its intellectual, its moral, and its religious culture makes it. Without Educational Institutions, missionary and charitable ones, would plainly, either have no existence at all, or at most, but a very feeble and precarious one. The tree must be judged by its fruits. The claims of these institutions must be determined by their effects upon society.

Charitable Institutions accomplish their object by the relief of individual suffering, or by the cure of disease, or the correction of evil habits. In their nature they are *remedial* and *corrective*. However noble and however Christian, they leave scarcely any trace upon the growth of society. They add to the comfort of its poor; and they do a most valuable work in cultivating and developing a noble Christian sympathy, which blesses alike him who gives, and him who receives. The moral lesson which springs from them is of the utmost value. In this respect they educate. But this is an incidental and reflex blessing, as all good deeds throw out their waves of influence in every direction. They do not educate and train the mental powers. They exert no formative influence in moulding the character of a people. They do not enter into the very groundwork of society. A great curative hospital is a noble institution of which any Christian community may be justly proud. It does much for the relief of suffering. By its curative agency it does something for the aggregate of productive industry; but it does little to quicken and instruct the intellect, little to stimulate genius, little to awaken the powers of invention, little to give man the mastery over nature.

Missionary Institutions may almost be said to be the adjuncts of education. Without the previous results of education they would hardly exist at all. And any existence which they might have would be but feeble and unproductive. Who but educated men could translate the Bible? To whom can we look for an adequate exposition of the sacred word; for a healthful Christian literature, permeating every part of our social organization, but to men of learning? Whom shall we send to translate the Scriptures into foreign languages, and preach in them the everlasting Gospel; so that the heathen of every dark region of the earth may hear in their own tongues in which they were born, the unsearchable riches of Christ;—whom, I say, shall we send to do this? Plainly men of broad and thorough education, men trained in language and literature, in philology; and especially men versed in the critical interpretation of the Greek and Hebrew Scriptures; but such men emanate from our institutions of learning, and are hardly found, and certainly not to be expected without them. It is not too much therefore to say, in looking at the true relation of things, that our Missionary institutions are the result and out-growth of our education; and I may add that they must be constantly fed and replenished with the best fruits of our schools of Theology, or they will decline in power and fail of their great object.

It is worth while now to look a little more narrowly at our Educational institutions to see what they have done, and what they are doing, in order that we may judge the more truly what claims they have upon our support.

To many it must seem a work of supererogation to attempt any formal statement of the advantages of education or of educational institutions, for the two may here be regarded as one. It would seem like pointing out the difference between knowledge and ignorance, between civilization and barbarism, between the social condition of a nation governed by wise and wholesome laws; where the rights of persons and property are defined and protected, and one, where brute force is the only law, and, where everything in the form of justice is dependent upon the will of an ignorant, capricious despot. Yet it may not, perhaps, be altogether useless to glance at the subject.

It is sometimes of advantage to know not only what events have come to pass, but what agency has produced them. In the question before us, it is obvious in the first place from the nature of the case, that education must have a controlling influence in determining the condition and progress of a people. By discipline the intellect is quickened, the powers of observation, of reasoning, of invention, of imagination, are all strengthened and developed. The cultivated mind from the high "vantage ground" of knowledge, looks out upon the panorama of life, discovers and watches the action of natural laws, studies their combinations and capabilities, and yokes them to its mechanism, and makes them do the work of millions of hands. It seeks out the subtle laws of vegetable growth and nutrition, and clothes the sterile field with a rich harvest. But I need not recapitulate instances familiar to you all. The Steamboat and the Telegraph have ceased to be wonders. All the signal achievements of our modern civilization are the joint results of the human intelligence and the human will, and these again are fashioned and directed by education.

But again, look at the subject from another point of view. Let the facts of history come to our aid. What has given to the old Bay State—to Massachusetts,—such a preponderating influence in the councils of this Republic ever since the days of the odious Stamp Act?

What has turned her rivers of water into mechanical agents of almost unlimited power? What is the secret of her unrivalled industrial prosperity? What has stimulated the inventive genius of her people, and made it productive beyond, perhaps, all former example in the records of history? What has dotted over her hills and valleys with ten thousand manufactories which crowd the markets of the land with their products? What has made Boston the Athens of America? We may answer, the intelligence and enterprise of her people. But this is only another name for her education and her educational institutions. Historically, Massachusetts owes her marked pre-eminence to Harvard College. Her common schools have done much, very much, towards a good beginning, but without the College the beginning would have been the end. None of the grand results could ever have been achieved. Indeed without the college the common schools would not have been what they are. The college has been constantly lifting them to higher and higher grades of excellence.

By selecting Massachusetts as an example, I mean no disparagement to other States. It is only that she was first in the field, and has led the van. It is not that her citizens have been born to a nobler inheritance of intellect and genius than the citizens of other states. It is not that the felicities of soil and climate have aided their success. Far otherwise. These only compelled them to diligence and hardihood. They owe their high position to their high education. This is the conclusion to which, I think, any careful inquirer will be led. Other colleges, with more restricted means, but with equally noble purposes, have followed in the footsteps of Harvard.

What has not Brown University done for Rhode Island, and Yale College for Connecticut, and Princeton for New Jersey; not to mention the University of Pennsylvania, and William and Mary in Virginia, and one or two others which took a conspicuous part in the cause of education before the Revolutionary war?

Can there any longer be a doubt as to what are the claims of these institutions on the benefactions of the public? If we would have skill in our industries, if we would have virtue and honesty in our citizens, if we would have learning and ability in our professions, if we would have unsullied and incorruptible justice in our Courts of Law, if we would have wisdom and statesmanship in our public councils, if we would perpetuate Republican government, and guard the sacred immunities of civil and religious liberty, let us cherish our institutions of learning. But how shall we cherish them? First and mainly by securing for them adequate endowments.

Our Academies require endowments for two reasons: first, to give them permanency; second, to diminish the cost of education. An institution must have permanency in order to give it prestige and influence. It must be able to command the best talent in its corps of teachers. It cannot be left to depend alone upon the popularity and enterprise of its principal for the time being; to rank with first-class institutions of its kind, it must have convenient buildings; it must have funds sufficient to meet a portion of the current expenses, independently of the variable income derived from tuition; and sufficient also to warrant putting the tuition so low, as to bring the benefits of education within the means of the great mass of the people.

Considering our numbers and our wealth, and the welfare of our children, we ought not to be satisfied till we locate Academies well furnished, at all our centres of population. They should be of such an order and such a character, combining the best intellectual training with the best moral and religious culture, as to preclude the inquiry where shall we send our children to be educated.

Still more do our Colleges need this kind of aid. They are quite sufficient, and perhaps, more than sufficient in number; but there is not one of them adequately endowed.

At this age of the world, and at the present state of intellectual growth, a first-class College is a great institution. It ranges over a vast field of knowledge, and a constantly widening field. It must have its buildings, its ample library, its varied apparatus for the illustration of physical science, its large collections in Natural History, to facilitate the boundless study of organic nature. It must have, above all, its full corps of professors, each proficient in his own department; each able to conduct his class through his own field of research, in the best and ablest manner. He must induct them into the best methods of study, and give them the largest amount of knowledge compatible with time allotted him. All this involves a large expenditure, but anything less than this falls below what should be the aim of a first-class college. And anything less than this falls below what we ought to covet for our children. A full and rounded education will be worth a hundred times more to them and to the public, than an inheritance in lands, and stocks and bonds, which will not be sure to build them up in virtuous character and public esteem; but which on the contrary, without the safe-guard and directive power of educational discipline, may tempt them to extravagance, and to vice, to ultimate ruin.

Our Colleges want endowments not only for the purposes before indicated, but for another of equal practical importance. We want more ample provision, in the form of scholarships or Aid Funds than we now have, for the assistance of indigent, meritorious students. This question enters more deeply into the prosperity of our schools, the welfare of our churches, and the success of our missionary enterprises, than most persons suppose. Our teachers, our ministers, our missionaries,—and we want them by hundreds every year,—are not likely to be supplied from the wealthier portion of our community. They will come as a general thing, from the middling and poorer classes. Many a young man with sterling mental endowments, is born to poverty. Such is the ordering of Divine Providence; but with a little timely aid his poverty is no bar to a splendid career of usefulness in the noblest departments of human labor. To aid such an one is simply sowing the seed upon good ground which shall bring forth fruit an hundred fold. The importance of this question is too obvious to need further discussion. I am sure it must commend itself to every thoughtful hearer. So much for colleges. The same course of remark is substantially applicable to our Theological Schools.

We are annually raising hundreds of thousands of dollars for Missionary purposes, and we raise none too much. But to what purpose is all this, if our schools do not furnish the men fitted for this great and peculiar work? We are annually spending millions of dollars in the erection of costly Churches, and I take it for granted that we need them all; but where are we to look for the ministers, who will acceptably preach in them the unsearchable riches of Christ, "rightly dividing the word?"

There is still another aspect of this matter too important to be overlooked. The offence of the cross has not yet ceased. The Church is still militant. The battle-ground is changed from time to time, but the conflict still rages. The denunciations of the skeptic and the scoffer are still repeated, just as if they had never been shown to be groundless and futile. The danger now is from the profound and subtle scientist. He is endeavoring to show that the inevitable deductions of science undermine the very foundations of our religious belief. Those scientific tendencies, or what are claimed to be *scientific* tendencies, are all drifting into what Huxley calls "crass materialism."

Now in view of these tendencies and these allegations, we may declare our belief that the foundations of revealed religion will stand secure against the assaults of science, as they have hitherto against the assaults of infidelity. We may say that we have not a shadow of doubt that there must be some gross fallacy, either in the assumptions or in the reasonings, which lead to the conclusion that there is no difference between mind and matter, between the intelligence which thinks and wills, and the material universe which is the subject of its analysis. But the declaration of our doubts or beliefs settles nothing. We must explore the same field of research with the scientist. We must follow him step by step, and cross-question his witnesses at every point, and show precisely where the fallacy lies, and wherein the conclusion is unscientific and untrustworthy. The public demands this of Christian scholars, who are set for the defence of the truth as it is in Jesus. But the preparation for this task requires all the culture which our best resources can furnish.

It is plain from all these considerations that we are blind to our own interests if we do not see the paramount importance of having our educational institutions liberally endowed. They have a primary claim upon our benefactions. I cannot but think that we shall fail in our duty to the cause of Christian progress if this great work is delayed much longer. There is only one other question which remains to be considered, and that is pressed upon us by all that precedes. Who will have the honor of doing this work? As a large and influential denomination we cannot say, and we are not disposed to say, let others have the charge of Education. It is a responsibility which rests upon us; and this question is narrowed down to this: Who of us will assume this responsibility? Those who have no means, however valuable their services may be in other respects, cannot become the patrons and benefactors of colleges. We are left then as the last resort, to ask whether there are among us, men and women, disciples of Christ, of ample means and large hearts, who will feel it a duty, and an honor, and a pleasure to make provision for these much needed endowments? A great responsibility evidently rests upon these stewards of the Lord. What nobler use can they make of a portion of the surplus wealth which God has given them, than to provide for the higher Christian education of the generations that are to come after them? What more fitting memorial of far-reaching wisdom and liberality can they leave behind them? Looking at the subject in the light of Divine Providence, may we not almost say, that for this very purpose, for this very work, have they been raised up?

Most worthy and honored names among those who have finished their work and left us, point the way and lure them on. To say nothing of others, the names of Nicholas Brown, of Nathaniel R. Cobb, of Matthew Vassar, and of John P. Crozer, will long stand as examples of Christian munificence worthy of all imitation. The friends of education all over the world, and especially the friends of our own institutions, will hold them in grateful remembrance, so long as history shall perpetuate the memory of generous deeds. I leave you, brethren, to recall as you will the names of living benefactors, who happily have not completed their work, and are only waiting to see what more their hand shall find to do in honor of the Master, and in the furtherance of his cause.

The PRESIDENT: According to the decision of the Convention before the close of the afternoon session, we are to proceed at once to the discussion of the report, which was laid on the table at the adjournment. President Bailey, of California, had the floor at the moment of adjournment.

Pres. BAILEY: I have come a long distance to be here during these sessions. I have come because we want your influence in California. I have come because I am afraid you do not understand our wants; because I am afraid you do not understand the character of California. Most of you know how California was settled. You know the sort of people that went there. They were the worshippers of Mammon. The Christian element is weak, the world strong, wealth strong. We have wealth for our half million or more of population such as belongs usually to a million. The wealth of California, with a little over half a million of inhabitants, is such as belongs to Michigan, Kentucky, and two or three other states, with a million of inhabitants. We are the weakest Baptist state in the Union. We are the weakest in number, with one exception possibly. We have but one Baptist to 155 who are not Baptists in that state. The little state of Delaware is the only state that we surpass, Delaware having but one Baptist to 160 who are not Baptists. We are also more isolated. For educational purposes, students from Wisconsin may go to the University of Chicago. You in this state may go to Providence. But for us to send our students to either of these institutions, the mere traveling expenses would probably cost as much as the tuition for three years. We cannot send our students east to be educated. And there is the same difficulty in getting teachers to go to California. I have been making an effort, as requested by our Board of Trustees, with some of the gentlemen connected with this Convention, to get a young man to go out and teach during the coming year. I am told, that the young men in our institutions of learning in the east are unwilling to go so far. What I wish to present here is, that California needs just the organization that is proposed here for your adoption. We are in agony in California for just that influence that we hope will come from this Convention. As one of the brethren remarked in California, "We want to get hold of the eastern hand. We want the warmth, the strength, the vigor, the energy, that may come from the great mass of our denomination to the very weak of our denomination."

Dr. FISH: I think this brother from California has given us the key to our inquiries and our action in his closing words: "We want to get hold of the hand of the East." Now, sir, we can all take up that word. We want to get hold of the hand of the West. [Applause.] We want to get hold of the hand of the South; we want to get hold of the hand of the North; in fine, we want to get hold of each other's hands all around. [Applause.] That is what we want. It was said here this afternoon, and I never felt more like shouting like a good Methodist, that there were some things that are hard to die. He said, we should be careful about going into this organization, because it might be difficult for it to die. My heart said, Yes and amen, and may it be hard to die! But, sir, I know it is not born to die. Why do I know it? Because I have watched it from its beginning; kept my eye on it, and close to it; and among the honors of my life, I shall count it as one, that I have been a member of the incipient and provisional organization, which now commits its destiny to your keeping. I say to this great audience to night; to these thinkers and teachers; to this body of Christian men, there is no layman who is living with the privilege God gave him, with two open eyes and ears, who uses his faculties as he ought to use them, who does not know that this has been a mighty power for the last few years. It has not been five years since this first began. It was laid on the heart at first of our worthy secretary, and it came into form in October, 1867. It commenced in the New York Baptist State Convention, and it is not four years and six months now since it begun in its operations; but the lines of its influence have gone out all over our churches, all over these United States. It has created an educational sentiment in the denomination that shows that it was of God. I thought to-day again and again of what they say of Columbus when he was amusing the sailors by the experiment of trying to make an egg stand on one end. After they had all failed, Columbus finally took the egg, and, breaking the end, set it up, and it stood. Oh! they said, any body could do that. Yes, said Columbus, if you had happened to have thought of it. And I said, why haven't we thought of something of this sort until the years 1867 and 1868? I have seen what that grand organization, the College Society for the West, has done for the Congregationalists and Presbyterians, and I agree with the remark of some brother here to-day, that if we had been up and doing as we now are, and feeling this thing deeply in our hearts, we should have had ten schools well endowed and doing glorious work for God and humanity, where we have one now. We are slow; we are late. Now, what has it cost to do what has been done? Perhaps $3,000 a year. Will any brother on this floor point out an investment so cheap? Less than $15,000 to do all this work. Now, it is proposed to do better than this. I believe there are gentlemen on this floor, or have been during the session, who, with gentlemen who are not here, will find it in their hearts to pay the running expenses of this organization for time to come, so that it will not be a tax upon the denomination generally at all. Now, what a grand work this is! (If there is anything I am nervous over, it is the fear of hearing that tap on the table, admonishing me that I have used my time.) And I say as I said when I begun, we want to get hold of each other's hands. It is a fault with our denomination, that we do not get hold of each other's hands enough. Every one is working on his own field. To-day, sir, when I looked over this company of educators and of gentlemen, who have given years to the cause of education, I felt proud of my denomination; not because I was ignorant of the denomination before, but because I had never seen them together before, as in their Conventions. Nor have you, Mr. Chairman, nor Mr. Secretary, nor any man on this floor. Our young students in the Theological Seminaries say, Why are not our professors in sympathy with the denomination as others are? There are reasons for it; but one reason is this: we have no platform upon which we come together in this capacity, and it is worth all it costs to bring out our professors, bring out our Presidents, all of them, and let us see their faces, and know their names, and be able to identify them, and let the ministers, these pastors, and these educators, see one another. A man said to me to-day, Will you point out Dr. Kendrick to me? And when I showed him to him, he said: "I have known that man, and known what a mighty power he is; but I had not seen him before." It is worth something that we should come together and know each other; and let us organize for all time the American Baptist Educational Commission. [Applause.]

Prof. GREENE, of Brown University: I want to say one or two words upon the formation of the national society. And the key-note with me is this: Not long since it was my experience—I will not say privilege—to solicit funds for the purpose of endowing one of our institutions. And I took the liberty of calling upon a gentleman who had had the advantage of the institution and yet was not of our denomination. I applied to him because he was once a pupil in that institution and I believed that he might have some sympathy with it. He had wealth, and I hoped he would bestow some of it upon that institution. He said to me, "I will think of it. I am rather inclined to think I shall do something for you." At the same time he said, "What are you Baptists about; here is Amherst receiving its $100,000, its $500,000. Here is Yale receiving its large endowments. Here are Princeton and Cambridge receiving large endowments and yet you are doing nothing. The Baptists are asleep." And that is the key-note. That is what I wish to direct your attention to. This came from one who was intelligent, one who knew the importance of our institutions, one who was ready to give and who did give; and this remark he made, "I believe every denomination should take care of its own institutions." Yet he said to me "Come again." I intend to see him again. I shall not be repulsed by that remark of his. I believe that what he said has been to a very great extent true—that the Baptists have been asleep in regard to the institutions which belong to our higher education. I wish the expression in the preamble had been rather than the endowment of "colleges," the endowment of "our higher institutions of learning." I wish it had been that for the reason that it selects one out of the grade while we have three, and we must have regard for the third grade of our higher institutions when we look to a system of education. It is exceedingly important that we should organize a system of education that shall reach down to the people, and take hold of the people, that we may educate our sons and daughters in institutions suited their capacities and wants.

The PRESIDENT: That clause is already amended, by consent, to "institutions of higher learning."

Prof. GREENE: I am very glad to know it. We need academies in every section of our country, and these academies should be fostered by the churches, and by the ministers, and by every intelligent man in the denomination. These academies will receive young men who may not intend to go higher than the academy, but who will be prepared, directed, and stimulated, perhaps to go into the higher institutions because they have been in the academy and have received there the impulse which shall carry them forward.

I wish to direct the attention of our brethren present to one consideration which seems to me the most important of all. We are here as educators. We represent the different institutions of our country. But the great mass of the Baptist people, the great mass of the wealth of the Baptist people is not represented here. How shall that object be reached? I say to you, it must be reached by educating the Baptist people and showing them that we must have our institutions brought into a vigorous condition before we can expect that they will lay hold as we desire of sympathy and support. We must educate the intelligent, and in fact we must educate the masses of the people in respect to education. I know of cases since the recent movement, of men who looked upon our whole system of education with indifference. By kindly instruction, by private conversation, by holding the system of education before them they have been led to embrace it with all their hearts and have been ready to give their money to the work. And this work of enlightening and directing must be done by such brethren as I see now before me. He who takes hold of the wealthy brother and explains to him the importance of our institutions, the growth of our denomination and the growth of religion among us is doing a good work. And that pastor who shall take hold of the members of his congregation who are willing and able to give and shall awaken in them a spirit of interest in our institutions and shall instruct them as to the wants of our institutions—that pastor will do a noble work. And let me say to you I hope that we shall go forth from this place to do that work. Our people are wanting in enlightened and concentrated interest, and that is why I am in favor of the continuance of these influences which are now beginning to affect the people. Let us have a national society. Let us go forth and continue this work until it shall reach the mass of our people and they shall feel its power and we shall feel its influence in our institutions. [Applause.]

Dr. J. A. SMITH: Mr. President, I feel a very great deal of hesitation in rising to speak in the presence of this audience, and the more as I am in doubt whether the thoughts which have been growing in my own mind, are altogether in line with the thoughts of the majority of those composing this Convention, and of very many in whose judgment I confide far more than I do in my own. But I take it that there is a desire, that there should be here, a very frank expression of opinion that there is no reason why we should keep back convictions that we honestly hold, but abundant reason why we should speak in a fraternal spirit to each other just what we think. I confess to you Mr. President, as I have thought more of this matter, since the discussion here in the afternoon, I have been increasingly of the persuasion, that it might be best, for this Convention not at the present time to attempt the organization that is here proposed, but that we continue to work in the same direction, upon the same basis, which we have used during the last five years, and that a better plan than to form such an organization as is proposed, might be to simply reconstitute the Commission. I am not persuaded myself that it is necessary to have a central treasury, where funds should be gathered and from which they should be disbursed. I am not satisfied that it is best to have this central Board. It seems to me that the two things we need in regard to educational work in the denomination, are simply advice and inspiration. We have had both these during the period of the existence of this Commission. I yield to no one in my appreciation of the important work which the Commission has accomplished. It seems to me that our ends can be realized in a still larger measure, by simply reconstituting the instrumentality which we have already used. I make these suggestions, however, Mr. President, with a great deal of diffidence, and simply because I am pressed to do so from my own convictions, and perhaps because it might be well for one who lives in the West, to stand and speak as I am now doing. It seems to me possible that in trying to do more we may do too much, and that it may be well under the present circumstances, to let well enough alone. I wish to allude to another point as suggested in a remark this afternoon, in allusion to the West. I presume none are as sensitive to criticism as those who are conscious of being, in a greater or less degree, open to criticism. That is my position

Yet I feel that some opinions unfavorable to the West, may have been expressed which would not be altogether just. I remark that there are many here, who are not so well informed, as perhaps most of the Convention are with reference to the history of denominational interests in the West. I shall very soon have lived twenty years on western ground; during the whole of that time, having connection with educational interests in the West. I think I know western men, in their connection with educational work through and through. And I wish to say here, that if it was the intention by any remarks made here this afternoon, to imply that it was customary in the West for funds to be used injudiciously, without a proper appreciation of the sacredness of such trusts, it is altogether a mistaken impression. [Applause.] I have also been a member of College Boards in the east, and I can say I have never known men more true to those trusts than western men. We have had occasion often to encounter the pinch of financial revulsions, and if we have been disappointed, if we have come short of our aims, we are entitled to the sympathy of the friends of education throughout the whole country. And let me assure you, that in any attempt or disposition, to censure the management of western educational interests, over and above what may be due to lack of judgment, such as is common to human nature, you do us great injustice. Let me say farther, in allusion to the very pleasant and humorous method of speech, adopted by one of the speakers this afternoon—I allude to the address of Dr. WAYLAND—it was a caricature of the West. Those things belong to the past, and are not true of any instance of the present that may be named. I may say, sir, that we are as fully advanced as any part of the country, in regard to our appreciation of what is necessary to constitute a first class school, of what is necessary also in the management of Educational affairs.

Dr. TURNBULL: I rise to say a few words of encouragement, in regard to the progress we have made in all respects, and particularly in regard to this matter of education. I have been impressed with it all the ay long, as I have looked upon this intelligent audience; the change during thirty years is immense. We have done nobly. I know that we Baptists have a chronic habit of finding fault with ourselves. But in comparison with other denominations we have made remarkable progress. I met a President of one of the Episcopal colleges, and he made inquiry in regard to this very matter. I stated what I knew of what we were doing, and I referred him to Dr. CUTTING, for further information. "Sir," he said, "you are fifty years ahead of us." This was said by a distinguished clergyman, President of a college. I state this by way of encouragement. As to the main question at issue, I have had certain questionings as to whereunto this thing would grow. It has been expressed here today, whatever is of God will last, whatever is of man will come to an end, and die by and by. But as to this thing, I am satisfied it comes from the providence of God, and it is destined to live (Applause.) Because it is a vital power, and all our hearts, I have not a question, I judge you by myself, my friends, all our hearts respond to this, I know. Dr. SMITH will go for it. He merely wanted deliberation, and discussion, and I hope he will have an opportunity. I like his caution, and it is very well to look at all the objections. I had another, and it remained upon my mind up to the time Dr. Taylor spoke, and I regarded him as a representative of our most important institution, the Home Mission Society. I was glad he took a noble stand at the very commencement of the organization of this body, and I thank you for the noble sentiments he has clearly and eloquently expressed. We need organization everywhere. Our great want has been want of organization. This necessity is being supplied by the Spirit of God, inspiring us and bringing us together, heart to heart, and hand to hand. We do clasp each other's hands; our hearts flow together in this very thing. I regard it as one of the most auspicious occasions, which I ever had an opportunity of attending. I think it is the beginning of one of the most glorious days in our denominational interests; especially of the cause of higher education, which grows out of it. I traveled a little in the west a few years ago, and was struck with one thing especially; everywhere the Catholics had planted institutions of learning, that are to tell upon the destiny of this country in all coming time. We must do the same thing and with the same spirit, only with a higher regard to the glory of God, and to the grand underlying principles of freedom: freedom to worship God; freedom as Baptists to carry out the great principles upon which we stand, namely, soul-liberty and the love of God for God's sake, by the free soul born from above, born again, symbolized in the great act which begins our Christian life, and which gives us our name, baptism, in the name of the Father, the Son, and the Holy Spirit. I believe this thing is of God. I thank Dr. CUTTING for what he has done; the Lord has put him in this place I trust, and I believe the Lord will keep him there, and I trust we shall join in this matter, and take a long pull, and a strong pull, and a pull altogether.

Dr. STONE, I regret one remark that has been made here I do dislike exceedingly to have our denomination disparaged needlessly. I regret the remark which was made that we have been asleep, when two millions have been added to the funds of our colleges for active use within the last five or six years.

I desire to say a few words in regard to the necessity for this organization. I sympathize with the view taken by Dr. SMITH, that the Commission has been of great use. It has prepared us for a further step. But the Commission as it is can never do the work that needs to be done. It is out of the question. It must necessarily be local. It will be liable to the charge of partiality from its local position. We want an institution organized that will have such a general and catholic character and such a position as will command the confidence of the entire nation. One great fault has been that multitudes of men, though with honest and good intentions have originated schools where sound practical wisdom and experience in educational affairs would not have dictated that they should have been planted. We want some sort of a body to which questions of location may be referred, and which may give practical wisdom to those who have none. Any one who has been over the West to any considerable extent knows that there are remnants of a great many schools which were organized under the name of Colleges; some of which lived a few years, spent a great deal of money and then perished. Some are still dragging out a wretched existence, and keeping some other locality and some other community from planning something that might be permanent. It has been said that this institution would tend to centralization—and bring about a failure that we wish as a denomination to avoid. Some degree of centralization in a denomination like ours cannot be avoided, sir. We want institutions of learning in many and in perhaps all the states. I do not sympathize with the idea that the multiplication of institutions is an evil. If you will examine the facts you will find that the colleges of this country are almost wholly dependent upon local patronage. I examined into that matter last spring, and found that there were but very few colleges that derived any considerable portion of their patronage from beyond a radius of one hundred miles. Some scholars of course will come from a greater distance, but the number is comparatively small. We shall need at least one college in nearly every state. Colleges will be built and men will undertake honestly to build them. And they will undertake to build them in wrong places. And you ask how shall we stop them? We may create an institution that will itself establish a tendency to leave questions of this sort to persons who have had experience in college-building. We want boards located so that there will be some intelligence in these committees in regard to questions that shall come up.

My opinion is that there is one mistake in the drafting of the constitution which has been presented. There should be another Advisory Committee at Memphis or Nashville, so that that locality will be represented and the actual wants and condition of the people will be understood. It should be understood by the people that we have a local committee who are interested in our success. I believe five local committees of twelve each would be decidedly better than three. Then the whole country will be under the supervision of committees who will see that no more money is wasted upon our institutions of learning; that no more buildings are erected for the rats, and no more efforts to endow institutions of learning shall be made and disgraceful failures result, to be the cause of a number of other disgraceful failures. If we go to a man of wealth and tell him we want an endowment for such an institution he says "What security have I? Over yonder is a fine institution that was erected for a college and nothing has come of it. Yonder is another and yonder is another. I have no security at all that my money will not be wasted. Give me some pledge that I can rely upon, that what is done will be done forever." But let twelve men, chosen for their experience and judgment in educational affairs be called to decide questions of locality, and they will carry with their decision a degree of confidence that will insure them success when they ask for a subscription. And I would say that not a single effort at endowment should be tolerated by the Commission that had not the endorsement of these local boards.

We cannot afford, as a denomination, to be delayed much longer in the accomplishment of this great work of planting institutions permanently. But it must be done under circumstances that will make the people have confidence that when a thing is attempted it will be carried out wisely.

Dr. J. WHEATON SMITH: When I uttered my quiet questioning of the wisdom of this measure in advance, I did it with the purpose of silently acquiescing in what I supposed would undoubtedly be the result. But fearful that I may have been misunderstood in the frank utterance of that questioning, and encouraged by this very fraternal interchange of views, I desire to add a word to the little which I said this afternoon. In passing, let me say it has rarely been my privilege to have been present at a meeting of my own, or any other denomination, where questions of so great moment were discussed, in a manner and in a spirit so evidently proper. I desire to yield to no one of my brethren present, in appreciation of the labor which has thus far been performed. I agreed entirely with my namesake from the west, that what we needed was advice and inspiration. I believe we have received both. But it should not be forgotten that in so far as you establish the success of efforts that are past, you establish the fact that there is no necessity for the change that is proposed to-night. Why not continue to do all this good work as we have done it? Why run fearful risks in attempting the establishment of what, not impossibly, may retard instead of advancing the great work which we all have so much at our hearts? Brethren, it may be that the experience of the last week at [the anniversaries of our denomination in New York,] has something to do with my caution. I am not old enough yet to be conservative, but the fact is that some of us have been busy in deciding what to do with the anniversaries we have, and just at the time, when the old societies are sloughing off life-memberships, or trying to do so, you come in with an establishment of a new kind. At the time when we are beset behind and before, as we attempt to create a representative body, for the management of our great national work, by the fact that we have sold out the rights of a representative body in advance for a few dollars to each individual man, you come in with a principlė vicious in policy, vicious in its nature, proposing to sell a man, for the sum of five hundred dollars, the right of perpetual membership, in the management of interests as vital as these. You propose to establish an institution which should be the recognized organ of the churches, without a single representative from a church upon this floor. You propose, brethren, to enter upon this work in the hope that you can control it. Imagine for a moment, a council sitting in New York, buttressed if you please by three advisory councils in the country, attempting to control the people in the North-West, in the management of their educational interests, and I think the council will have a difficult time of it, in just so far as they come into contact with the people of the North-West. I have come to the conclusion that there is very rarely a man, in the fullness of his heart attempts to help a good cause, that an eye more far-seeing than his own, does not discover a bright future. They tell us of our fearful blunder at Lewisburg, when for twenty years, we had been sending our young men out of the state for education, and the result was if they were good for anything somebody else got them, and if they were not good for anything they came back to us. [Laughter.] And we established a college where we had to go by stage and canal to get to it, and a fearful blunder they called it, but a good blunder it was, and God has given us as the result in a central place, an institution which is making all around it to bud and blossom as the rose. [Applause] Crozer Theological Seminary was not built for a Seminary, but its sainted founder had seized on it, thought of a neighborhood school and established it—to find it a failure. The facilities he furnished for a first class education there, were used by those who were abundantly able to pay for such facilities everywhere, and the building became a hospital, and sheltered the wounded and the dying through the war, and then, in God's own good time, when the man went home to his fathers, there came out of the blunder an institution that stepped into full growth, between the rising of the sun and the shadow of the coming evening. I have done weeping and wailing over Baptist blunders. [Applause and laughter]. But I cannot sit down, Brother President, without specially guarding against this conclusion. It may be that I am suspected of lacking favor to this enterprise, on the ground that it is so largely national. It may be becoming in me, therefore, to say that I judge that to be one of its chief recommendations. I am glad amid the revolutions of States, oftentimes discordant, and belligerent, to see back again the dear old friends of my college life, glad to welcome, at least in one national meeting, those who from all parts of the country came up to consider with us these great interests. I can hardly tell you, gentlemen, what is the motto on the shield of my native state, hardly the motto on that of this, the state of my adoption; but there is one motto I remember, one banner that floats above me alway, in the visions of my brightest noon-day, in the dreams of my shortest sleep. That flag

> "Whose mingling rays, unite
> One blended flood of braided light,
> The red that fires the Southern rose,
> The spotless white of Northern snows,
> And spangled o'er its azure sea
> The sister stars of liberty." [Applause.]

Rev. Mr. PIERCE: It seems to me that the Territories have an interest in this matter. I suppose we all know that our land is only half developed; that New England is away in one corner, that Philadelphia is down on the Eastern shore; that the Missouri and not the Mississippi, runs nearer the centre of our land. That in ten territories west of the Missouri River, lies the vast undeveloped better-half of America. Now, I speak in behalf of my better-half to-night. [Laughter.] I say that we need some organization in the Baptist denomination to gain time. That is what we want. I have lived up there in the mountains and I have seen the Presbyterian general missionary pass through our town west, east, south and north, having general supervision of Colorado, Wyoming, Utah, New Mexico and Arizona, putting his hand on every purse which he could get hold of, and saying, "Gentlemen, our society will back you in schools, in churches, in whatever you wish; only come with us." And I have felt my blood start in me—notwithstanding we are warned not to speak of Baptist mistakes—I have felt my blood start when I found that I could not travel over that vast region, and hold my own ground. I say when I see these things, I feel that we ought to have a place somewhere, and I would say let this association be organized, and send the Secretary by the first train, and take hold of Dacotah, where the Rev. G. W. FREEMAN has already called a meeting to see what can be done. Let him climb over the mountain by stage to Montana, and if Helena is to be the place, claim it for Baptist ground. So gentlemen wherever the best place can be found where a railroad comes through, give it to us and we will make a school there. I would have him go into the mountainous districts of Idaho, and say there: "Gentlemen the Baptists have come; they have a warm hand, and a warm heart and they will give it to you." I would have him go to Oregon. I received a letter from Portland, a few weeks since, saying, that they had thirty thousand dollars worth of Baptist property there, and no minister to preach. I would have him go to Washington Territory, and if I could learn where the Western terminus of the Northern Pacific Railroad would be, I would have him go there.

Now we say, if you wait for men to come from those territories to ask for your help, they will never come until the Presbyterians, Catholics, Methodists and Episcopalians have the best ground in the territory, and you may take up with about fourth best. No, send your men and take it.

Now I come in behalf of another little Territory up there, with a few Indians, some white people and a good many cattle in it, and where the Baptists have secured the first foothold. [Applause]. And we have an institution there,—young as it is, scarcely out of swaddling clothes yet; yet we have an institution there into whose treasury men of other denominations who are to-day working for their daily bread have paid their money. Why? Because they say, "We are live men and we will work with the first one that comes." I say put them up there in Laramie, on the plains where riches lie spread beneath your feet on the ground, where the coal veins lie just beneath the surface, where the golden sands flow down the sides of the mountains, and where above all the goddess of health sits supreme upon her throne 7000 feet above the level of the sea.

I am sent here by a body of Trustees to ask the Baptist denomination if they will help us, with the understanding that if I do not secure my favor there is a certain lady not a thousand miles from here, who while she proposes to keep off from our track, yet says that if the Presbyterians will lift up a school there she will give $10.000. Now we ask whether you want the ground or whether you wish to give it up.

Just a moment with regard to another point. I would say that I thank God there is one place in the Western Country where the Baptists are fairly ahead; and that is in Greeley—not the man but the town! [Laughter]. Where the Congregationalists, the Episcopalians, the Methodists, the Unitarians had all formed their churches while the Baptists were lying asleep, until one consumptive brother who had come out there to save his life—and did save it—said, "I will go out and see if I can find one Baptist in town." And strangely enough he found twenty-six. He telegraphed to me and said, "Come down and see what we can do." We went down and held the first Baptist Prayer-meeting ever held in the Territory. The next morning they had a subscription paper on the ground, and in two weeks from that time they let the contract for the first Baptist Church of the town of Greeley.

A few years ago when I was a boy, I learned that the Great American Desert lay between the Missouri River and the Pacific Ocean, and we all supposed that that was good for nothing and ought to be forced out of the world. But we have learned lately that Alaska is good for something besides an ice-house; that Oregon contains the country that is to be the garden of the world; that Montana and Dacotah are splendid farming countries; that Utah cannot be excluded and taken full possession of by Brigham Young because of its rich silver mines; and we will learn bye-and-bye that Wyoming is good for something besides a sheep-pasture—although it is splendid for that. All along those heights are splendid places for fortifications. Let the Baptists take possession of those fortifications by educational institutions and churches. Or will you wait until the German with his infidelity, the Irishman with his love for the

Pope, and the follower of Confucius shall come there and take possession of the fortresses and then take your muskets and try to drive them out? It remains for you to say whether you can afford the three years that have been asked for before completing this organization.

The hour of adjournment having arrived, it was voted to continue the discussion till 10 o'clock.

Prof. LINCOLN : I should not have arisen at all, sir, if I had any idea it was so late. I have been so extremely interested in the remarks that have been made, that the time has gone by without my knowing it was so late in the evening. But I feel for one, a very great interest in the question that is now before us, and I believe that is, the adoption of this report. I feel, for one, a very strong interest in this matter, though I have much less acquaintance with this whole subject than many, perhaps most of those who are here present. But I came here with a very earnest wish that something at least might be done that would carry forward the great and good work which has already been done by this Educational Commission. I was moved both this evening and this afternoon to say a word or two after listening to the words of my young friend and very much esteemed pupil, Dr. SMITH, (of Philadelphia) whose words I am sure we are all interested in, as we certainly would be interested, in any word which he utters so well. As a graduate of our college he of course speaks well, but I want to say a word upon that matter of *blunders*, and to congratulate him that he had come to the conclusion not to bewail any further Baptist blunders, and it occurred to me then feeling as I did, and as I have already said I have been feeling to-day that we might make a much worse blunder as Baptists than to form this national society. [Applause].

Moreover, I thought I might encourage my young friend, being an older man than he, to have some faith to believe that, if it were a blunder it would be a blunder like the Lewisburg University that he recited to you, as so overruled for good to the whole denomination. [Applause].

Sir, I was disappointed, I confess I was not prepared for it. I suppose I do not understand the matter, and that I am urged forward by my great interest in this whole business of our Denominational education, so that perhaps I do not understand what these objections are and what these difficulties are, that have been touched upon, hinted, and surmised, especially by my friend, Dr. SMITH. I did not expect the very instant that the motion was made on this report that we should have a note of discontent. I did not expect these doubts and fears. I was not prepared for them. Why, my young brother seemed to feel that there was coming up by and by in the future, some dreadful thing to harm us all; indeed he indicated by those words always impressive, familiar as they are, that there would be something by and by come up that would not down at our bidding.

But I did not intend to dwell upon this, sir. I only want to say, I am sure we want to do something that will give us an onward movement in this good path that, under the leading of my respected friend, Dr. CUTTING, we have begun, and I want, for one, to respond to everything that has been said to-night, especially that which was said by Dr. WOOD. I appreciate the good work that our brother has done—done so wisely and so well. I thank him for it—for the wisdom and intelligence with which he planned these measures, and for the energy, the untiring energy, with which he has carried them out. And now to think we are to come to a dead stand! And now to think we are to do nothing more, but stop here and think of something or other, nobody knows what, that is going to rise up by and by and stare at us if we make something of a permanent organization to carry on further our educational interests. Why, sir, I thought as I was listening of something which was called up by looking at you, sir, and remembering your lamented father. I remember his saying about an excellent friend, that he had observed that he never got into a position where he was already doing well, with promises of prosperity and happiness and usefulness, but that with a certain dread of worldly prosperity and a certain desire to have always the feeling that he was a pilgrim and a stranger here, he was sure to break up his tents, and, as he used to say, go off to work in some other part of the field, and I was afraid we should be doing just so; we were doing so well, and had made such excellent progress in such a short time, we should be afraid we were doing too well and would stop. Why, sir, having this evidence from all parts of the country of the good work that this Commission has done, and having these prophecies in all this testimony of the good work yet to be done for us all, north, south, east and west, as a denomination in the furtherance of our educational interests, let us be doing something, sir.

Dr. ROBINSON: No man here feels more gratitude to Dr. CUTTING for the work which he has accomplished in the past five years than myself. It was a needed work—a work the value of which we shall hardly estimate in this century. I have, however, some apprehension in respect to the organization here proposed. It has been asked, What objection can be alleged against it? We call ourselves Baptists. I claim to be pre-eminently a Baptist. One fundamental principle of our churches is absolute church independence. Absolute church independence! We will brook no interference from any quarter. I read here, that it is proposed to form a National Society, which shall be the recognized organ of the churches through which funds can be wisely applied in helping men to help themselves. Who are we? Is there a man in this Convention representing a church? I am not representing a church here. I don't know of any here who are. Many of us are sent here by corporate institutions—institutions of learning—education societies. But it is further on recommended, that we proceed to organize; that "*we* proceed to organize a national society on the basis of the following constitution." One object of this organization, it is said, will be the suppression of needless institutions and the encouragement of those that promise well for the future. There are many of our states that have two or three, some more, institutions claiming to be colleges. It is hopeless to expect perpetuation of these colleges. It is deliberately proposed—it is announced as the intention of this organization to suppress all needless institutions and encourage such as promise well. Who founded these institutions? The churches. The churches paid for them. The churches have given not only their money, but their prayers, to these institutions. Can we suppress them according to our church polity? Is it to be a practicable thing? Try it. Try it in the State of Iowa where there are three colleges. Say to them: "We will suppress these institutions." They will ask you, who you are. They have a right to ask that question. So there are other institutions over the land. I don't understand how, with our church polity, this institution can be made to work practically and successfully. I may be mistaken. I have lived somewhat out of the world; but I do understand something of church independence. And I propose to cling to it in the fullest sense, anywhere and everywhere, and at any hazard. [Applause.]

But I see possibly rising up before me a moneyed institution. Here are to be invested funds. Is it to be a banking institution? One friend suggested waggishly a limitation. One suggested seven millions, and the other thought it might possibly be eight. Is this to be a banking institution? Who is to be responsible for these funds? How are they to be appropriated? I read a little further on over in the constitution here about certain institutions that are to be under the care of the society. I don't know what that means. I don't know how much it means. Is this organized corporation to take charge of and have under its care these colleges that receive its advice and assistance? I read certain words respecting the advice. I read here again respecting *care.* A good many other things of that kind suggest themselves to me. The hour is getting late. I think it is very likely a foregone conclusion, that we are to have this organization. I respond most heartily to all that has been said about the wise use of funds and about institutions that we need. And perhaps this is possibly the best means of accomplishing that. But I am not sufficiently informed as yet.

DR. BURROUGHS moved that the report be recommitted to the same Committee, to have it under consideration until 11 o'clock to-morrow morning, and that it be made the special order for that time.

Dr. HAGUE: I would like any one to try to put down one or two of those colleges in Iowa. I wished some ten or fifteen years there was a way to do it in a Baptist fashion. We are all jealous of church independence. The way to do it is a way consistent with the spirit of Christ.

Where there is a will, there is a way; where there is a thing to be done, there is a way to reach it, and it is for the wisdom of this body and for you to solve that problem. I believe it may be solved, let me add. If we had only done this ten years ago, it has been said, we might have had ten institutions where we have one now. Now, it is well worthy of remark, that nothing could be done of this sort ten years ago. At the meeting in Brooklyn the editor of the *Independent* came to me, asking me to write an article to review that body. I did so in a column and a half, and that article brought me into communication with some of the leading minds of the Congregational Churches of the country. They said, it presented to their minds the dawn of a new era. You know that for thirty years the north, south, east and west could not have met in such a convention to discuss such a subject. Till the war had closed, it was impossible for our other societies to meet. All minds, north, south, east and west, answered to the call of the educators that are to determine the future. A leading gentleman stated to me: "You are ahead of all the rest, and your convention is prophetic of a grand future to you. If your denomination can do such a thing as that, and bring together the leading minds of California, South Carolina and Virginia, from the Atlantic to the Pacific, the Gulf of Mexico to the St. Lawrence, you have a grand future." Do not mar it; do not depreciate it. [Applause.] Recommit this report. The objections are such as can be easily removed, and present a document that your children and children's children shall delight to read.

The PRESIDENT: The motion is that the report be recommitted to the committee, with a request that the committee report at 11 o'clock to-morrow morning, at which time it shall be the order of the day for discussion.

Dr. CUTTING: Before that question is put, I want to say that that hour has been particularly reserved for another subject. We have the expectation of a report, in which I am sure the Convention will be deeply interested, on the relation of our colleges to the public life of the nation. It was intended for that particular hour. I move as an amendment that instead of eleven, the hour be 9 o'clock to-morrow morning.

The Rev. Mr. GRAVES read the report of the Committee on Enrollment, which was accepted.

The Convention thereupon adjourned to Thursday, May 30th, at 9 A. M.

THURSDAY MORNING SESSION.

The Convention reassembled at 9 o'clock.

The proceedings were opened with prayer by Rev. ALVAH HOVEY, D.D.

The Rev. Dr. HOVEY read the report of the Committee on the Relation of our Colleges to the Education of Women.

REPORT.

Your committee take pleasure in commending to the Convention the well-considered views expressed in the paper read by President Kendall Brooks, of Kalamazoo, and feel some hesitation in attempting to go over again, even in the briefest way possible, the topics so instructively discussed in that paper.

Yet certain questions in respect to the best education for woman, and the best way of securing it, are so important at the present time, as to justify in our opinion, a few words from your committee.

They are fully persuaded that the time has come when the benefits of liberal culture, in the accepted use of that expression, should be placed within the reach of young women as well as of young men, and they believe, that if this is done, a considerable number will appropriate those benefits.

Convinced that women are as capable of profiting by liberal studies as men, they are also satisfied that the best course of discipline and instruction for them will be found to differ very little, if at all, from the one required for the good of men. For as it is with food, air, light, and exercise for the body, so it is with knowledge and training for the mind; what is adapted to one of the sexes is adapted to the other likewise. Woman does not cease to be herself, more beautiful and delicate in form than man, because she is nourished by the same kind of material food as her rougher brother; nor will she cease to be woman in mind and heart, and taste, should she receive into her spiritual being the same truth which quickens, invigorates, and delights him.

So far then, as variations in the prescribed course of study are concerned, your committee are of the opinion that young women may be educated without serious difficulty in the same colleges with young men; with a reasonable number of elective studies for the last two years, persons of both sexes could pursue the same course and be trained by the same teachers.

They also believe that the education of the sexes together, in the higher branches of good learning, would be very likely to improve the discipline and scholarship of our colleges, and to give to young men and women juster views of each other and of human life. In making this remark it is of course assumed that suitable provision would be made for what may be called the home life of young ladies while in college.

The question of co-education, however, is one which can only be answered satisfactorily and finally by trial; but so great would be the advantages of such education in point of expense and of the mutual influence of the sexes on each other, that your Committee have no doubt of the wisdom of bringing the question to the test of careful experiment.

For the Committee,

A. HOVEY, *Chairman.*

On motion of the Rev. Dr. Boardman the report was accepted and adopted.

The Chairman of the Committee on Organization stated that the Committee were in session, but were not yet prepared to make a report, and asked for further time, which was granted.

Prof. A. C. KENDRICK, D. D., LL.D., from the Committee to introduce a resolution on the death of the Hon. Wm. Kelly, made the following report:

REPORT.

The Committee to whom was referred the presenting of a resolution regarding the death of the Hon. William Kelly, President of the First National Baptist Educational Convention, and of the American Baptist Educational Commission, respectfully submit the following:

Resolved, That in the death of William Kelly we deplore the loss of one whose singular urbanity of manners, rare mental endowments and culture, purity of character and life, and enlightened devotion to public interests, secular and sacred, won for him our love and admiration.

Dr. KENDRICK: I did not contemplate making any remarks upon

this occasion, and this subject, but I cannot refrain from saying a word, expressive of the very warm love, and of the very high admiration with which the life and character of Mr. KELLY always inspired me, and of the profound sorrow with which I received, as we all did, the tidings of his death. I feel that it was one of the privileges of my life, to be acquainted with Mr. KELLY. I feel that it was an honor and a benefit to know him; to meet that genial smile, to meet that unfailing gentlemanliness, and urbanity of manner with which you were sure to be always greeted, and to come into contact with a character that, in every relation, alike public and private, seemed to me to be as near perfection as any character with which it has been my privilege in life to become acquainted. His home was an earthly paradise, alike in its external appointments, and in the sweet and gentle influence that presided over it. From that home radiated, and went forth an influence in every direction, of which it would be difficult to say, whether it was more potent or more benignant. I have no words now. I felt in drawing up this resolution that anything which expressed adequately my own feelings would seem in a public resolution, improperly hyperbolical. Our educational interests and all our public interests, except as the event is over-ruled by the Providence of God, and others are raised up, as we trust they will be, to supply his place, seemed to have suffered an irreparable calamity. But he is gone. He has terminated the record of a bright, pure, noble, useful Christian life, and I doubt not, is enjoying the reward of that life through grace in the better world.

Dr. CUTTING: I cannot refrain from adding a few words, to those which have been so fittingly spoken by the Chairman of the committee, in reference to the great loss which the cause of education has sustained, in the death of the Hon. WILLIAM KELLY. It was likewise my privilege to enjoy his friendship, and to know in the relations of that friendship the purity, the completeness, and the beauty of his character and of his life. And what is to the special purpose in an assembly like this, it was my happiness to know as I learned it in one way and another, the history of his relations to the cause of education. To illustrate how early his interest in the cause of education commenced; among those who were present at his funeral, was an honored and distinguished pastor of one of our important churches who, more than forty years ago, was in the academy with me at South Reading, and for a time shared the same room with me, a most worthy young man, as he has been a most faithful minister of Christ. I well remember how suitably he was in every respect provided for; how comfortable his condition was, as compared with that of many of the students at that time in the academy, who were candidates for the ministry. Two or three years ago, this pastor told me how it happened that his condition was so comfortable at that time. Said he

"Mr. KELLY"—and Mr. KELLY was a young man then, of not more than twenty-two or twenty-three years of age,—"Mr. KELLY took me by the hand and gave me counsel; he advised me to prepare for Newton Theological Seminary; he furnished the money for my preparation; he sustained me while I was at Newton, and when I graduated, he sent me a suit of clothes in which to make my public appearance; and when I was ordained he said quietly to me, that a little money to start me in my profession would not be amiss, and placed a hundred dollars in my hand." Just about the same time, youth as he was, he made his first subscription to the cause of education, in giving his name to the library fund of Brown University, the first considerable sum raised by that university, after Dr. WAYLAND became the president. From that time on, successful merchant, retired Christian gentleman, always he has been modestly and quietly, but persistently the friend and benefactor of education. He was the President of the Board of Trustees of Rochester University, the President of the Board of Trustees of Vassar College, as well as the President of our Educational Commission, in which from the first he took the profoundest, most tender and most earnest interest. One of the last things he did before he went away, on the voyage from which he did not return, was to make a subscription of fifteen thousand dollars to the funds of the University of Rochester. And I know that it was in his heart, and there are those here who know it was among his purposes, to aid Richmond College in its most laudable attempts to rise from its depression, and to diffuse its blessings over Virginia and the south. Always and everywhere, from youth to age, he was thus the friend and the benefactor of the cause of education. It is fitting then, that we record this memorial of his character and his work.

Dr. HAGUE: I beg leave to add one word. No one of this company, probably, remembers Wm. KELLY as far back as myself. It was my great regret to have been away from home so as not to have known the time of his funeral, and on that account to have been absent therefrom, and to have lost the delight of listening to those tributes to his character which were given at that time by those who knew and loved him. I will take this opportunity, therefore, to say that I loved him, and loved him not merely as a man and a benefactor, but I loved him as a boy and a schoolmate. And he was then relatively what he has been ever since to the community. I am often reminded in thinking of such a life, of the reply of the mother of Washington when Lafayette had been praising her son: "Well General, George always was a good boy." And so in looking back we see in Wm. KELLY as the boy at school, the germ of his manhood. He always was the same. He and I with my brother and his brother were playmates on Wednesday and Saturday afternoons on Brooklyn Heights near where his father lived, and so I watched his growing up. I loved him then as a well-balanced studious boy. But I forbear to amplify in the direction that my feelings would prompt me, remembering the hour, and what is to come. I only add one word, but it is a subject germain to our line of thought—what advice to give to rich men in reference to their sons when preparing for business. Shall they not have a liberal education? Wm. KELLY had virtually a liberal education. In Wheaton School, Chatham Square, we had all that pertained to the breadth of the high school. From my place in one corner as a little boy I used to look across the room and see there a friend bending closely over his book and all absorbed—it was Wm. R. WILLIAMS. And right by his side another boy more blithe and more social, Robert KELLY. And not far from him in another department, my young friend and playmate, Wm. KELLY. When Robert KELLY graduated, William, who had most of all that pertains to an English high school student life, joined his brother in going into business. William and Robert KELLY were masters of business. In six years William KELLY had acquired a fortune. In 1836 they anticipated the crash of 1837; they furled their sails and went out of business before the crash came, and there was William KELLY, with his fortune invested in Rhinebeck. Robert KELLY lived in New York enjoying the confidence of the people, holding himself ready to be the servant of the public and of his country; became connected with the Board of Trustees of the University of Rochester, and was Chamberlain of New York, occupying a wide sphere of social, religious and political power. I say, Mr. President, that the lives of these two men are vocal with instruction.

Prof. HARRIS: These brethren who have spoken, knew Mr. KELLY intimately. I speak as one who never saw him, but yet I loved him. I rise just to say that, though modest and unobtrusive, by those actions which speak louder than words, he had made his name a household word with us in Virginia.

Prof. F. O. MARSH: I want to add one word as a lesson from the just remarks made by Dr. HAGUE, that education does not disqualify a man for business. A. T. STEWART was educated for the ministry. I have the following statement from a man who carefully gathered the facts a few years ago; of the merchants of New York for the past fifty years, there have been only about seven per cent that have absolutely gone into bankruptcy during the history of their business lives. Of the ninety-three per cent. who have not gone into bankruptcy over fifty per cent. were graduates of the colleges of the United States. I want simply to state that fact as a lesson for men who imagine that education spoils a man for business life—and especially if it has been an education for the ministry.

Rev. Dr. BOARDMAN moved the adoption of the report as the sense of the Convention, and that a copy of the resolution be sent to the family of deceased, which was unanimously agreed to.

The Rev. CRAWFORD H. TOY, D. D., read a paper on

THE PLACE OF THEOLOGICAL SCIENCE IN THE SCIENCES COMPRISED IN A LIBERAL EDUCATION.

In a sense it is true that the study of Theology is, and must necessarily be, the most generally diffused of all studies. Theology is concerned with interests which all men feel to be the highest, and its subject matter is at hand in every human breast, and forever asserting its claim to serious consideration. In this respect it differs on the one hand, from physical science and language which require outward apparatus, and on the other from psychology, which does not usually commend itself as of immediate practical importance. Whatever man's theory of the Universe may be, there are some questions which he cannot avoid—What am I? What is my relation to the power or powers of the Universe? What is my destiny? These questions the Hindoo and the Greek studied in their national poetry, the Egyptian and the Assyrian in their monumental inscriptions, all ancient nations in their daily religious service, and to-day among peoples civilized and uncivilized, among classes cultivated and uncultivated, believers and skeptics, theists and atheists, they have no small share of men's thoughts.

This is especially true among ourselves of those persons who either heartily embrace Christianity, or are seriously investigating its claims. Christians, particularly, must be students of Theology. They are constant readers of the book which teaches its principles. They are constantly listening to announcements and explanations of these principles. Their minds naturally dwell on theological facts and doctrines. The Pulpit and the Sunday-School are theological schools. Many a man who has had no other training is well versed in exegesis and dogmatics. This has been so from those early days when persecution concentrated and intensified Bible-study to the middle ages, when thousands of young men thronged to the great Universities to hear Abelard and his successors, and to our own times when sermons, books, and periodicals, bring every day to our doors the same material for thought.

But, while we are thankful for so great diffusion of Christian knowledge, we cannot disguise from ourselves that there is painfully wide-spread and great ignorance. There is much superficial knowledge—there is very little accurate knowledge. The few may reach clear conceptions of Scripture-teachings,—the many will content themselves with vague views. This evil, grounded in human nature, and to be expected everywhere and at all times, is not lessened by the boldly practical tendencies and impatient temper of our age. The masses are not intelligent hearers and readers of the truth. The cardinal facts of the Gospel, indeed, they grasp, but they are without wide and clear knowledge. The more cultivated rely on newspapers, and manuals, and compendious dictionaries, and commentaries. The preacher must often be aware that his attempts at exact statements are unappreciated, that his nicer excellencies as well as his nicer faults pass unnoticed, and this tends to lower the standard of ministerial effort. There is a grievous lack of keen interest in the broader aspects and minuter distinctions of divine truth.

And this at a time when we particularly need fulness and distinctness of knowledge and belief. Human science is growing daily in extent and clearness, and popularity, and, as it grows, tends to set itself up as the antagonist of Christianity. The more clearly it sees its own truth the greater its disposition to judge all truth by its own standard. This growth of science is the expression of the growth of the world. It is a part of the general advance to self-consciousness, which is attended by sharper and sharper self-questioning. The race is striving to bring itself face to face with all the questions which affect it, and to render account to itself of all its beliefs. It brings this disposition into the domain of religion. The man who believes holds his belief under the condition of investigation and intelligent apprehension. As the mature man, though he may believe as really as the child, must attain his faith by more elaborate processes, and hold it in more complex form, so does each advancing age of the world show more manifoldness in processes and forms of religious belief. Nor can we expect to escape from the spirit of our age. We breathe its atmosphere, we exist and think under its conditions, we believe and act according to its laws.

These considerations show the need of the general diffusion of broad and clear religious knowledge. The masses ought to be reached, and the Christian, world is attempting to reach them by its Sunday-schools, and periodical literature, and missionaries. But is impossible now to make liberal culture universal. Would God that all the Lord's people were prophets. But it seems probable that the conditions of life will always restrict the mass of men to that moderate culture (constantly enlarging, it is true,) which is compatible with daily toil for bread. However this may be, the best means of reaching the many is highly to educate the few. The University is the creator and maintainer of colleges, academies and schools. Culture descends with ever-widening sphere and lessening depth from the scholar to the people. Universal shallowness will remain shallow to the end. The impulse to thought and investigation must come from minds heated to enthusiasm by fulness of knowledge and laborious thought. Our true policy is to give to our best men the most liberal culture that time and appliances permit, and to send them forth to rouse and lead our people.

Thus much in respect to the peculiar circumstances of our times. It may be added more generally that society, and especially Christian society, is to be a revelation of God, and fulfils its end in so far as it glorifies him by the manifestation of his being, his attributes, and the laws of his government. To do this, it needs knowledge, and every member of society must recognize the obligation to acquaint himself with God to the extent of his ability.

To come now to purely educational grounds, there seems to be no good reason why theological science should not take its place among the other sciences as equally essential to liberal culture. Thorough education requires universality of study both in order that the special discipline of every department of thought may be received, and that the thought material may be acquired which is necessary to produce sympathy with all human interests and efforts. The word 'universal' must indeed be taken in a modified sense. We cannot master all facts and sciences. But we can master enough to bring us in contact with all modes of reasoning and classes of interests. Further, the connection of all branches of knowledge makes acquaintance with one an aid to a fuller acquaintance with all others. If then, as we may here assume, theology represents definite and peculiar systems of facts and modes of thought, which are of universal interest and importance, we ought to give theological science a place in our higher curricula. Several objections which naturally present themselves to this view may be briefly considered.

To some persons what is here proposed may seem to confound liberal and technical studies. 'Ask our young men who do not intend entering the ministry to study Theology!' As well ask them to study Law and Medicine! There are two satisfactory answers to this objection—one based on the differences between Theology and the other professional sciences, the other applicable to all these sciences.

There are two important differences between Law and Medicine on the one hand, and Theology on the other. The first is, that the material of the former is more shifting and lies more remote from ordinary life and study than that of the latter. Legislative enactments and judicial decisions are constantly accumulating and passing away, and require constant study that one may maintain one's self in sympathy with the profession. Discoveries and inventions in Medicine make up a literature by themselves. Then the material of these sciences, anatomy, pathology, legal principles and enactments, rarely force themselves on the attention of an unprofessional man. But theology remains unchanged by time, and its material is in our hearts and lives, in our ordinary books of study, and is necessarily an object of attention to every thinking man. The second difference is that we may safely entrust our lives and property to men in whose honesty and capacity we have confidence, while necessity is laid on every man in respect to his soul and to God, to have an independent opinion and ground of independent action. It is at his peril that he surrenders these to any man or class of men, and the practical question is whether he is to form his opinions on full or on slender knowledge.

The other answer to the objection applies to all the sciences. While there is a real distinction between technical and liberal studies, it must not be pressed too far. In every profession or science, besides the strictly technical details, there is a large mass of matter in which the professional differs from the general student only in the extent to which he carries his studies. In all there are subjects which may, and often do, form part of a general course. Our Colleges and Universities have unprofessional courses of Constitutional and International Law, Rules of Evidence, Blackstone's Commentaries, Physiology, Comparative Anatomy, and Medical Jurisprudence.

We have a natural interest in all knowledge, and we find in every department an infinite number of grades. How far we shall go in any direction is matter of time, opportunity and capacity. The student who spends twenty years on Latin looks back on his respectable college-learning as little better than ignorance. We encourage the boy at school to do what he can with Æschylus, though we know that he cannot enter on the criticism of the text or appreciate the poet's higher moral and poetical excellencies. In a word, in all branches of knowledge there are special and general courses. There is nothing which may not become technical, there is nothing which may not be made general. While therefore, there will be a sufficient field for the wider and maturer studies of the preacher, the unprofessional student may find much in theology becoming and practicable for him as a man of culture to know.

In respect to the difficulty of finding time for such study, it may be said that too little time is given by young men as a rule to their preparatory studies, that the topics here referred to would attach themselves easily to subjects now embraced in curricula, that it might be a question whether it would not be judicious to substitute these for some others, and finally, that if it be shown that they are of supreme importance, the time to prosecute them must be taken, even though it should touch on that which custom has assigned to the material interests of life.

To some persons it may seem of doubtful propriety that any but Christians should thus devote themselves to the study of Theology. The teaching of the Scriptures can be properly apprehended, it is said, only through the guidance of the Holy Ghost, and a merely secular study will lead to misunderstanding and perversion, and perhaps to an unconverted ministry. It is true that divine teaching is needed to understand the Bible. It is also true that the obligation to study and understand the Scriptures is universal, and further that men do actually form opinions right or wrong, and must be helped to attain as much as possible of the truth. It is clear that this objection, if consistently urged, would lead to withholding the gospel entirely from the unconverted. Truth is always a test and discipline. It may become a savor of life or of death. We must accept the possibility of perversion and evil, and do what we can to guard against it. It must be the care of the churches jealously to guard their doors, to scrutinize all who ask for entrance, and above all to see that unworthy men do not press into the ministry of the word.

Having said thus much in support of the claim of Theology to an equal place with the other sciences, let us ask what are its special claims to consideration, It may be well to state distinctly that we are here concerned with believing study only. There is no lack in the world of philosophical examination and sharp criticism of Christianity as a system of belief. Nor would we put any obstacle in the way of investigation. We invite the closest scrutiny of the Bible, its faith, its morality, its history, geography and chronology. We do not object to a Science of Religion, provided it have the elements of a science. But here we are speaking of the study of Theology by men who accept the Bible as divine, who have made what investigation may be necessary and are convinced.

And first, our cultivated young men ought to make special and accurate study of theological topics, because they will thus lay hold more distinctly of cardinal facts and principles of all knowledge. The Universe without God is a hopeless mystery, and science, which is only a classified statement of the phenomena of the Universe, is, without the science of God, defective and eccentric. It is true, that particular parts of the field may be worked, and many important partial results gained without acknowledgment of the centre and source. Strictly speaking, pure human science is absolutely independent of theology, though in fact it generally advances by means of hypotheses which take their color from the latter. But Philosophy which stands above science, which uses the results of science as its material for the construction of an all-embracing system, has always stood in the closest relation with Theology. The philosophers of the world have always been theologians. God is the centre of all things, and to ignore him or misapprehend his relations to the creation is to distort the moral Universe as the Ptolemaic astronomy distorted the solar system. Against such distortions, so prevalent now, our youth must be fortified by clear knowledge of God's revelation of himself in the Scriptures.

Human thought, which is the expression of the relation between facts, must be controlled by its starting-points or axioms. What will be the result if the fundamental axiom be ignored, if the fact on which all others depend be omitted or misunderstood?

Influenced, as we necessarily are, by the modes of thought of our time, we are constantly in danger of admitting into our philosophy of life ungodly elements which retard our Christian progress and hinder our usefulness.

In order therefore, that the controlling axioms and material of thought may be sound and true, our young men need thorough theological training.

Secondly, the valuable mental discipline given by theological studies, furnishes another reason for their general prosecution. Whatever is said in this respect in behalf of the classics may be said in higher degree of the interpretation of the Scriptures in the original tongues, and in an important sense of their interpretation in the vernacular.

The qualities of thought and mental habits engendered or developed by Metaphysics are called forth by Dogmatics and Polemics. Accuracy of historical investigation, careful discrimination of ideas and words, cautious balancing of arguments, discriminating application of principles—all these are brought into play by the study of the ordinary topics of Theology.

But, without dwelling on this generally admitted fact, I may refer briefly to certain important elements of thought, which are peculiarly nourished by these studies.

One of these is humility, a quality without which it is not possible to reach the highest excellence in thought, inasmuch as the thinker must always feel himself to be simply the interpreter of the facts given him by observation. Let Isaac Newton and Auguste Comte be compared in this respect. Now, the student of Theology finds himself constantly in the presence of facts and persons greater than himself—an authoritative presence before which he bows his head, and to which he submits his mind. His submission is not slavish cringing, not abandonment of individuality and prerogative, but a free and glad recognition of and faith in something above him, out of which comes the disposition to accept God and his universe as guides—a disposition which, carried into other departments of thought will be of lasting importance to him.

Then, from this humility springs calmness, engendered by the conviction that there is a sovereign righteous ruler who orders all things well, and an eternal truth which will manifest itself and prevail. Our impatient struggles cease in the presence of this conviction, and our minds assume the attitude best suited to the reception and comprehension of truth.

And this leads to patience in investigation, which may well be called the highest of intellectual virtues. Unpretending as it usually seems, and lacking in grandeur, we owe to it more triumphs of thought than to anything else. Perhaps no age or people ever needed it more than we. And surely if there are any studies that tend to foster it, it is these that we are considering. All the complexities and difficulties of the matter combine with the reverence and love it calls forth, with the sense of its supreme dignity and the supreme importance of our decisions to cultivate stillness and persistent labor. Here the motives are the fear of God, the love of man, the everlasting future. If these do not develop patience, nothing will.

Finally, (for I can only barely mention these things), breadth of thought is a direct product of theological study. It has been affirmed of theologians that they are the most narrow-minded of men, and the odium theologicum, as a result of this narrowness, has become proverbial. But this hatred, when it exists, is the result not so much of narrowness of view as of intense conviction of the supreme importance of the views held. The true theologian, he who imbibes the spirit of the Bible, is not narrow. He is firm in his maintenance of truth, but he is broad because truth is broad, he is liberal because he is humble, he is catholic because the Bible is catholic. Narrowness is egotistic—the student of theology is led to sink self in the truth. Breadth of view is the result of a true conception of the vastness of truth, and a true regard for the dignity of man, and both of these will come from genuine study of Scripture.

These qualities, humility, calmness and patience and breadth give tone to thinking, and theological study, which best secures them, stands thus as the best counteracting influence against the arrogant and narrow tendencies of human science. It impresses us with the reality of spiritual agency, and cultivates the spiritual logical faculty, which has for its materials the deeper spiritual instincts of the heart, and whose method and matter are ignored by human logic.

The value of the literary and scientific material given by the study of theology, is too obvious to need illustration. Judaism and Christianity represent a great fact in the development of the world, which it is necessary for the student of general history to comprehend. No one can be said to be up with the times who is ignorant of the questions respecting the origin of the Pentateuch, the genuineness of Isaiah and the Gospel of John, and the criticism of the text of the New Testament. As to the alleged controversies between the Bible and science, if the theologians have erred through ignorance of science, the scientists have also erred through ignorance of the Bible and theology.

All these purely disciplinary and literary benefits, however, are to be regarded as incidental advantages, and not as primary motives to the study of theology. While this study, for reasons already given, is not to be restricted to Christians, we must insist on the reverent and religious spirit which is appropriate to the study of the word of God. And our plea for its general diffusion would be valueless if we could not add that we may expect from its prevalence increase of piety and efficiency in the Christian youth of the day, and therefore in the whole Christian world. A general impulse will be given to the study of the Scriptures, a livelier interest excited in evangelical subjects, and in the progress of the truth, there will be more intelligent apprehension of the Gospel, and profounder views will be gained by the continuous meditation which will thus be induced.

We may anticipate a polenical advantage also from the better acquaintance which our people will thus gain with our peculiar views and the grounds on which they rest, not urging this in any selfish sectarian spirit, but from the conviction that the whole truth must be known and maintained.

If it thus appears that theology in its disciplinary and literary aspects is entitled to as much attention in a liberal course of study as any other science, that it supplies fundamental material and develops essential qualities of thought, that it opposes itself to injurious tendencies of human science, and that it nourishes piety and Christian efficiency, it remains to inquire whether any practicable scheme presents itself for making it generally accessible to the men who aim at the acquisition of more or less thorough culture.

I have not defined the term "theological science," because its general import is plain. It is intended to embrace all that is taught, or that ought to be taught, in our Theological Seminaries, with the exception, perhaps, of the purely technical branches as Homiletics and Pastoral Duties. It is the study of the Bible, and all that is immediately connected with it.

As already suggested, these studies ought to engage the attention of all Christians as far as they have capacity and opportunity to pursue them. Many of our Church-members are reading men, versed in current literature, with some capacity for connected thought, and interested in scientific and literary matters. This class of men might be directed by the pastors and other competent persons to books of biblical and systematic theology, ecclesiastical history, biblical introduction and other theological subjects, and stimulated and aided in reading and study. The effort need not be confined to church-members—persons who make no profession of faith in Christ may be interested in such studies, and so brought in contact with evangelical truth. The young men, particularly, of all classes may thus be reached. We have books of different grades of fullness and difficulty to suit the cases of men of widely different culture. This will entail labor on the pastor, but it will increase his own knowledge and culture, widen his sphere of usefulness by giving him a peculiarly strong hold on an important class of his hearers, and increase the efficiency of the church.

To come, however, to more systematic instruction, we may begin by affirming that such instruction must be denominational, and that theology had better be excluded from all the state-establishments, whether common schools or Universities. Theology is necessarily sectarian or individual. Even the more general branches, as Ecclesiastical History or Introduction, must take color from the peculiar views of the instructor, and such presentation would not be tolerated in this country. But, if an instructor could be found so colorless or so adroit as to teach Dogmatics and Bible Interpretation with perfect satisfaction to all classes of opinions, there is a decisive objection to such a plan. There could be, according to the constitution of our public institutions, no standard or guarantee of orthodoxy. The occupant of an important chair might embrace and teach fundamental error, and yet keep his position because there was no authority interested in guarding the truth assailed. If we may judge by the history of theological thought in the German Universities, skepticism and rationalism would inevitably follow from such state-appointments of theological teachers. I believe the experiment has never been fairly tried in this country, and it is to be hoped that it never will be tried.

Excluding then, this method, we are restricted to Theological Seminaries and Denominational Colleges as instruments of theological culture. Of both of these, (especially of the former) it is true that their theological complexion is known and guarded. The student is at liberty to differ from the Professor as widely as he pleases, is invited to form his own opinions, but the influence of the Institution is given in behalf of interpretations of Scripture recognized by some body of Christians, and scrupulously watched over by them.

It will be quite practicable for theological seminaries to arrange courses adapted to the wants of general students, whether the studies be proscriptive or elective, though the elective will have decidedly the advantage. In one session a man tolerably well trained may gain such knowledge of the Old Testament, the New Testament, Dogmatics, Church polity, and Ecclesiastical History, as will put him in close sympathy with these branches, and give impetus to his studies throughout his life. Students will be more likely to undertake such study when the College and the Seminary are connected or contiguous.

Let them be encouraged to do so, let our Seminaries make special provision for them, and let the attention of young men be directed to this point, by college professors, pastors, and the public prints.

But, while we hope that many may be induced to make more or less full study at the seminaries, the practical difficulty of inducing graduates of colleges to continue their studies at other institutions will be very great, and we must therefore look to the colleges themselves to furnish the means of theological study. Let it be understood that we are not advocating theological chairs or departments in colleges. These have been tried, and though directed by men of ability, have failed, because, they being practically restricted to ministerial students, it has been impossible with the resources of our denominational institutions, to give them much fullness or depth. What is here suggested is that the instruction in theology stand alongside of the instruction in other sciences as equally entitled to the attention of cultivated men, and equally accessible to all, recognized and offered as part of a liberal course of study.

Something has already been done in this direction. There are chairs of Natural Theology and Evidences of Christianity, and they are usually not the least popular of the College-classes. Recently in a Baptist college in this country, instruction has been given in Biblical History and Theology as a purely collegiate course, and the course might no doubt be extended without difficulty so as to embrace other theological subjects.

The objection to the introduction of theological instruction into State-institutions does not apply to the original languages of the Bible. Provision for the study of Hebrew and New Testament Greek, might be made everywhere. The Professor of Greek could by syllabus, lectures, or text-book, give to his classes the main grammatical and lexicographical points of difference between the Classics and the New Testament, and would find in the language of the latter much that is worthy of study from a purely linguistic point of view. Hebrew is entitled to far greater attention than it has received. Its grammar is a very interesting one, and its vocabulary is remarkable. It is desirable that our colleges should afford our young men the opportunity of becoming acquainted with at least one of the Shemitic family of languages, and the Hebrew has peculiar claims on us. As Christian students and defenders of the faith, there is a serious obligation laid on us to understand the very words of the Prophets and Patriarchs. A chair of Hebrew is a desideratum in every college. If the language were once fairly brought before our young men, we may be certain that they would pursue it with enthusiasm.

I cannot here enter into the details of the instruction. It will not be difficult even with the present form of our Colleges to make a beginning, though it will be necessary to proceed cautiously. A Professor of History could have a course of Biblical and Ecclesiastical History. The Department of Metaphysics and Ethics might include Dogmatics and Polemics. With Hebrew and Greek might be combined in the Denominational Colleges, the interpretation of the Old and New Testaments. Other topics might be introduced as opportunity offered. But thoroughness is better than extensiveness. One theological branch well-taught, will be more useful than a superficial sketch of the whole science.

I close with two or three suggestions.

It is important that the theological training here contemplated be presented to the young men in our Colleges as a necessity for every man who aspires to thorough culture, and that they be encouraged and stimulated to reach it. The effect of a general diffusion of this culture will be to swell the ranks of the ministry, and to draw ministers and people together in closer sympathy.

At the same time, the study should be carried on in a reverent spirit. It must not be a school-task, but the free effort of men who appreciate its seriousness and value. It will therefore be better that the special character and the extent of theological study be left to the choice of the student himself. This freedom will not, however, prevent the use of such aids to study as examinations, diplomas, and prizes.

There will be no conflict between the college-courses and the Theological Seminaries. The latter now have to do much elementary work, and will be heartily obliged to the Colleges if they will send them students tolerably well prepared in all theological branches. The result of this will be to extend the courses of the Seminaries, and to raise the standard of ministerial education.

Finally, if the suggestions here made be approved, it will be well to begin this work immediately. Wisdom must be learned from experience. The best methods will be found by actual trial. We have no model before us. So far as I know, the experiment has not been made in modern times. Our own needs must be our guide. And here, as in all things looking to the up-building of the Kingdom of Christ, let us not forget our entire dependence on the guidance of the Holy Spirit of God.

Dr. BOYCE: I have not felt before, in this meeting, as much regret at the physical difficulty under which I am suffering as I do at the present moment; I have very earnestly desired to say some things in connection with the topic presented in the very able paper of —I was going to say my colleague, but I am very much better pleased to do like Dr. HOVEY, and call him my pupil. He has got ahead of me, as Dr. HOVEY says of his pupil. I feel that there is, at the present time, a very great call upon our denomination for the instruction of our laymen in Theological science. There is a work which lies before our laymen and which opens up immense fields of usefulness to them, if they can only be properly instructed. I think I see also in this a means of wide-spread increase in the ministry in the right direction; an increase not in numbers alone, but in men of ability, men fitted for the work; and the manner in which many men may be brought with more light into the ministry of the Gospel, from the direction which their minds have taken from a taste formed in earlier times and a preparation which has been obtained in that way. I believe we do very great injustice to our people in this country, and Christian people elsewhere, when we lead them to suppose that all that is needed, so far as instruction in the Bible is concerned, is such as is obtained by mere reading of the English Bible with an occasional commentary or so, such as is received in prayer meetings, and in connection with Bible classes.

I do not know of but one single illustrious instance—there may be others at the North—of a man who had not himself decided upon the position of a preacher who entered the Theological Seminary, and that man was Dr. JUDSON. I have known of two cases in the South within my own experience in connection with our Seminary. One of those who staid with us without any connection at all with the ministry, with no prospective connection; simply taking such studies as he pleased for his own gratification, is now living in California. I received a letter from him some months ago. He spoke of his earnest desire to return and spend another year or two, because he found the instruction he had received from us helped him to do a work there which there was no one else to do.

I have a very large Bible class, first commencing with some twenty or thirty pupils, then running up to seventy, then filling the room, then dividing and growing again to seventy. If I had room, I could have at least one hundred males and as many females, for the purposes of instruction; to whom I am accustomed to deliver very much the same sort of instruction upon Biblical Interpretation, which I delivered, during the absence of Dr. BROADUS in Europe, to a class before whom I lectured for him. I found that the people of the town composed of doctors, lawyers, merchants, some old men who had hardly ever had any instruction at all; one of them an ignorant man of eighty years of age; from that going down to young men of sixteen or seventeen in the University; all equally seemed to be interested in this lecture on Sunday morning. I lectured to them an hour and a quarter, and I don't think, that I very frequently saw any one yawn or show any sign of weariness.

The first year I ever tried that course, I tried it with a company of ladies, of all classes. I took up the book of Genesis, and they were astonished that there was anything to be learned in connection with Genesis. They thought Genesis was just a little account of the creation, and that was the end of it. Taking that now as an indication of what is felt everywhere, and then take the fact, that men of culture love culture and love literature, why shouldn't men love to find out the beauties of Hebrew poetry, as well as the beauties of Latin or English poetry? Why should a man be stirred by the Odes of Pindar or Horace, and not be influenced by the Psalms of David or the visions of Isaiah? Why should a man be stirred by the Philosophy of Bacon, the pointed, pithy sentences which mark that great Philosopher, and not in like manner be stirred by that most wonderful wisdom, that most excellent of all wisdom so far as philosophy is concerned, with which there is nothing to be found in all the history of literature to compare, the Proverbs of Solomon? [Applause.] Who reads them? How many persons know them? It was wisdom, not simply because it was inspired, but wisdom if it had not come to us from inspiration. More than that, I think there are some men fond of systems, some men who like to see things fit together, see that they have a relation, and that they are not mere facts, who gratify their taste sometimes in the direction of botany, going over the world, and finding here and there scattered flowers of all kinds, and discerning more excellence and beauty in the work of the Creator's hands. Men who study botany merely as boys or school-girls study it, merely to say something about it, will realize nothing of the beauty of such things, which a man will realize who masters it as a science, and rejoices in the beauty and harmony which he sees developed, and in the means we have of knowing God with all the glory and greatness which belong to Him We discover such manifestation of order, relation and correlation, among the doctrines of truth that are linked together in such a perfect system, that the man who once begins to see it in the glory of its excellence, to recognize in its wonderful harmony the fitting in of its doctrines, feels with amazement in his heart, a deep gratitude to God for the evidence which has come to him from the system of Theology, that it has come from God whose system is to be found everywhere.

Dr. JONES: I was much pleased with the paper to which we have just listened. Every one who aspires to a broad and generous culture, must not wholly neglect theological science. We all say that any one who aspires to a broad and generous culture, must have some acquaintance with medical science, some acquaintance with legal science. And yet who says, and who feels that one to be a true scholar, must be familiar with the word of God, and with the sciences developed from it? Why sir, theological science, it were but a truism to say, is chief of the sciences —the science of God. To know God, is to know everything; and to be ignorant of him, is really not to know anything as we ought to know it. The gentleman who gave us the paper said that God is the centre of all things. So he is. Now, if we take possession of the study of God, if we stand close to him in his light, we see light; but until we know God and until we come into the charmed circle, by which he is surrounded, we have no clearness and no strength of vision. Standing near to God, looking up into his loving eye, and catching the light that pours from his radiant face, our whole soul is illuminated with the genial light, and inspired with the warmth he thus gives us, and all our powers are energized. Now, sir, let us encourage theological study, not on the part of ministers alone, but on the part of our leading lay scholars, on the part of our young men—nay, on the part of our young women.

Dr. BLISS: As a College professor I beg for a couple of minutes of this crowded time, before we leave the subject now before us, I have listened with great admiration to the essay of Professor Toy, as setting forth clearly and in logical order, the essential branches of theological science, and as urging very impressively their importance in an ideal scheme of liberal education. But, having regard to the practicability of his views, from the position of a College professor, I have listened to him, at some points, with unbounded amazement. A liberal education is, in one aspect, the work of a life-time, and as such doubtless requires and gives room for, all that has been here proposed. In that elementary stage of it, however, which lies within the college curriculum, where the time is now pitifully crowded with tasks scarcely possible to be performed, yet not possible to be omitted, here to think of adding a range of studiess which might almost double our burden, strikes me as passing strange. Even the proposition, so eloquently advocated yesterday, to introduce the Hebrew language, (a small fraction of theological study), as a profitable branch of general, collegiate education, seemed to me to imply such a conception of what may be done by colleges, that I could only wonder where gentlemen had learned to hope that these can accomplish what seems to me so unattainable.

I have some doubt about the expediency of attempting to bring theological science into the college curriculum, but do not think of discussing the matter, under any aspect, now. I only wish to express my conviction that the finite capacity of that curriculum must of necessity exclude many subjects of study of the greatest intrinsic importance, and theology, as well as law or medicine, among them.

Dr. KENDRICK: I would be glad to offer a few words in relation to this subject. I have listened with exceeding interest, sir, and I will say, as my friend and former pupil, Prof. BLISS, has said, I have listened with admiration to the paper and the suggestions which it makes in regard to the importance of Theological education in its various branches. Our minds and hearts all feel responsive, as also to the very great desirableness of introducing the Hebrew language, one at least of the Semitic languages, and of all others the Hebrew, to the knowledge of our young men in a course of liberal education, and especially of our Christian young men preparing for the ministry. Now, our brother who read the paper yesterday, Dr. PEPPER, I think, intimated that the reason why we exclude the Hebrew is because it is not quite heathenish enough. Had it treated of Apollo and Diana and Venus and Bacchus, I suppose Dr. PEPPER would take for granted that the college faculty, somehow or other would work it in. [Laughter]. But inasmuch as it gives the Ten Commandments and some other doctrines—the doctrines of the one, only God,—why, it was not quite palatable, quite so acceptable, either to the professors or to the students. I don't know where Dr. PEPPER was educated. [Laughter]. I don't know what kind of testimony he was intending to bear to the character of the college of which he was a graduate, and of the professors under whom he sat in receiving instruction. But I don't believe that they would be willing quite, to allow the implied testimony in relation to their moral proclivities, in the very delicate and ingenious and eloquent intimation which he made in regard to their instruction. This, however, by the way.

I have only to say in relation to the University of Rochester, we should be exceedingly glad to introduce the Hebrew into our course of instruction. From the beginning of our Greek course, from the time when I first take my Greek classes, which is usually with the commencement of the last term of the Freshmen year, down to the last term of the Senior year, in which I have students at all, every Monday morning is the recitation in the Greek Testament. I begin, generally, with a few chapters of Matthew, the first chapter, because I want to make some general remarks in regard to the miracles that cluster around the Incarnation; the reason of those miracles, the propriety of them, and some general considerations of that character. I go on to the Sermon on the Mount, which I endeavor to make rather a means of getting to the bottom of those profound and most important instructions. After that, we go over to such portions of the New Testament as we may choose, sometimes the Epistle to the Romans—filled with the profoundest philosophy that is embodied in any book that was ever written on the face of this earth, within the same limits. I mention this, however, simply as an indication that it is not because the Hebrew Scriptures are not heathen that they are ruled out of our Rochester course. But what are we to do? Now we want something of the Hebrew, we want some of the Greek New Testament, we want some of its theology. I am as perfectly convinced as the gentleman who read the paper, or as any gentleman can be, of the importance of theological instruction to every well regulated, well disciplined mind, and of its importance in a course of liberal education. What are we to do? Prof. BLISS has suggested the almost overwhelming difficulty with the case as it stands. We should have accumulated upon a college course which is now groaning under its weight, as much more matter almost. Well, I suppose we have got to meet these questions in part, by optional courses. I take Prof. BLISS' position with a qualification. Instead of saying that *every* liberally educated student must take a course of theology, I would have this perhaps one alongside of a number of higher courses, all of which might stand upon a level. Not this tabooed in any way; not this appropriated especially to the ministry, but a certain well organized, well selected course of theological instruction alongside of other courses. And when we have lifted up our college course, when we have got one additional year of preparation from our academies—*from such academies as we are to have,*—then I don't see but that it may be possible to make some compromise like this, and to introduce some portion of theological instruction into our collegiate system. But permit me to say, Mr. President, I think there is one of our colleges in which, it seems to me, there is a very admirable chance of making some experiment, a fair experiment. We are about to have one of the ablest theological instructors in the country taking the headship of one of our oldest and best colleges. And if the experiment can be made successful anywhere, I should suppose it could be made there. And I want to say I think if something like this could be done, we might, perhaps, add to the chances of multiplying and increasing our students for the ministry—of increasing the number and increasing the quality of our students for the ministry. I should like to see the barriers a little thrown down, a little less marked between our colleges and our theological seminaries. On the one hand I should like to see a little more elementary theological instruction introduced into the later stages of the college course, and I should like to push our collegiate instruction into the theological institutions. In this way, instead of standing on the boundary line and demanding of a man that he shall be a candidate for the ministry and bring certificates from the church of his being in good standing, &c.,—instead of repelling every other one—open your arms, throw out your inducements, induce every Christian young man to enter upon the theological course. I think there are very many of these young men who would enter that course who are not yet prepared to make up their minds to enter the ministry, and who, in the course of that process would receive the inspiration, upon whom the Spirit of God would descend, and we should have a larger number of that class of young men who, it has been justly lamented, do not just now enter the ministry, but who would enter it if we would throw open the doors of our theological institutions and open the courses of our theological instruction and win them in—draw them in instead of repelling them. And then let them form their resolution under the inspiration of these studies to enter the sacred ministry. [Applause.]

Prof. ANDREWS: It is with great diffidence that I express myself upon this subject, but it seems to me that to make provision for this want which has been so ably set forth by Dr. Toy, in the way which was suggested by his paper, is open to one serious objection. If there should be provided in the college curriculum an optional course of theological study there is one great reason to fear, if I may judge from the little experience and observation which I have had, that some young men, either through ardent zeal, not sufficiently regulated by knowledge, or attracted by some of the pleasures of an early settlement, might be induced to branch off too soon from that general literary and scholastic culture that must be at the base of all, and take this optional theological course, instead of taking a full theological course. I was about to rise as Dr. Hovey* brought out the point which in part covers the view that I shall express. I believe that the whole college curriculum, with possibly the exception of pure mathematics, may be permeated with such an influence and spirit as shall secure in great measure for every class of young men who fill our colleges, just what we desire. No man can adequately teach ancient languages and literatures without ability to defend the great truths of Reve-

* The remarks of Dr. Hovey are missing from the reporter's notes.

lation, the profound facts of theology in connection with those questions which so naturally suggest themselves and force themselves upon every thinking student and upon every true instructor in teaching the classics. I thank God that the time has come when the teaching of the classics is no longer heathen. I don't believe there is a Baptist college represented here in which the classics are taught in a heathen spirit. Christian study of the classics is, I believe, pursued in all our institutions. Never have I felt myself so thrown back upon what little theological attainment it was permitted me to make, as I have been in the teaching of the Greek language and literature. No man can adequately teach Homer, much less can any man with any sort of adequacy teach Plato, who is not profoundly interested at least, in the truths of theology. I have never found a class that did not respond to what feeble attempts I may have made to defend the great truths of religion, as one has such abundant opportunity to do in the teaching of classics, and so, I believe, it is with English literature. Much more is it so in the departments of metaphysics and ethics. There is abundant opportunity all along the curriculum of our students for the competent instructor to meet for every class of young men, these great questions that are stirring the thought of our age. [Applause.]

Dr. PEPPER: There is an exceedingly important question raised here, and I desire to say a few words in this connection. Whenever I see and hear Dr. KENDRICK I am sorry that I did not graduate at Rochester. [Applause] Whenever I see and hear Prof. LINCOLN, I am sorry I did not graduate at Brown. Whenever I hear my Baptist brethren in almost any capacity like this, I am sorry that I did not graduate at a Baptist college. I did graduate at a college which is not Baptist. I graduated at a college, however, which should be known from the Professor of Latin, —the gentleman who was my Professor in Latin and who has become known to us all recently, Prof. JEWETT. In other words, I graduated at Amherst. We all of us I supposed had learned long ago to adopt the sentiment of our poet Longfellow when he says that: "Things are not what they seem." Now I did not say that the reason why Hebrew was not introduced into our college course was that its classics were not heathen. I said that would seem to be the reason. I did not mean to imply that Latin and Greek are taught in a heathen spirit. I know that they are not so taught in our colleges, in our Baptist colleges, and in the college at which I graduated. I would not have them in any respect receive less attention than they do. I am exceedingly gratified that Prof. KENDRICK had beforehand settled the question how the Hebrew might be introduced, in having said in his most charming, delightful and able paper, that he would have the first two years of the college course compulsory, if I remember aright, and in the last two years he would have something more of option. It seems to me he has entirely settled the question for us. As this question has come up in this form, if there ever is again a convention of this sort, and God shall spare the life of Prof. CONANT until that time, I trust he will have the privilege, and it shall be laid upon him as a duty, to prepare and read a paper at that time upon this subject

Dr. ROBINSON: I suppose that our colleges, as well as our theological seminaries, have felt the difficulty of persuading young men to continue their regular courses of study before entrance upon the Christian ministry. I think I can say very plainly that if Hebrew and certain theological studies become a part of the college curriculum, there is an end of all prospect of holding theological students, when they shall have graduated at the colleges. Any attempt to reconstruct our present method will be fatal unless there shall be general co-operation among colleges throughout the country. Every theological seminary has graduates from a great variety of colleges. There must be some uniformity of study. One has attended to Hebrew, and another to a portion of the New Testament Greek, another to a little of dogmatic theology. He goes to a theological seminary for a year. He wishes to select his course. You find at the very outset that he is ignorant of the first principles of grammar and rhetoric. Ask any of the Professors in our medical schools where young men come with slight preparation and propose the study of medicine, ask them as to the rhetoric, style and skill of the papers presented for examination. Have we so much time now in our colleges that we can forego rhetoric, forego logic, abandon mathematics, mix the professional with the college course? Woe the day when we attempt it. [Applause.] The best men to whom it has been my privilege to teach theology, were men who have come from the colleges ignorant, I might say, of the New Testament, except what they had learned in their mother tongue, ignorant of Hebrew, ignorant of dogmatic theology, coming with the simple purpose to learn. My deliberate conviction is that the best possible course of preparation for a successful theological study or study in the theological seminary is to compel the young men who are proposing to enter the ministry to pursue the same curriculum as they pursue who propose to enter law or medicine. I don't understand how there can be any possibility for dispute here. With our present organization I can see no possibility of making such a change in the college curriculum without a thorough reconstruction of the curriculum of students in the theological seminary.

Dr. DODGE: It seems to me we should have our college curriculum, not in reference to the Theological seminary exclusively, nor in reference to law, nor in reference to medicine, but in reference to life. That the thing to be done is to make a man, to bring out all there is in him, and therefore, I say, the Bible must have ts place, not solely because it is a book of God, but because it is a book of man. [Applause.] It is the highest, and profoundest, and richest of all human thinking and human feeling, and therefore that which I would like to suggest as to the paper would be to substitute the study of the Bible for the study of Theology, and therefore I quite approve of the study of Hebrew, because the Hebrew language embodies all that we have of Hebrew literature, and without the knowledge of the language, the life of the greatest of the nations, perhaps of the old world, greatest certainty in religion, is unknown and concealed. Prof. ANDREWS, the professor of Greek in Madison University, is accustomed every Monday to give instruction in the New Testament; and so we give a term and a-half to the Hebrew, not exclusively to prepare men for the Theological seminary, but to give them the broadest education that we can, and prepare them for life. [Applause.]

The report of the Committee on Organization was then presented by Mr. SAMUEL COLGATE.

Mr. COLGATE: The Committee on Organization, to which was recommitted the constitution that was presented yesterday, beg leave to make the following report. In explanation they would say that they find their time too limited to report a constitution which they think can be a permanent constitution. The work is one of great magnitude. A constitution to embrace the educational interests of the Baptist denomination of the United States should be very carefully drawn. It requires great consideration and much time. We have been in session since half-past 8 this morning, and we have come to the following conclusion: that the work of the present Educational Commission has been well performed,—that it has accomplished a great work under its present constitution. The nature of the report this morning is to recommend the continuance of the work under the present constitution, with the exception of the first and second articles. That is the substance of the report.

The report was then read.*

It was moved and seconded that the Report be adopted.

Dr. MOSS moved as an amendment that the first and second articles as reported be amended so as to read as the first article of the constitution of the old Commission reads. The amendment was seconded.

Dr. BROADUS: I beg leave merely to say, sir, that while I don't know anything particularly about this matter, it is plain to me that this proposition leaves us just where we were after the committee and the secretary had been at work, and proposed to us what, I presume, they considered makes some little advance, to which I see no objection at all. I don't see how we gain anything by staying where we are. I like a little change, anyhow, because it looks like progress, even if there be no progress.

* This Report is not preserved in the Minutes.

Dr. SEARS: I was about to speak on the same point. This looks to me like carrying out the suggestion: "Why not let well enough alone?" If I understand the import of this, it is to remain as we were. I don't see what alteration there is. I don't see what is done by all the labor that has been bestowed by the committee to whom it was recommitted, upon this new constitution, and from some points of view I should be glad to do so. I like the present organization of this Society because it is so congenial to all our institutions. My tendencies lead me to like it if I could. I would say, let us stand by this if we could afford to do it. But that is the trouble. I think we cannot afford to stay just exactly where we are. Old Dr. BOLLES told me when me when I was a young man what I think is very pertinent to our present position. He was a prudent man, and I profess to be a prudent man. Said he: "The most imprudent thing in the world is extreme prudence." [Laughter and Applause.] And I think we are just there. I agree with all the cautions that have been thrown out, and yet I say in spite of them, we have got to face it. There is no security against the abuse of power, but the trouble is we can not afford to stay just where we are now. There is the work to be done. All that has been done is admirable and is safe. We must do a little more that is as admirable, and may or may not be as safe. We must have caution, but it must be caution in the right direction. I will tell a little story which is a very old one, and for that reason may be a new one to some of you. A man met a boy in great trouble on the road, who had upset his load of hay, and tried to comfort the boy. The boy said: "I should not take on so if my father wasn't under the load." There is the trouble in waiting three years. "Wait three years and we can get a good constitution." Why, the German Empire was made in three years, and the French Empire destroyed in less than three years. What do our brethren from the Western Territories and States say about waiting three years? Our Western institutions cannot wait three years. Why, we ought to show magnificent results in three years. And old as I am, I don't want to go so slow as that. [Applause.] I hold a peculiar position—I am a go-ahead conservative! Do the thing and run a little risk. Why, the society may become a dangerous power, it is said. To be sure, and what cannot become a dangerous power? My personal liberty is a dangerous power. Our political liberty is a dangerous power. The liberty of the Baptist churches may be abused as well as any other. The *independence* of the Baptist churches may ruin the interests of the Baptist churches because it is abused. I go for the independence of the Baptist churches. I risk it, and I run a tremendous risk to do so. The Fabian policy is what an old man talks of,—that is, under certain circumstances. It is sometimes the best and sometimes the worst.

Dr. MOSS: If it will be in order for me, I would like to explain why

I offered the amendment. I wish to say that I heartily agree with all that has been said by our respected instructor, Dr. SEARS, and also all that was said by Dr. BROADUS. And I agree most heartily with all that was contained in the articles as reported by the committee. No man on this floor who knows me at all, but knows I am whole-hearted, in my desire to see this American Baptist Educational Commission organized here to-day. But it has seemed to me that we ought to make this constitution just as simple and just as brief as possible, that these suggestions which have come to us from the committee on organization may be very well made to the Advisory Board, or the Executive Committee, or whatever they may be called, and adopted by them and incorporated by them in their by-laws, and that other such suggestions may be so considered and adopted. But I would not have a constitution adopted here to-day, that, by its excessive detail and by its numerous restrictions should, in any wise, impair the action of the Executive Committee. I wish that it may cover the whole ground of our secondary and higher education without exclusive reference to the ministry; without exclusive reference to any class, but inclusive of all classes and of the entire work of our higher education. So that I would have it simply read that its object is the promotion of education and the increase of the ministry. My simple object in making this amendment was not to interfere with advance, but to make room for much greater advance than would be possible if we were restricted by these restricting clauses of the constitution.

Dr. CALDWELL: I wish to propose an amendment at the proper time. The terms of the report of the committee confine any aid given directly or indirectly to periods of the infancy of our institutions. I think there is a time when the college suffers a great deal more than it does at an early period of its existence, and I wish to propose at the proper time that during periods of special emergency aid may be given which would include any time when a college gets into a feeble condition and wants to be helped over a hard place.

[The suggestion of Dr. CALDWELL was adopted, when the Constitution was taken up for action on its articles.]

Mr. COLGATE: The amendment offered by Dr. CALDWELL is in spirit with the ideas of the committee. But I would say in reply to what Dr. Moss has said that if the Educational Commission is left where it is now, we have no powers to increase our work. The members of the Educational Commission for the past two or three years have not felt that they have had any power to procure or receive funds for other objects than simply their own maintenance, and to diffuse intelligence and to stir up interest in educational affairs. We wish to make progress, and under this report we have a field opened to us to make progress, and when the triennial convention is called we think the subject of education in our denomination will be better understood. And at that time a perfect constitution can be reported. We feel if we attempt at this meeting to propose a constitution, it will be imperfect, that it is better to work in this imperfect manner under the old constitution, and come prepared in three years to endorse something that will last, than to have an imperfect constitution at the present time. The resolution which has been offered with the recommendations that have been made, will furnish all that the committee require to do the work that will be necessary for the coming three years.

Dr. MOSS withdrew his amendment.

Dr. CUTTING: I want to say a few things about this matter of organization, and I may as well, by your leave, say them here and now. Many years ago a book written by Dr. WAYLAND—less known than I wish it was—entitled, "The Limitations of Human Responsibility," made an impression upon my mind which has never left me. And so far as regards the spheres and limits of my duties, I have found more light in that book than in any book I ever read, except the Bible. Under that view of the limitations of human responsibility,—that we owe duties and that there are limits to them,—I prepared a paper, such as I thought it was becoming in me to prepare, not officially, but upon the basis of my knowledge and experience in regard to the work of the Educational Commission, intending to place that paper in the hands of the committee which might be here formed on the subject of organization. By your vote that paper was read to this body, and was referred to that committee. I likewise regarded it as my duty in aiding the purposes of that committee to write a constitution, which I did write and placed in their hands, a large part of which is in the constitution which was printed yesterday. There were changes and amendments made which were not in accordance with my judgment. In preparing that paper—in writing that constitution, I felt that I had done my duty, and that what remained to be done was to be done by you. I have not the slightest desire or wish to control in any manner the action which you shall take. I have personal friends here—a good many of them. I would not have one of those friends vote in favor of perpetuating this work because I desire it. I would not have them fail to vote against the whole thing if they do not like it. I want only that which is best, and I confide more in your judgment than I do in my own.

Then there is another thing. I don't wish that any member on this floor should give a vote on this subject connected in anyway in his own mind with my official relation to the Commission, because I shall not live always, and I am liable to disability at any time. And so far as my personal desire is concerned, you could not do a thing to please me so much as to give me the humblest place on the Board of Councillors, and appoint a secretary who has the vigor of manhood, who has hope before him and who is prepared to do his work better, far better, than I can do it. You remember, Mr. President, for you have seen it, the Aurora of Guercino, less celebrated than its wonderful rival by Guido Reni, but more true to the mythological representation, by the introduction of the husband of the goddess. You remember that when Tithonus, a mortal, espoused the beautiful Aurora, he was in his youth. And that he had the privilege of asking whatever he pleased of the gods. He asked for immortality, but forgot to ask for immortal youth. So he grew old, and older, and ever older until he was but "a gray-haired shadow," while Aurora was still young and blooming and ever beautiful. And all he asked at last was the privilege to die. Now, sir, this cause of education is the young and beautiful and ever-blooming aurora, while I am but that old Tithonus —though I can hardly call myself "a gray-haired shadow." [Laughter]. I will not pretend even that I am an extremely ancient man, but, sir, I have no confidence in my power to carry forward this work a single month. I have performed all that I have done under physical difficulties of the most serious character. And when I have been advised over and over by my physician to abandon it, I have adhered to my task because I love it, and because I believe the ends to which it looks to be the hope of the Baptist denomination. [Applause]. We must be an educating people or we are a lost people—and we ought to be. In the middle of the nineteenth century, with a population sometimes estimated at from five to seven millions, with 18,000 churches, shall we suffer our institutions of learning to be feeble and decrepit? If we do not multiply them according to the necessities of new states, if we do not make them strong in the old states, if we do not educate our young men for our ministry, if we do not bring all that there is in the human being to bear upon the progress of Christianity, the glory of our Redeemer, the advancement and triumph of religion in the world—if we fail to do these things, we are not worthy of a place among the people of God. [Applause]. I now desire that we should be in a condition to cast this work on somebody that can do it better than I can do it. I fear if you leave this merely where it is, it cannot be done. There ought to be freedom in regard to that matter. I am willing to accept the report of this committee, though it is not all that I desire. I did desire that you should organize this work, and take it up with a determination to make your influence and power felt all over this land. [Applause]. And if you are not prepared to do all that, then take this report. What I had hoped was to see this constitution adopted after you had made the alterations in the second article, which are proposed in the amendments that have been offered this morning.

Dr. BRIGHT: Our friend CUTTING's modesty is excessive; it always was, and never was more finely developed than this afternoon. But there is one thing about him, notwithstanding his modesty, he is always to be relied upon to fill an emergency when it comes. [Applause]. He always did it, and always will do it. I am sorry he slandered himself so much, and took so much pains to do it, as to go to Rome for that very damaging illustration of the way in which he is unworthy of the blessed and rising institution. [Applause]. I think this institution need not stand still even if it had adopted the amendment offered by Dr. Moss, and I don't think need stand still if it adopts the report of the committee. I never heard in any Baptist organization such reliance, such trust in a constitutional amendment as I have heard here to-day. Why, one would suppose that the whole life of the thing is in its constitution. Now my opinion is, when we are not perfectly agreed we should hit upon the best compromise we can.

A basket of flowers, brought into the church at this moment, was presented to Dr. Cutting.

Dr. BRIGHT (addressing Dr. Cutting): Doctor, do you think you are worn out and old? That is an offering from Aurora, sir. [Applause and laughter].

The very least you can do with the constitution this year, the better it is with all concerned. The less the better, and why? For this reason. It is not an easy thing for any Baptist organization to hit upon just the constitution, just the organization that is best adapted to the work that is before it. Now, how to raise means and how to apply them, how to foster institutions and how to repress them, is one of the most difficult things that American Baptists have undertaken to do. Now the simple fact is that the constitution that my brother Cutting drew up was not the best piece of his workmanship. He did it in a hurry, and did it as well as under the circumstances he could, but it hasn't the marks on it of the fine workmanship that he knows how to put on such an instrument. Then what shall we do? I say we had better wait one, or two, or three years, and put more life into the Commission under its present organization. Take time. Let the committee have time, and when they have got their plans thoroughly matured, then let them bring the result to us, and I have no doubt it will be cordially and unanimously adopted. But we are not ready to do that. This morning, I think, there were some five or six things brought forward, and the committee had about twenty minutes to decide upon them all. This that has come is a compromise. It is the best thing the committee could do under the circumstances. By-and-by, I have no doubt, we shall have something wiser, maturer, and better, but in the meantime let us work under the constitution the committee have proposed.

Allow me to ask Dr. Cutting a question. Has not the Commission of this thirty or forty men the power to amend and change this constitution as it chooses?

Dr. CUTTING: Exactly, sir.

Dr. BRIGHT: Has not the Commission the power to take as much of this printed document as it pleases and adopt it as part of that constitution?

Dr. CUTTING: Yes, sir.

Dr. BRIGHT: Now the simple question is whether it is better to leave a Commission of thirty intelligent men, with weeks or months before them, as it may be, to mature its constitution to meet all our exigencies, or to rush it through in the short time that is before this meeting. I say, refer it to the present Commission, rather than bring it here to a meeting where we have not time to consider it.

Dr. BOYCE: I expressed to-day a desire that the report which should come back from this committee should be simply the report that it originally presented. When a different report came from the committee this morning, I felt inclined at first to allow it to pass without any further objections, because I supposed that these brethren who had been most deeply interested in the getting up of this Commission, and the working of it in the past, preferred to put it in that form, and I therefore did not feel inclined to put myself in the way of their action. Now, sir, from the language that has been used by Dr. CUTTING and others, I feel as though that has not been the case, and consequently I am in favor of working upon the constitution of the original report, instead of the one that has been proposed this morning in the new report of the committee. I believe, sir, that yesterday the body of this Convention were in favor of the report then before us. I believe that the persons who had objections to it were but a handful; that, taking it as a whole, most of us felt that this was the best thing that could have been done. And I believe that if we had gone on yesterday without recommitting that report, and taken it up article by article, we should have had no trouble in reaching a conclusion long since. I believe that we can now put it in such a form that it will be generally acceptable throughout the house. [Applause].

Now, sir, one great objection that is made to forming a permanent organization at the present time is this: that we start out, it is supposed, with a sort of fixed law, like the laws of the Medes and Persians, that can never be changed. Now, what is the case? The case is that this constitution is one which can be changed at any time by the vote of two-thirds of the members present at the triennial meeting, provided that no change be made in regard to the main object of the Commission. Now that is the only limitation here, and if it is desirable so far as that article is concerned, it might be changed now so as to make it only a two-thirds vote at the next meeting. If we can put this organization in a practical form now and can see it work for three years under the guidance of the secretary—

he understands what he is about—and not under the charge of a new secretary whom we may have appointed, at the end of the three years we shall learn what we ought to have as a Commission, and then we can change the constitution without any difficulty whatever.

I would move that the report of the committee, after the word "resolved," be stricken out, and that the constitution originally proposed shall be adopted as a substitute.

Dr. J. WHEATON SMITH: I do not rise for any extended remarks, but rather to take an obstacle out of your way. I find that in what was possibly my too great caution of yesterday, though expressed as it was, I am a little misunderstood in this matter, and may unfortunately have left the impression upon your minds that I am not favorable to the organization and its relation to education. If so, I am very unfortunate indeed. I do not object to the organization, but long for it. I only want it to be of the right kind, and come from the bosom of the churches. I did hope that some of the gentlemen who spoke last evening would give us some reasons for the organization as now proposed. I heard of none.

If I could be persuaded that this paper answered the purpose, and that our method of organization was a wise and good one, I certainly would vote for its adoption. I beg my brethren to remember that slight as the impediment may be, it certainly shall not be brought in the face of what may be considered any wise method of organization. But I do want our churches to have something to do with this matter. I do want a matter so vital to spring directly from their bosoms. Not a church is represented on this floor.

Dr. MOSS: For the purpose of making a motion that shall bring before us the question: "Shall we organize a National Society?" I move that this whole subject be laid upon the table.

Carried.

Dr. MOSS: I now move that we proceed to organize a national educational association, to be known as the American Baptist Educational Commission.

Carried unanimously.

Dr. BOYCE: I now move that we take from the table the proposed substitute, that is, the constitution contained in the original report of the committee.

Carried.

[The notes of the reporter fail at this point. In the Minutes of the Secretaries, it is said: "The substitute proposed by Dr. BOYCE now being in order, the Doctor moved to amend the substitute by putting in the place of Article Second of the Constitution, proposed by the Committee in their original report, the Second Article of the Constitution offered in their revised report. An earnest discussion ensued, participated in by Dr. SEARS, Dr. BRIGHT, Dr. CUTTING, and Dr. BOYCE.

The hour of adjournment having arrived, the question before the Convention was made the order of the day for 2 o'clock, P. M."] Adjourned.

THURSDAY AFTERNOON SESSION.

The Convention re-assembled at two o'clock, and was opened with prayer by Rev. J. WHEATON SMITH, D. D.

On motion of Rev. G. S. BAILEY, D. D., of Illinois, the Convention proceeded to take up the Constitution article by article, including the substitution of the second article of the revised report, as moved by Dr. BOYCE at the close of the morning session, and with various amendments the articles were severally so adopted, and then the Constitution was adopted as a whole. [The Constitution will be found in the Addenda.]

The further consideration of organization was postponed to the evening session.

It was voted that the Committee on Organization be a Committee to nominate the officers of the American Baptist Educational Commission.

The Convention adjourned at an early hour in pursuance of the vote accepting the invitation to visit the Crozer Theological Seminary. Adjourned.

THURSDAY EVENING SESSION.

The Convention re-assembled at a quarter before eight o'clock, the Rev. Dr. J. P. BOYCE in the chair. Prayer was offered by Rev. O. O. STEARNS.

Members from the sections where Advisory Committees were to be appointed, were added to the Committee on Nominations, viz.: Rev. G. S. BAILEY, D. D., Rev. O. O. STEARNS, Pres. L. A. DUNN, Pres. R. C. BURLESON, D. D., Prof. H. H. HARRIS, Rev. J. A. BROADUS, D.D, LL.D., Prof. J. L. LINCOLN, LL.D., Rev. C. W. ANABLE, D.D., Rev. R. TURNBULL, D.D.

On motion of Dr. HOVEY the following resolution was adopted:

Resolved, That the thanks of this Convention are hereby tendered to the daily papers of this city for the full reports they have given of our proceedings.

A paper was then read by Rev. T. G. JONES, D. D., of Nashville, Tennessee,

ON LIMITING THE NUMBER OF OUR INSTITUTIONS BY OUR POWER TO MAKE THEM STRONG.

To meet the requirements of education, institutions of learning of various grades are needed. But our ability to establish and sustain such institutions is limited. If we multiply them, we must, as we have only a certain measure of capacity, in the same degree diminish their proportions and lessen their efficiency. Hence arises the question, Whether it is wiser to attempt to meet the demands upon us by increasing the number, or by enlarging the proportions and adding to the strength of our institutions of learning.

In favor of their indefinite multiplication is sometimes urged the common maxim of universal application, that competition is the life of trade. It is said that to increase the number of our schools, is to promote their efficiency. It excites emulation and generous rivalry. It diffuses light, promotes popular appreciation of education, increases the aggregate of those who enjoy its benefits, enlarges, through them, the number of the friends of the schools, and strengthens and stimulates the public interest in their prosperity. Thus, it is said, an increased demand is caused by an increased supply, and the advantages of education are multiplied and extended.

Another consideration sometimes urged in favor of the multiplication of institutions of learning, even though they should be of very limited proportions, is drawn from the supposed disadvantages incident to the concentration of great strength and influence in any one corporation or locality. It is thought necessary sedulously to guard against monopolizing tendencies. A very strong establishment of overshadowing influence might oppress and embarrass weaker but highly important and useful institutions. It might discourage local enterprises necessary to the educational and other interests of many communities. Like other monopolies, it might arbitrarily control education in its methods, in its quality, in its range, and in its cost. It might too, it is feared, through personal favoritisms, intrigues, and other influences, give, in some instances, fixed control of education and its interests to a few, and those not always the best qualified and most deserving persons.

It is also suggested that a few great, overshadowing institutions of learning might make education in its shape and hue, so to speak, too uniform, too stereotyped, too strongly impressed by special, local and individual influences, to suit the multiform character and widely different circumstances and interests of so many distinct individuals and communities, localities and sections, as exist in a vast country like ours. There is thought to be danger of forestalling nature, of sacrificing individuality, and all distinctiveness of character. And it were absurd, it is said, to call that education by which the most marked and important part of our individual and personal being, is not only not developed, but obscured, or neutralized and lost. In this view, it has been thought by some that the strength which has been concentrated on a celebrated institution of learning with whose character and position all present are familiar, much as that institution has honored its founders and supporters, might have been more usefully employed, if it had been divided and judiciously distributed between several establishments in different sections of the land. The same locality, surroundings, and influences, the same instructions, the same methods, the same curriculum, produce, it is insisted, too much sameness of type. Every one is too much like his fellow. There is not variety enough for the diverse departments, phases, tastes, wants of society and of life. Not only is diversity of talent required, but diversity of development as well. When one thinks of the average man of that distinguished and venerable institution to which I have just referred, he is apt to picture to himself, it is said, a dead-level man, stiff, prim, and precise, and a dry, angular, spectacled man; a man who has been stretched on the bed of Procrustes and made shorter or longer according to the most approved pattern of the school to which he belongs. One would know him, it is affirmed, if, as is not at all likely, he should, under the inspiration of temporary whim or caprice, don the broad brim of the Quaker, or the curiously-cut coat of the ancient Methodists, the robe of the Churchman, or the cowl of the Benedictine Monk. He is a stereotyped man, and one has only to observe his port and mien, and hear his voice, at once to recognize him. An old Scotch Covenanter, or a grim-visaged English Ironside were as easily mistaken. This great establishment has been powerful enough to dictate and fix the style, within its own ecclesiastical connection, for a continent; but, with all its learning and all its piety, that has not been, it is averred "the highest style," for living power and popular effect.

Again, it is asked, if large educational establishments, as well as other corporations, on which are concentrated great wealth, and other means of power occupying commanding positions, and wielding, of course, vast influence, be not essentially opposed to the genius and spirit of that great denomination of Christian people, in behalf of whose educational interests especially this Convention is assembled? Might not the heads of such powerful corporations come to have an undue and dangerous ascendency, giving to the churches and to the people, if not the law, yet, in virtue of their eminent positions and commanding influence, authoritative interpretations of the law? Nay, it is even asked, might not some Baptist Hildebrand, climbing up to the highest seat in some splendidly endowed grand central establishment, give us, if not nominally, yet really, for some vast section of our Baptist domain, a Baptist pope, by the breath of whose nostrils, nod of whose head, wave of whose hand, might be set up one and plucked down another, and by whose word might be dispensed or withheld ecclesiastical and theological honors and emoluments? Or might there not be, at the very least, some real and hurtful weakening of the hold with which our people cling to the precious privilege of private judgment and the independence of the churches? Is it not now true, to some extent, say some very zealous and jealous defenders of individual and ecclesiastical rights, that the heads of some of our more prominent and influential schools of the prophets, while having, perhaps, nothing at all of the spirit of usurpation or autocracy, do yet, in virtue of their peculiar positions, as well as high character, exercise, by the very invitation of the churches, some of the functions of diocesan episcopacy? It is, perhaps, admitted that so far there may have arisen no serious evils from it, that it may, indeed, have been only a benefit, and a great benefit; but where is the guaranty, it is asked, that it will always be so? Might not men less wise, less disinterested and devoted in their places, exert a far different and a deeply deleterious influence? Might they not exercise controlling power in putting into the most conspicuous and important places, their own flatterers and favorites, to the exclusion of the ablest and most meritorious men? Many zealously competing institutions, weaker though they were, might do much by their jealous vigilance, exercising a healthy and restraining influence upon each other to counteract the evil tendencies so greatly feared.

And now, as opposed to the objections just indicated, what are the reasons for limiting the number of our institutions by our ability adequately to endow and equip them, and to make them really efficient? Without attempting to adduce all the considerations that might be urged, I will state only the more important of those that have occurred to me. And in what I shall say, as in what I have said, I shall have reference mainly to our higher institutions of learning, though the general argument will apply equally to the humbler. Elementary and academic education, as well as the higher and more advanced requires the service of strong men and the help of all useful appliances. It were a great mistake to suppose that our schools of inferior grade might safely be put in charge of weak men, and that the elements of learning may be properly taught by men of inferior parts and imperfect education. Weak men cannot efficiently conduct establishments of even the humblest class. No one can properly impart the elements of learning who cannot impart a great deal more. A weak and untrained man educate and train others! The supposition were absurd! Beginners, more than any others, need the best trained and most competent instructors. Start them right. Put them on the right course, and they will go on safely and well—their future way will widen, and rise, and brighten as they advance. Start them wrong—put them on the wrong course, and their progress will be retrogression. They will have to be turned back. They will have to unlearn their learning. They will be obstructed, embarrassed, weakened, discouraged in all their future career.

If we had fewer but better endowed institutions of learning, rather than so many ill-appointed and weak ones, the cost of education, while more extended and thorough, would be lessened, and its benefits diffused among a larger number of persons. Weak institutions are unable to do the work that wins reputation. Without reputation they will have little patronage. With little patronage they cannot afford to make even their inferior instruction cheap. On the other hand, institutions whose appliances are the most complete, whose course of study is the most extended, whose methods are the most efficient and highly approved, and whose standard of attainment is the highest and the most rigidly enforced, will have the most extensive patronage. Their halls will be crowded with students, and they will be able safely, and even profitably, to reduce the fees of instruction, and other expenses of the student, to the minimum amount. For, it is with institutions of learning, as with all other business establishments—where the products are increased, the prices are lessened; where the sales are great, the profits may be small.

In large and well-appointed institutions not only is the range of subjects in which instruction is given wider, but the instruction, while of greater scope in respect to each subject is, at the same time, likely to be much more detailed, minute and correct. Each instructor has his specialty, to which he gives all time and energies. Hence he masters it and handles it with facility. He is no man-of-all-work. He does not attempt, like many a pretentious pedagogue, and alas! like many a more modest and meritorious man, the drudge and pack-horse of our poor and weak institutions, deficient in the number as well as attainments of their teachers, to give instruction in Latin and Greek, and Mathematics, in all the modern tongues, and the whole circle of the sciences. If Shakspeare and Coleridge were myriad-minded, if Joseph Scaliger and Sir William Hamilton knew everything, there are not many like them. To effect the utmost, the mind must not be too discursive. It must concentrate its powers, it must focalize its light. In other words it must recognize the great principle, so well understood and so potentially applied in the physical world, of the division of labor. And this can be and is done, practically, in large and well-endowed institutions of learning as it can never be done in small and deficiently-endowed ones.

To secure for our professional chairs the highest talents and attainments, whether at home or abroad, is a matter of cardinal importance. One thoroughly accomplished and competent professor is worth many inferior ones. One such man will give character to a college or university, while any number of weak and incompetent ones will never do it. He will, too, reproduce himself in his pupils, and thus multiply himself indefinitely. He will fire them with his own spirit, and nerve them with his own power. Only institutions of high grade and commanding position can secure the services of such men. Poor and obscure ones can never do it.

In the various processes of education, as conducted in our higher institutions of learning, many important adjuncts and appliances are required by the instructors. They must have philosophical and scientific apparatus, cabinets, libraries, museums, gymnasia, (for the body is to be educated as well as the mind), with ample grounds and commodious buildings. Now, all these things, when complete, and of superior quality, require the expenditure of large sums. We cannot afford to furnish them to a great number of small institutions. And yet the instruction and training given without them is very defective and unsatisfactory. Concentrating our resources, however, upon a few well-organized and judiciously located institutions, we could easily supply them with all this apparatus of instruction.

In addition to the heavy expense entailed in procuring this extensive and costly apparatus, other considerable expenditures are required thoroughly to equip institutions of the highest grade. They should have foundations for scholarships and for fellowships, teaching the especially meritorious and gifted, yet indigent, without charge. and stimulating and sustaining the aspirations and efforts of those who, eminently studious and capable, wish to prosecute their literary and scientific pursuits beyond the range of the common curriculum. Thus would they raise up a class of superior scholars, to meet the demands of the ever-advancing age, and to fill, with ability and honor, the chairs of the leading colleges and universities of our own and other lands. Further still, our institutions of learning, whatever their name or grade, but especially the higher, ought to be able to offer valuable prizes, "solid rewards," as some one has well said, "as well as other distinctions." But, for these, too, they must have fixed foundations—foundations to *encourage* and *stimulate*, as well as to *support* learning.

Having mentioned buildings, I trust I shall be pardoned for saying a few words further respecting them. I cannot agree with those who think the architecture of our higher institutions of learning a matter of comparatively little importance. On the contrary, I believe it to be of great and far-reaching importance. At the Educational Convention, held two years since, in the city of Brooklyn, a distinguished member of that body told a somewhat amusing anecdote of, as he said, "the three B's—brains, books, and bricks." And then he insisted that we must have brains. He also insisted that we must have books. But he said not a word on behalf of bricks. Now, notwithstanding this high authority, and the great success of the German, and some other celebrated seats of learning, with few or no bricks, I am half disposed to take the part of the bricks, and almost to invert the order, as he ranked them, of the B's. Extensive and imposing buildings have an elevating and inspiring effect upon students, professors, patrons—indeed, upon all who behold them. We are all, as the great Webster said in his first Bunker Hill oration, beings of taste, of sentiment, and of imagination, as well as of judgment and of reason. And the former have immense if not controlling influence over us. Please the taste, arouse the sentiment, enkindle the imagination of men, and you have their sympathy, their heart, and with that you command all their energies and resources. Sentiment is the inspiration of high character and bold endeavor. The martyr is a man of sentiment. So, too, the great worker, as well as the great sufferer, is a man of sentiment. He is no mere utilitarian. He lives and labors for a great idea. To him, the highest real is the divine ideal. Beauty, grandeur, the sublime, the magnificent, are elements of utility. We Baptist people have not sufficiently recognized these high and potent principles. We are too baldly and bleakly literal, too strict-construction, too narrow, meager, common place, too dryly utilitarian.

Alas! that it should be so! It has prevented us from subsidizing and laying under tribute to our cause, some of the noblest influences and mightiest forces that affect and control mankind. The Parthenon of the Greeks, the Coliseum of the Romans, the magnificent mosque of the Mussulman, the costly and richly-adorned pagoda of the Hindoo, the temple at Jerusalem, St. Peter's at Rome, the old and classic piles at Oxford and at Cambridge, proud old baronial halls and feudal castles, have wrought a wonderful influence upon the world—have given tone to its philosophy, its poetry, eloquence, science, art; have given shape and hue to its life—have done much to form its morals, as well as its taste; to fix its religion, to form and control its government—to determine, indeed, the destinies of men. The Jew fought the Roman, while the temple stood. When it was fired, he rushed forward frantically to its rescue. When that perished, perished with it his pride, his hope, and all his prowess. When that fell, fell with it the venerable nationality of Israel. It had consolidated and kept together the chosen people. Henceforth they were to be "scattered and peeled" among the nations. While St. Peter's stands, it is hard for the Romish hierarchy to fall. The papacy will scarcely perish utterly, while that glorious pile, as the chief seat of its wondrous worship, still lifts its imposing front to Heaven, and displays its graceful and its grand proportion to the fascinated gaze of man. Superior architectural structures fix interest, and give it stability and permanence. That distinguished seat of learning, which is the pride of the Old Dominion, and of the South, the University of Virginia, would never have achieved its high reputation, and exerted its wide and commanding influence, if its buildings had been incommodious and inferior. Though not particularly elegant or symmetrical, they are extensive and imposing, and occupy a commanding site, in the midst of beautiful and attractive grounds. They have localized and concentrated interest. They have fixed the educational centre of the State in a small interior town, that otherwise, and but for the shadow of a great name could never have commanded and controlled it. The magnificent national capitol, and other costly and superb public structures, notwithstanding the powerful gravitations towards the geographical centre, and the centre of population, have fixed, for this generation, perhaps for our whole national life, the seat of the national government at Washington. That we may avail ourselves to a greater extent than otherwise would be practicable of this great help of architecture, let us concentrate our resources on fewer educational establishments.

Another objection to the multiplication of weak institutions, is that they discredit learning, and disparage its friends. Strength wins respect and admiration, while weakness is pitied or contemned. And yet there are cases in which weakness is more to be feared than strength. "Be more afraid of a fool than of a knave," said a man of great sagacity. "The weakness of the one is more formidable than the strength of the other." So, let those who are apprehensive that strong institutions of learning may damage the denomination, be more afraid that weak ones will do it. They disparage us in the view of others, and greatly lessen our moral force in the general community. They lessen, too, our own self-respect, and thus increase the tendency, already too strong among us, to self-disparagement. We ought to have, certainly in some respects, more self-appreciation, more self-assertion, and in nothing more, perhaps, than in the great matter of education, in behalf of which our people have great zeal, and in promotion of which they have done much of which they may well be proud.

And yet we are constrained to confess, that many of our institutions of learning are inferior—so inferior that many among us cannot be induced to patronize them. Our people are possessed of strong sense, as well as zeal. When our schools are really good, they readily recognize their excellence, and patronize them in preference to all others. But they cannot be led, and ought not to be expected so to stultify themselves, whatever their denominational zeal, as to think them superior when they are manifestly and deplorably inferior. Baptists may sometimes show a reprehensible lack, as we often think they do, of *esprit du corps;* but that is not, by any means, the whole nor the main reason of their failure, in so many instances, to sustain their own institutions.

The fact is, they lack respect for many of them. I certainly would not intentionally disparage any body or any thing; but I must say, that we have institutions calling themselves colleges, or even universities, and, by a great stretch of charity and courtesy, so called by others, that ought to be called academies. Taking the higher name, they are led to profess to do, perhaps to attempt, the higher work. But it is a mere sham. They impose, perhaps, on themselves, and they impose on others. In trying to do the work of a college, they do not even do well the work of an academy.

We all know what an awkward figure an individual cuts who attempts to do what he cannot do, what is manifestly above his capacity. Making such an attempt, an institution of learning makes a yet more ungainly and ridiculous figure. Call such an establishment a college, a university, and a quiet, sarcastic smile plays over the face of every intelligent, well-educated man you meet. Call their half-educated pedagogues scholars, and you commit a calumny upon one of the noblest of the learned professions. You lower the respectability of learning, you degrade the conception of higher education, you compromise and mortify and weaken its truest and best friends.

In this connection, I cannot refrain from adding, that in the interest of those capable and excellent men who, amiable and tractable, from various causes sometimes become connected with such weak and ricketty establishments, as well as on behalf of higher education itself, we should resist the tendency to multiply them. What a pitiable spectacle do those men for whom is invoked the sympathy of every more fortunate scholar sometimes present! With talents and attainments that might adorn nobler spheres, and be eminently useful in them, hidden or obscured in some out-of-the-way place, immured in the unfurnished, dirty, comfortless rooms of some poor, dilapidated, ruinous old building, long innocent of paint, or even white-wash, the very sight of which, with its miserable surroundings, sinks and keeps down the brightest and most buoyant spirits! With a nominal salary ridiculously small, yet not promptly paid, if paid at all! Expected to make brick without straw! to train up accomplished scholars and men of science, without any of the apparatus of instruction; without libraries, laboratories—anything! To form men of taste, of high and generous culture, wide-minded and lofty, with everything about them, in their susceptible and plastic youth, little and low, and poor and mean!

Another objection to the mistaken policy we are considering is, that weak institutions relax and corrupt discipline. And thus do they not only fail to effect, but they obstruct the highest ends of education. For he is not educated who has no proper habits of study, no proper recognition of authority, no self-control, no moral tone, no mastery of moods, and whims, and passions, and caprices. Discipline is of the very essence of education. But the weak school, or college, or university, or whatever else you may call it, is not strong enough for discipline. It is controlled not by its faculty or board of trustees, but by its thoughtless, wayward, lawless students, or its uninformed and injudicious patrons.

Again, too great multiplication of institutions of learning unwisely divides, and thus weakens, the energies and resources of the friends and promoters of education, and causes the use, unproductively, of large sums of money.

Further still, such multiplication constantly and powerfully tends to the depression of the standard of attainment; an evil than which none that I have mentioned is of greater magnitude. Against it, all, in these times, and especially Baptists, should most sedulously guard. This is an age of great mental activity, of great breadth and variety, and of no little depth, of culture. If we would keep abreast of it, we must have men of high and varied, broad and deep scholarship. False religion, a counterfeit Christianity, intrenching itself behind the bulwarks of ages, having vast resources of strategy, of numbers, and of wealth, compassing earth and hell, time and eternity, laying sacrilegious hand upon the truth of God, profaning the sanctities of heaven, subsidizing the world, and human nature, and all the forces of learning, and art and science and philosophy, and laying them all under tribute to its cause, is to be exposed and put to shame in presence of and contrast with the true. Skepticism, wide-spread and intense, armed with all the force of culture, talent, genius, and always having the sympathy—if latent and undeclared—of the unregenerate heart, is to be met and vanquished. Piety and zeal, unaided, are unequal to the task. The church of God, then, must have men of might, thoroughly armed and equipped, among her sons. The rank and file must be enlightened to be properly loyal to high leadership, and to make that leadership successful. Divisions weaken the force of the hosts of God. Error, developing itself in false principle and foul spirit, is the source of division, as truth is the basis and bond of unity. As Baptists, we profess to be champions of truth, and leaders of lovers of truth. A genuine, sanctified Christian scholarship, is the touchstone of truth. We, then, specially need it. Let us vindicate our high claims by our high scholarship. We appeal from tradition, however hoary and venerable; we appeal from ecclesiastical prescription, however solemn and imposing; we appeal from every thing, directly and only to the word of God. But that word is in learned and no longer living languages. Upon it rests the mists of ages. It has passed through many and violent vicissitudes. It has been perverted, wasted and covered with false glosses, by zealotical and wicked partizanship. It has been diluted and attenuated, and bereft of its spirit and power, in many instances, by weak and vapid, unscholarly and unphilosophical criticism, commentary and exposition. It has been often incorrectly rendered, by a pitiable mental imbecility, or a grossly defective erudition, or a narrow and selfish bigotry. To restore it, and rightly render it, to illustrate it, and enforce it, the highest and most advanced Christian scholarship is imperatively required. The production of such scholarship is incompatible with any lowering of the standard of attainment in our institutions of learning. Indeed, on many accounts, it requires that that standard shall be constantly advanced, and raised higher, and yet higher.

For all the reasons I have suggested, and for others that the time will not allow me to urge, but which will readily occur to every thoughtful mind, we should eschew the folly of dividing and diffusing our strength in futile efforts to sustain an indefinite number of institutions of learning, and concentrate it upon only so many as we may be able thoroughly to equip, and to conduct with full efficiency. To this end, let us, at as early a day as may be practicable, form a national educational union, or some sort of league, strong and efficient, whose object shall be to concentrate, consolidate and properly centralize our educational forces. Among us, as a Christian denomination, the injudicious multiplication of weak educational establishments, is doubtless due, in no inconsiderable degree, to a perversion and overstraining of the great principle of individualism. We have a very high and enthusiastic appreciation of the independence of the churches, and of the personal importance of the individual members of the churches. A church is a church, say we, with all the rights and prerogatives of a church, however small and weak it may be. It will not concede pre-eminence to any other ecclesiastical organization, whether association or convention, synod or council. It will not be absorbed or overborne by any of them. In any important issue it will maintain its ground against them. And if it shall see fit, it will spiritedly and promptly secede from any sort of confederation it may have formed with any of them. So, too, the individual man is a man, however humble and obscure, and he will not be absorbed or overborne by the church. His is the sacred right of private judgment. The ultimate appeal is to himself. In an issue he will maintain his ground against deacon, and pastor, and church. And if it seem good in his own eyes, he will secede and set up for himself, and draw along with himself all others of kindred type. Now, under the influence of this perversion of a great and Scriptural principle, we divide and sub-divide indefinitely and ruinously. We would almost seem ambitious to furnish the completest and most striking demonstration of the doctrine of the infinite divisibility of all things. Thus we scatter our resources and divide and waste our energies, and forestall progress, and make impossible any grand achievement. In our horror of hierarchy, and great ecclesiastical establishments, and of all centralization, we forego the advantages of a just and reasonable, as well as Scriptural, concentration and consolidation of our powers. Hence, we have never accomplished, outwardly, at least, with all that we have done and suffered, any thing worthy our divine principles and our sublime mission. We are afraid of every thing that is on a grand scale. We have never recovered from the great fright the colossal hierarchy gave us ages ago. We are afraid of the union that is strength, because, while tending to grandeur of proportions, as well as grandeur of effort and grandeur of result, it implies what we deem a dangerous concentration. We forget or overlook the fact that as in the natural, so in the moral world, there is a centripetal as well as a centrifugal force. Hence, instead of following the wisdom of nature, which is the wisdom of God, in accumulating strength at the centre, and sending it forth along the innumerable radii of a great and sublime circle, we fly off perpetually, and diffuse and waste our energies along the lines of a boundless circumference. We have the *ra-*

tionale of Baptist inefficiency in Baptist lack of concentration, as seen in their unwise multiplication of weak churches, associations, presses, schools, colleges, and all other institutions. To avoid the evils resulting so largely from the perversion of a great and noble principle, let our brethren, without yielding or in any degree compromising that principle, cease to pervert it. Let them study a wider and closer union, and greater compactness of organization. Let them, eschewing local and sectional prejudices and predilections, with all unworthy aspirations for individual and personal pre-eminence, so concentrate their vast resources and their mighty energies, as to have the strength necessary to carry forward grandly the grand work committed to their hands

In closing the paper which I now respectfully submit, let me state that in nothing I have said would I be understood as opposed to meeting the demand for institutions of learning with an adequate supply, in respect to their number, more than in respect to their efficiency. I would multiply throughout the land, and over all the earth, well-appointed judiciously located primary schools, high schools, academies, colleges, and universities, up to the fullest measure of the demand for them. I certainly would not so limit the number of our institutions, as that any considerable portion of our youth should, on that account, fail altogether of the advantages of education. It is better, doubtless, where it is impracticable to have superior schools, and where such as exist in other places are inaccessible, to have inferior ones, than none. But these are exceptional cases. In general, the proposition holds good that we should limit the number of our institutions of learning by our power to make them strong, that is, really efficient. The many and great advantages of strong over weak institutions, will draw students and patronage from every remote and destitute district, and thus render it unnecessary in those districts to establish inefficient schools. It is a good as well as common maxim, that whatever is worth doing at all, is worth doing well. The work of education is surely worth doing. It is, with emphasis let me say it, worth doing well. Let it then be done well. But it can only be so done, by well-equipped and efficient institutions. Such institutions, and such only, on the whole, really advance and secure the best interests of true education.

Dr. WOODS: I would like to say one word in relation to this topic. It is a very important subject, indeed—the limitation of our institutions to our ability to endow them properly. It is a point to which we should direct our attention more than has been done by the denomination. Instead of being compelled as we have been, even within my remembrance, in order to obtain the best education, to send our sons to academies, and colleges, and seminaries of other denominations, there is no reason why we should not make all our institutions of learning equal to the very best, both in the amplitude of their endowments, and in the skill and in the varied learning of their professors. Should we do this, students would be attracted to our institutions of learning from many a family where there is now criminal neglect of education. We ought to have a course of training and a corps of teachers sufficient, not only for all our institutions of learning for all classes, but a corps of teachers sufficient to supply our share of the teachers of all the non-denominational schools in the land, the private school, the public school, the common school in all its grades, the normal school, the institute, the college There is no reason why we should not place teachers of our denomination in places of influence. I was much gratified by hearing the father of a young man who graduated recently at Brown University, one of the first scholars of his class, declare that his son was to be a teacher. This is next to the office of the sacred ministry. I know of no calling by which our influence as a denomination can be so successfully wielded as by training up first-class teachers for all the institutions of the land.

Voted to take from the table all unfinished business.

On motion of Dr. BOYCE the Preamble of the Constitution was adopted. [The Preamble will be found with the Constitution in the Addenda.]

On motion of Rev. Dr. CALDWELL the following resolution was unanimously adopted:

Resolved, That this Convention, received and provided for with most generous hospitality by the friends of education in Philadelphia, appreciates the kindness, the thoughtfulness, and the efficiency of the arrangements made for its convenience, and hereby expresses its particular obligations to the Joint Committee of Arrangements of the Pennsylvania Baptist Education Society, the Philadelphia Conference of Baptist Ministers, and the Trustees of the Crozer Theological Seminary, by which provision has been made for the reception of delegates, and for reporting the proceedings of the Convention.

On motion of Rev. Dr. HOVEY the following was unanimously adopted:—

Resolved, That the thanks of this Convention are hereby expressed to the friends of education connected with the Crozer Theological Seminary, for the pleasant excursion and generous entertainment given to the members of this body.

The Rev. Dr. CALDWELL, from the Committee on Libraries, presented his report, which report was adopted.*

REPORT.

The Committee appointed to consider the subject of Libraries in our Institutions of Learning offer their report:

They have received no instructions from the Convention, and the subject has had no place in its discussions or prepared papers. They have no special or exact information in regard to existing libraries. They are therefore obliged to present the subject to the Convention in its more obvious lights, with such suggestions as occur, and to leave it to make such impression as its natural importance is calculated to create.

The Library certainly has an important and hardly a secondary place and function in the system of public education. Indeed, the Free Public Library seems to be a necessary part of the complete system of popular education. Certainly no college or professional school can be complete, nor can it be efficient without it. Universities and libraries have always gone together; the library generally gathering at the college, the college never existing long, never doing its work well without the library. The library is not the living teacher, and cannot supply his place; but it is his ally, his inspiration, his own teacher. It helps him learn, and it helps him teach. In it are accumulated and preserved the results of ages of thought; all the previous knowledge of the race. It is the arsenal, the reservoir, the bank, the invested fund, on which intellectual inquiry constantly drains. It supplies a considerable share of the intellectual forces which move through the halls of a college. Teachers and pupils resort to it not alone for immediate tuition. They find light there for every path of research. But

* The remarks of Prof. Matthews on this report are not found in the reporter's notes.

who grows familiar with a great library, and does not feel upon the mind an influence which is not always knowledge, but which is the breath and exhalation of its treasured thought? There sit "the dead but sceptred sovereigns who still rule our spirits from their urns." The presence, the atmosphere, is felt. It communicates impulse to generous scholarship. And beyond that, it becomes to the college an attraction and a privilege. Better than lawns and groves and bowered walks, or even stately architecture, are the alcoves upon whose shelves are laid up the student's pleasantest recollections, and which are to the world the visible signs of the employments of the place. And

"Hither, as to their fountain, other stars
Repairing, in their golden urns draw light."

The use of the library depends upon those who know how to use it, and also upon its quality. Its value is not according to its magnitude. It may be, like too many of our collections gathered by indiscriminate gift, a heap of books, good and bad, mostly worthless, constructed on no scientific principle, with no proportion in its departments, and with no reference to the ends of a high and ample education. Few libraries, if any, are perfect. Those approach the ideally complete library which have originated in a large and sufficient fund at the start, and have grown unhampered by any considerations of expense, after a law of their own, and with a defined and grand aim.

Most of our institutions of liberal learning, however, have postponed, perhaps from absolute necessity, the construction of a library, till every other want is provided for. When grounds are secured, and buildings erected, and professorships endowed, then last a library is projected, and the scraps and savings of the college are given to it. But it comes to nothing useful or even respectable till it has a permanent fund yielding a constant income. Then it can be built upon some plan. Then books can be bought which are not for immediate use, but which constitute the intellectual reserves, ready for any emergency. For that is a too narrow theory of the library, however plausible, and although held by men who have learned to trust to their own brains rather than books, which holds that it should be composed only of such books as are necessary for the ordinary purposes of instruction. There are books which may wait for years for the eyes which shall look after their contents. But let them be read for the inquirer when he comes, that there may be no fact in the vast record of the world's thought and life which he may not be able to verify. Some books are for daily use, and for all students. Some are for the single and special student, who may appear only once in four years, it may be in a generation. Whatever he wants to study, whatever path of knowledge he wants to pursue, leading into whatever remote and dark corner, let him have the means of prosecuting his work; let him have the original sources of information, that he may not be obliged to resort to encyclopedias, and take his learning at second or fortieth hand.

This Convention has no call, perhaps, to make any new or special deliverance upon the subject of libraries for our higher institutions. It need not, as it cannot with its limited time, lay down any principles in regard to their construction and management. And yet it may properly, it ought even, to emphasize the call which almost all our institutions make upon their benefactors for large and generous foundations for libraries. There are men, there are women, who have money to give, or money to leave at death, who can especially appreciate the satisfaction there is in bestowing it so that years and ages after they are gone, a few thousand dollars are turned into a permanent intellectual investment, a spring of intellectual life, not a dead monument of stone, but of living truth, which stands amidst the coming and departing generations, if not to speak for the giver, at least to carry forward his beneficent influence, making it immortal as the thirst for knowledge or the works in which truth is embalmed, and, as Milton says, "treasured up for a life beyond life."

For the Committee, S. L. Caldwell.

The Committee on Nominations, through Rev. Dr. Jeffrey, reported, making nomination of officers for the American Baptist Educational Commission, and such officers were elected by acclamation. [For Officers see Addenda.]

The report of the Committee on Professional Schools was then read by President E. G. ROBINSON, D. D., LL.D., and, on motion, adopted.

REPORT.

The Committee to whom was referred the question, How far is it desirable to add special or professional schools to our existing college system? beg leave to report as follows:

The American college is a distinctively American institution; the product of our Christianity and the source of our civilization. Our Christianity and our civilization being what they are, our college system could not differ essentially from what it now is. The type of the American college, with all its unimportant variations in different parts of our country, is everywhere in reality one and the same.

In our existing collegiate system, your Committee see no need of any special change. It seems sufficiently flexible for all practical purposes. And as in the past it has kept pace with the progress of the national life, so in the future it may be trusted to the silent operation of the inevitable laws of growth. Any attempt at radical, arbitrary changes we cannot but regard as certain to result in manifold mischief.

How far any special Schools of Science and the Arts may, under the same college government, be advantageously associated with the established collegiate system, is a most difficult question to answer satisfactorily. Your Committee are, however, unanimously of the opinion, that such schools are not needed to supply any deficiencies in the existing college curriculum. That curriculum, as it now exists, is both as complete in itself and as ample a preparation for the various courses of professional study as the limited time now allowed for it will admit. And even for those special pursuits contemplated in special schools of science, we cannot but regard the regular college course as a most desirable a .d, for the best results, an indispensable preparation. If special schools are to lure young men from the regular college course, we must regard them as calculated to lower the standard of education and to lead to a rapid declension of every species of culture and in every department of learning. What we thus say of special schools of science, we think to be equally true of the professional schools of law, medicine and theology. No College can unite, under the same government and faculty, a collegiate and a professional department, without serious injury to both. We cannot combine the German gymnasium, which the American college more nearly resembles than it does any other institution, and the German University, to which our American professional schools in some respects correspond, without a virtual destruction of the distinguishing characteristics and the distinctive merits of each. Our settled conviction is, that it would be a disastrous day for all departments of learning in our country, if ever the type of the American college should be merged in that of an ideal American University. If, however, special schools of science and the arts can be so connected with the college curriculum as to leave it and its design intact, we see no objections to them; but our belief is, that our professional schools of medicine, law and divinity will thrive better, and will more effectually accomplish their designs when established as independent institutions either within or in the immediate neighborhood of those social and intellectual centres found only in our cities, than when closely connected with our colleges.

E. G. ROBINSON,
WM. HAGUE,
J. A. BROADUS.

The report of the Committee on Academies was read by Prof. J. L. LINCOLN, LL.D., and, on motion, adopted.

REPORT.

The Committee to whom was assigned for consideration the subject of Academies as the Base of our Denominational Institutions of Learning, ask leave to report:

The Committee are assured, that at this stage of our proceedings this subject requires no full unfolding or illustration at their hands. This work has been ably and completely done not only at this Convention in the opening paper of Dr. Sears, but also in other like papers presented at the earlier Conventions, and especially in the paper presented by Professor Greene in 1870 at Brooklyn. It seems, therefore, only needed at present to mention the conclusions which have been reached, and to ask that they be formally adopted by the Convention, and through the efforts of its members be realized in action.

It is much to know, that it is now recognized as an assured conviction that academies constitute the foundation of institutions of higher education in this country, and so of a well ordered system of denominational education, the necessity and desirableness of which are also recognized and acknowledged. Without academies as sources of a constant supply of students well educated by preparatory study and training, our colleges and theological schools not only could not thrive and flourish, but would soon cease to exist. Instead, therefore, of vainly endeavoring, as so often in the past, to build at the top of a system of higher education by a chief attention to colleges, we need most imperatively to lay its foundations broad and deep in the establishment of centrally located, well appointed and amply endowed academies.

We are also convinced, that the High School cannot do for us the work of the academy; and this because it is local in its character and uses, and also does not and cannot furnish the needful elements of a religious and truly Christian education. We must have academies, and academies of our own, and academies in all respects of the highest order. We must not be content that they can do good service, but that they do the best service which such an institution is capable of rendering. They must be so generously provided with teachers and with all means and appliances of instruction and training as to be able to furnish the best preparatory education both in quantity and in quality. There is needed in the instructors, and especially in the principal, an order of talent and attainments and character not inferior to that required in the highest scientific and literary institutions of the land.

Then, too, these academies ought to be set in practical vital relations to our colleges, and there ought to exist the fullest sympathy and co-operation on the part of all to whom belongs the conduct of both. The managers and teachers and friends of both should ever feel and act as co-laborers in a common cause, and one in which they have a common interest. The instructors in the academy should aim to send to the college students taught and trained most thoroughly for a college course, and the college instructors should teach and train such students with the same thoroughness and fidelity, and both rejoice together in the end in the good work of education in which they have together been laboring.

Finally, that academies may be established such as these, and capable of rendering such service, it is indispensable that they be amply endowed. It is only thus that these institutions can be rightly appointed and furnished with teachers and means of instruction, and can furnish instruction at such cost as may put their advantages within the reach of all, and it is only by such endowments that they can reach the requisite permanence in existence, and in fame and power.

For the Committee, J. L. LINCOLN.

The Rev. Dr. MOSS, from the Committee on the Publication of the Proceedings of the Convention, read his report, which was adopted.

REPORT.

The Committee on Publishing the Proceedings respectfully report:

1. The Joint Committee of Arrangements, which provided for the entertainment of this Convention, will pay the expenses of reporting its proceedings, and putting them in type.

2. Copies of the Proceedings can therefore be furnished at the cost of 30 cents in paper covers, and 50 cents in cloth binding.

On motion of the Rev. Dr. JEFFREY the thanks of the Convention were tendered to Hon. FRANCIS WAYLAND, for the able and courteous manner in which he had presided over their proceedings.

President JAMES C. WELLING, LL.D., Chairman of the Committee on Colleges and the Public Life of the Nation, having been under the necessity of leaving the city, it was voted that the report prepared by him be accepted without being read, and referred to the Executive Committee for publication in the Minutes.

REPORT OF COMMITTEE ON THE RELATION OF AMERICAN COLLEGES TO THE PUBLIC LIFE OF THE NATION.

"On my arrival in the United States," says De Tocqueville, in his treatise on "Democracy in America," "I was surprised to find so much distinguished talent among the subjects, and so little among the heads of the government." Writing in the year 1835 from personal observations made in the years 1831 and 1832, he reports it as "a constant fact, that the ablest men in the United States are rarely placed at the head of affairs; and it must be acknowledged," he adds, "that such has been the result in proportion as democracy has overstepped all its former limits. The race of American statesmen has evidently dwindled most remarkably in the course of the last fifty years."

A writer for the Princeton Review, in its number of July, 1842, commented at great length on "the aimless inefficiency and want of mental power" visible in the administration of our public affairs, and in view of this deplorable fact, he urged that the bequest of Smithson (not then appropriated) should be applied to the founding of a great "School of Politics" in the United States.

The Hon. Horace Greeley, in an address delivered before the Literary Societies of Hamilton College, N. Y., in the year 1844, held the following language:

"I have come naturally to the consideration of the position of the Educated Class in our existing society, and the influence they therein exert. Will any contend that this is what it should and must be? Is our public opinion usually shaped and directed by that of the most elaborately educated? I think no one will pretend it."

Mr. John Stuart Mill, in his "Considerations on Representative Government," published ten years ago, does but sum up the common judgment of intelligent observers at home and abroad when he says:

"It is an admitted fact, that in the American democracy the highly cultivated members of the community, except such of them as are willing to sacrifice their own opinions and modes of judgment, and become the servile mouth-pieces of their inferiors in knowledge, do not even offer themselves for Congress or the State Legislatures, so certain is it that they would have no chance of being returned. Political life is, indeed, in America a most valuable school; but it is a school from which the ablest teachers are excluded; the first minds of the country being as effectually shut out from the national representation and from public functions generally, as if they were under a formal disqualification."

Such are commonly supposed to be the facts in the case, as they lie upon the surface, patent to the observation of all. Admitting them to be correctly stated, we must also concede the justice of De Tocqueville's inference when he remarked that the race of American statesmen had evidently dwindled most remarkably in the course of "the last fifty years" anterior to the date when he wrote, and since that period there has been no arrest in this growing deterioration. And hence in order to ascertain the fountain and origin of the evil it becomes a fair subject of inquiry, whether it is the State which has fallen away from the educated mind of the country, or the educated mind of the country which has fallen away from the State. De Tocqueville and Mill hold to the former view of the facts involved in the case. Mr. Greeley inclines to the latter opinion, and avows the belief, in the Address before cited, that if "the educated class is far less potential than it should be, the mischief may be the country's, but the fault is primarily its own." In the former of these aspects, the question is one which revolves primarily in the sphere of social and political science. In the latter, it is a question of political ethics which still more directly addresses itself to us as men charged with the formation of a part of the educated mind of the country. In either aspect it is one which immediately concerns us as *educators*, called as we are to inculcate a true science of government and to impress on our pupils a sense of the obligations they owe to their fellow-men in the figure of civil society.

De Tocqueville undertakes to explain the divorce between our highest culture and the public life of the nation by a variety of considerations; but the most prominent among them is found in the fact, that our political institutes, under the constant mutation of parties in the United States, do not admit of anything like a "political career" deserving to take rank among the learned and liberal professions by the culture it demands and the honorable rewards it brings. And hence, as he justly remarks, the pursuit of wealth in our country "generally diverts men of great talents and strong passions from the pursuit of political power; and it frequently happens that a man does not undertake to direct the fortunes of the State until he has shown himself incompetent to conduct his own." And in his opinion "the vast number of very ordinary men who occupy public stations" in the United States is quite as much due to this cause as to the bad choice of the people, acting from ignorance or wilfulness.

Mr. Mill holds that the political phenomena in question are referable to the general tendencies of our modern civilization, which, in the distribution of its public functions, is coming day by day to depend more on the low average knowledge of the many than on the great intellectual supremacy of a few commanding minds. Modern society tends ever more and more toward "a collective mediocrity." And this tendency "is increased," he admits, "by all reductions of the [elective] franchise, and by all extensions of the suffrage—their effect being to place the principal power in the hands of classes more and more below the highest level of instruction in the community." But the tendency itself is undoubtedly organic in the whole frame-work of modern society—the "collective mediocrity" of the masses and of their political representatives being only one aspect that reveals the common "form and pressure of our times." This tendency, he thinks, cannot be arrested in the political world, as it "spins down the ringing grooves of change;" but its velocity and momentum can be modified and directed, yea, *must* be modified and directed if the highest culture of society is to exercise its due influence on the public life of the State. The only brake of which Mill can conceive as suited, in a measure, to check the natural rate of the downward progress visible in representative government, is to be found in the adoption of "some mode of plural voting which may assign to education, *as such*, the degree of superior influence due to it."

In the light of these general reflections, we may now be better prepared to consider and appreciate some special facts bearing on the subject in hand. It is proposed to take the last three Congresses of the United States, and to estimate the degree in which even a nominally educated mind may be said to have pervaded their deliberations. The statistics on this point are as follows:

The Senate of the Fortieth Congress consisted of 53 members, of whom 25, or 47 per cent., were college graduates. [The States of Alabama, Arkansas, Florida, Georgia, Louisiana, Mississippi, North Carolina and South Carolina were then unrepresented, and Maryland had but one member in that body.] The House of Representatives consisted of 188 members, of whom 61, or 32 per cent., were graduates of colleges.

The Senate of the Forty-first Congress consisted of 72 members, of whom 33, or 46 per cent. (very nearly), were college graduates. The House of Representatives consisted of 239 members, of whom 75, or 31 per cent., were college graduates.

The Senate of the Forty-Second Congress consisted of 74 members, of whom 34, or 46 per cent., were graduates of colleges. The House of Representatives consisted of 243 members, of whom 77, or 31 per cent., were graduates of colleges.

It will thus be seen that the contrast which so forcibly struck the mind of De Tocqueville, as he compared the Senate with the House of Representatives in point of culture, has not lost all its salient features since he wrote. Nearly one half of the Senate is composed of liberally educated men. Less than one-third of the House claims to belong to that category, and the different manner in which the members of the two bodies are elected is doubtless, as De Tocqueville suggests, the main reason of this difference between them.

It cannot be doubted that the influence of American colleges on the public life of the nation, as measured by the actual character of the education of our public men, is less now than it was forty years ago when De Tocqueville wrote, as it was less then than it had been at an earlier period in our civil history, when, if our colleges were fewer, the men whom they sent forth found a more ready access to places of public honor and trust.

Your Committee have not had time to compile or compute all the statistics relating to this point; but, in exhibition of the general direction in which it is supposed they would point, they need but cite the following observations from an Address delivered a few years ago before the Alumni of Princeton College by Prof. John S. Hart, at present Professor of Belles Lettres in that institution. Prof. Hart spoke as follows: "Not one generation back the singular spectacle was presented in the Senate of the United States, then in its palmiest days, of more than *one-sixth of its entire number of members being alumni of the College of New Jersey*." This statement is made by Prof. Hart on the authority of the late Senator Southard of New Jersey, who, being himself a graduate of Princeton College, "took note of the fact with honest pride."

Considered as a seat of learning, Princeton College has certainly not fallen from its high estate at the present day. But what at present is its representation in the Forty-second Congress? In the Senate it has three representatives; in the popular branch of Congress it has only one. In the Senate of the Forty-first Congress it had two representatives; in the House it had five. In the Senate of the Fortieth Congress it had no representative at all, and in the popular branch only four. Nor were her sister institutions, Yale College and Harvard University, any more fortunate than she in the relative number they respectively contributed to the National Congress, though both surpassing her in the number of their living graduates. The comparative statistics of the three colleges under this head during the last three Congresses are as follows:

	Fortieth Congress.			Forty-first Congress.			Forty-Second Congress.		
	Sen.	Ho Reps.	Both Ho.	Sen.	Ho Reps.	Both Ho.	Sen.	Ho Reps.	Both Ho.
Harvard	1	0	1	2	2	4	2	1	3
Yale	1	6	7	1	5	6	1	8	9
Princeton........	0	4	4	2	5	7	3	1	4
Aggregate of these three Colleges, 12						17			16

According to her triennial catalogue of the year 1868, Yale College had at that time 3,645 living alumni. [Deceased alumni, 4,104; total, 7,749.] According to her triennial catalogue of 1869, Harvard University then had 2,977 living alumni. [Deceased alumni, 5,033; total, 8,010.] According to her triennial catalogue of 1869, Princeton College then had 2,446 living alumni. [Deceased alumni, 1,901; total, 4,347.] Arranged according to the relative number of their living graduates, these three institutions would therefore stand as follows: 1st, Yale; 2d, Harvard; 3d, Princeton. Arranged according to their numerical representation in the last three Congresses, they stand as follows: 1st, Yale; 2d, Princeton; 3d, Harvard.

Besides these classifications, another suggests itself, based on the ratio which the number of graduates furnished by each to these three Congresses bears to the total number of the living graduates belonging to each College respectively. The statistics under this head are substantially as follows:

Ratio of graduates in Congress to the total number of living graduates belonging respectively to Yale, Harvard, and Princeton Colleges, at the dates of 1866, 1868, *and* 1870, *when the elections were held for members of the popular branch of Congress:*

	40TH CONGRESS.	41ST CONGRESS.	42D CONGRESS.
Yale...............	1:490	1:607	1:472
Harvard.........	1:2600	1:720	1:1030
Princeton........	1:550	1:337	1:631

Average ratio under this head during these three Congresses:

Yale...........1:508

Harvard......1:1450

Princeton...1:506

It will thus be seen that the ratio of Yale and Princeton under this head is substantially the same, while Harvard falls below both on this score still more decidedly than in point of the actual number contributed by each to this department of the public service.

And this fact naturally raises the question whether, from the statistics before us, we are warranted in drawing the inference that there is something found in the training of Yale and Princeton which has proved more conducive to success in the sphere of public life; as there certainly would seem to be something found in the training of Harvard which has proved more conducive than that of either Princeton or Yale to the nurture of literature, if we may judge from the relative contributions made to American letters by the graduates of each. Conceding the justice of this inference in the former case, while claiming the benefit of the inference drawn from the facts in the latter, the friends of Harvard would perhaps urge, in extenuation of her inferiority on this score, that, as things are in our country, it is the highest proof of superior intellectual culture among the graduates of Harvard, that they furnish the smallest quota to this body of representative politicians, composed, as it is, in the greater part, of men who have never received a liberal education. And to this apology might be added, perhaps, the just boast that in the person of Senator Sumner she has contributed to this branch of the public service the most scholarly of living American statesmen.

In measuring the actual influence of the American College on the public life of the nation, it is obviously more just to look for our standard in the small number furnished to our Federal Legislature by these three great institutions, than in the aggregate number of nominal college graduates found in the ranks of Congress. It may well be doubted whether the standard of education in some of the so-called "colleges" of the country, is high enough to ensure for their graduates any very marked intellectual pre-eminence over the graduates of the academy and private school, where the latter are under the conduct of able and efficient teachers.

There are several subsidiary inquiries which, in the line of this investigation, must suggest themselves to every thoughtful mind. Your Committee can but indicate a very few among the many that call for further research and elucidation:

1. What is the comparative political influence of the highest intellectual culture in a community where its exponents are few and greatly superior to the lower level of the popular mind, as contrasted with that which it is likely to exert in a community where the general diffusion of popular education has created the conditions of a "collective mediocrity?"

2. Which is safer—civil progress under the direction of the educated few, or civil progress under the direction of the "popularly educated" masses?

3. In the changed relations superinduced by the general diffusion of popular education, has the American college taken due care, by the quality and thoroughness of its discipline and instructions, to insure for its graduates a relative mental superiority among their con-

temporaries, equal to that which obtained before such general diffusion of "popular education?"

4. Is it the natural and normal necessity of representative institutions, under the forces impressed on modern civilization, that they must result in the greater and greater exclusion of superior minds from the direction of public affairs?

5. What measures, if any, can we take, as educators, to raise the standard of scholarship in the country, and at the same time restore to American colleges the relative patronage which, as compared with the growth of our population, they have been losing since the year 1838? [See tables of President Barnard in his Annual Report of 1870]. If we do not raise the standard of scholarship, what hope can we have of re-asserting the intellectual superiority formerly conceded to liberally educated minds by their less favored contemporaries, and if the number of college graduates does not keep pace with the growth of our population, how can the college expect to maintain its relative numerical representation in the public councils of the nation?

6. In view of the changed aspects of modern civilization, has not a new class of political studies come to demand a larger share of our attention as educators? The higher political studies of the present day, succeeding those of constitutional polity, which mainly engaged the thoughts of our predecessors, must obviously relate to questions of wider social science and of public economy. To these progressive studies every American college must devote itself, if it would keep pace with the growing demands of a progressive civilization, and lay the foundations of political promotion for its graduates. The Science of Political Economy holds in her hands the master-keys of future statesmanship.

Such are a few among the many affiliated questions suggested by this inquiry. Within the limits of this report it is possible only to state them, not to discuss them. But they are questions which address themselves to us no less as citizens, desiring to cherish a legitimate pride in the dignity and purity of our civil institutions, than as educators, bound to inculcate the truths of a sound political philosophy, to the end that, as Milton has expressed it in his tractate on education, we may contribute all that lies in our power to mould "not poor, shaken, uncertain reeds of a tottering conscience, but steadfast pillars of the State."

All of which is respectfully submitted.

JAMES C. WELLING, *Chairman*,
JAMES R. DOOLITTLE,
HORATIO G. JONES,
} *Committee, &c.*

The Rev. Dr. CALDWELL offered the following resolution, which was unanimously adopted:

Resolved, That before dissolving, this Convention takes occasion to urge upon the friends of education, and the associations entitled to constitute members of the Commission, to furnish the contributions required to carry on its operations.

Dr. CUTTING: I wish to say one word before we part to the gentlemen who have come together from all parts of the land, to take into consideration the topics that have engaged our attention. It is my conviction, after my observation and experience, that if an awakened interest in education in the Baptist denomination is to be sustained, and the proper fruits of it are to be gathered, there are two classes of men on whom rests the responsibility of the great work. These two classes are our educators and our pastors. It is my conviction that, taking the world as it is, the work of the educator is but half performed, when he has performed his best duty to the classes that are under his instruction. He owes a duty to the public. He is to be *the educator of the public in respect to education.*

He owes a duty to his own denomination or church. He is to be the educator of his own denomination, of his own church. And if there be any special defect which, to my judgment, works itself into the character of the educators of this time, it is to be found in the tendency to the confinement of their interests and their labors within the walls of their colleges or other schools, whatever they may be. They are not, to the extent to which they ought to be, *the leaders of their brethren in the work of education.*

And, as to the duty of pastors: I would like to point him out, if I could see him—he is in this assembly—the Rev. Mr. STEARNS, of Wisconsin. I knew him when he was a boy. His father was a Baptist minister. I do not believe he ever had a salary of $350 in his life. He preached in the distant regions of the north, to humble country congregations. He gave to that boy the inspiration which sent him to college under great difficulties. The boy graduated at Brown University. He in his turn has raised five boys and has sent every one of them to college. [Applause]. One of them is a Professor in a University, another is a Principal of an Academy; another is at the head of instruction in the Argentine Republic.

Now, it is true that, *as a class*, ministers educate their children better than do any other class, and my argument from that fact is this: what is good for a minister's son or daughter, is good for other people's sons or daughters; and that pastors who feel their responsibility in reference to the education of their own children, should be leaders of their people in reference to the education of theirs. So did the Scottish pastors, and it was they who placed Scotland in the position which Scotland occupies now in reference to the civilization of the world. So did New England pastors, and so New England reached the position which she holds in respect to the civilization of the world. At Associations, in State Conventions, I have urged these convictions upon the minds of my brethren in the ministry. I beseech you, brethren, remember your high mission in respect to this thing. It is the chief hope of the cause of education.

The President resumed the chair.

On motion of Rev. Dr. BOYCE, the following was unanimously adopted:

Resolved, That this Convention entertain a profound sense of the foresight and liberality of those gentlemen of the American Baptist Educational Commission, whose wisdom devised and whose contributions have sustained the operations of the Commission. Their names will be held in everlasting remembrance in the history of one of the most important epochs in the Baptist denomination.

Resolved, That to the Rev. S. S. CUTTING, D. D., are especially due the thanks of the Baptists of the entire country for the energy, faithfulness and self-sacrificing spirit with which, with so much wisdom and executive utility, he has brought the work intrusted to him to its present state of perfection.

Dr. CUTTING: I thank the brethren for this too generous recognition. And yet, so far as my wishes are concerned, I am unfortunate. It was my desire and hope, by a resolution expressing the appreciation of this Convention of the work done by the gentlemen of the Commission, whose liberality has sustained it, that that work would be recognized as you have recognized it in the first of the resolutions just passed. I would not have the force of this recognition abated by any reference to my own share in the work performed. As for myself, I have only to say this: First, that I could have done nothing except as I was sustained by these gentlemen, to whom reference has been made. Second, I could have done nothing except as I was sustained by such men as Dr. HOVEY, Dr. CALDWELL and others, whose time I have consumed, whose labors I have secured in every department of the work in which I have needed help. To them are due in great part the thanks which have been given to me. My service is an humble one. As I remarked two years ago, the hour had come, in the good providence of God, when it was but necessary to lift a voice and the voice would be heard throughout all our ranks.

Rather, Mr. President and brethren, would I have you remember those who have been associated with me, and the Infinite Being whom we delight to serve, and whose blessing has so crowned our endeavors. [Applause].

Prayer was offered by the Rev. Dr. KENDRICK, and the Convention adjourned *sine die*.

FRANCIS WAYLAND,
President.

WILLIAM H. EATON,
C. H. WINSTON,
D. H. COOLEY,
Secretaries.

ADDENDA.

CONSTITUTION

OF THE

American Baptist Educational Commission.

PREAMBLE.

WHEREAS the American Baptist Educational Commission has proposed to surrender to this Convention the further prosecution of its work, suggesting modifications as to the character and sphere of that work, and

Whereas, the Constitution of the Commission provides for the merging of the temporary and provisional body in one more comprehensive and permanent, now,

Therefore, this Convention, in order to perpetuate the work of the Commission, and to provide for its enlargement as the calls of Providence may seem to require, adopts the following

CONSTITUTION:

ARTICLE I. This Association shall be styled the American Baptist Educational Commission.

ART. II. This Commission shall have for its object, the promotion of Education and the Increase of the Ministry, in the Baptist denomination. It shall perform its work by forming centres of counsel and co-operation; by collecting and diffusing information in respect to the cause of education as connected with the Baptist denomination; by inducing and fostering the organized action of the denomination in behalf of its institutions of learning and the education of its youth; by endeavoring to awaken and sustain a profounder interest in the increase and education of the ministry.

It may perform its work further by collecting and appropriating funds for nourishing and sustaining during periods of special exigency unendowed or inadequately endowed institutions of higher learning in States or Territories requiring exterior aid, and may receive and hold in trust, moneys for the endowment of such institutions of learning, given under conditions, until such conditions permit their transfer to the institutions for which they are designed. It shall not take part in the work of raising endowment funds, except by advising the institutions how to proceed, so as not to interfere with each other, or make unreasonable demands on the friends of education.

Art. III. This Commission shall be composed, for the time being, of the subscribers to the original five years' fund of the Commission, and of the members of the present National Baptist Educational Convention, and hereafter, as follows:

1. Of delegates from incorporate institutions of learning, whose Boards of Control are wholly or chiefly of the Baptist denomination. Colleges, or Universities, having undergraduate classes or schools and conferring degrees, Theological Seminaries, and Education Societies of one or more States, may each send two delegates. Academies or Preparatory Schools may each send one delegate.

2. Of delegates from Baptist State Conventions or General Associations, and from Baptist State Pastoral Conferences. Each such Convention, General Association, or Pastoral Conference, may send two delegates.

3. Of persons or associations paying money into the treasury of the Commission, to promote its purposes, as follows: Any person paying $50 annually, shall be a member while so paying; any educational association formed to aid the purposes of the Commission, paying into its treasury not less than $100 annually, may appoint a delegate.

Art. IV. The officers of this Commission shall consist of a President, two Vice-Presidents, a Recording Secretary, a Treasurer, an Executive Committee of ten, whose seat shall be at New York, and four Advisory Committees of twelve each, whose seats shall be respectively at Boston, Chicago, Richmond and Nashville. These officers, when sitting together, shall constitute the Board of Councillors. This Board of Councillors shall appoint a Corresponding Secretary.

Art. V. The Executive Committee, of whom three shall be a quorum (except for the investment of money, or for its disbursement for the maintenance or endowment of institutions of learning, in which case the quorum shall be five), shall appoint such assistants or other agencies as may be necessary to carry out the purposes of the Second Article of this Constitution. It shall be intrusted with the administration of the Commission, it shall fix its own modes of procedure, and shall have power to fill vacancies occasioned by the resignation, removal or death of its members. In case of a vacancy it may appoint a Corresponding Secretary to hold office till the next annual meeting of the Board of Councillors. It shall call annual meetings of the Board of Councillors, to whom it shall make report in detail of its proceedings. It may also call special meetings of this Board, and all calls of such meetings, whether annual or special, shall be by written notice to each member, in which the object of the meeting shall be stated.

The Executive Committee may refer local questions to the Advisory Committees, and the Corresponding Secretary may call meetings of those Committees for the consideration of such questions. At such meetings four shall constitute a quorum.

Art. VI. The Board of Councillors shall hold annual meetings, as called by the Executive Committee, and shall determine the general policy of the Commission, but the care and disbursement of funds shall be entrusted solely to the Executive Committee. The Board shall have power to fill vacancies, other than those which may occur in the Executive Committee, and shall report triennially to the Commission. Eleven members shall constitute a quorum.

Art. VII. The Commission shall hold triennial meetings, which shall be called, and for which arrangements shall be made, by the Executive Committee. The officers above named shall be chosen at these meetings, provided that the Executive Committee shall be divided into two classes, five only (except to fill vacancies not filled as herein before named), to be chosen at any triennial meeting.

Art. VIII. Funds for the maintenance and endowment of institutions of learning, shall never be paid from the treasury of this Commission without satisfactory guarantees to secure the purposes of the donors and of this Commission against waste or perversion.

Art. IX. This Constitution may be altered or amended by a vote of two-thirds of the members present at a triennial meeting, provided that no change shall ever be made in the main object of the Commission, and provided further that none shall be at any time made in respect to the election or duties or powers of the Executive Committee, except by a two-thirds vote at two successive triennial meetings.

OFFICERS

OF THE

AMERICAN BAPTIST EDUCATIONAL COMMISSION,

ELECTED MAY 30th, 1872.

President.

REV. ALVAH HOVEY, D.D., of Massachusetts.

Vice Presidents.

HON. J. R. DOOLITTLE, LL.D., of Wisconsin.
REV. J. L. M. CURRY, D.D., LL.D., of Virginia.

Recording Secretary.

PROF. N. L. ANDREWS, of New York.

Corresponding Secretary.

REV. SEWALL S. CUTTING, D.D., of New York.

Treasurer.

JOHN M. BRUCE, ESQ., of New York.

Executive Committee.

SAMUEL COLGATE, Esq., N. J.; WILLIAM A. GELLATLY, Esq., N. J.; Rev. EDWARD LATHROP, D.D., Conn.; Rev. EDWARD BRIGHT, D.D., New York; A. B. CAPWELL, Esq., N. Y.; JAMES L. HOWARD, Esq., Conn.; SAMUEL A. CROZER, Esq., Pa.; Rev. HENRY C. FISH, D.D., N. J.; JACOB F. WYCKOFF, Esq., N. Y.; GARDNER R. COLBY, Esq., N. J.

Boston Advisory Committee.

Hon. J. WARREN MERRILL, Mass.; Rev. GALUSHA ANDERSON, D.D., Mass.; Rev. WILLIAM LAMSON, D.D., Mass.; GARDNER COLBY, Esq., Mass.; Rev. A. J. GORDON, Mass.; Rev. G. B. GOW, Mass.; Rev. E. G. ROBINSON, D.D., LL.D., R. I.; Rev. S. L. CALDWELL, D.D., R. I.; Rev. C. B. CRANE, D.D., Conn.; LAWRENCE BARNES, Esq., Vt.; Rev. W. H. EATON, D.D., N. H.; Rev. JOSEPH RICKER, D.D., Maine.

Chicago Advisory Committee.

Rev. J. A. SMITH, D.D., Ill.; Rev. G. W. NORTHROP, D.D., Ill.; Rev. JESSE B. THOMAS, D.D., Ill.; Rev. G. S. BAILEY, D.D., Ill.; Rev. KENDALL BROOKS, D.D., Mich.; Rev. SAMPSON TALBOT, D.D., Ohio; Rev. A. A. KENDRICK, D.D., Ill.; Rev. HENRY DAY, D.D., Ind.; Rev. JOHN H. GRIFFITH, Ill.; Rev. DEXTER P. SMITH, D.D., Iowa; Rev. DANIEL REED, LL.D., Minn.; MILO P. JEWETT, LL.D., Wisconsin.

Richmond Advisory Committee.

Rev. J. L. M. CURRY, D.D., LL.D., Va.; Rev. J. L. BURROWS, D.D., Va.; Rev. J. B. JETER, D.D., Va.; Prof. H. H. HARRIS, Va.; Rev. BARNAS SEARS, D.D., LL.D., Va.; Rev. WILLIAM T. BRANTLY, D.D., Md.; JAMES C. WELLING, LL.D., D. C.; Rev. W. P. WALKER, West Va.; Rev. W. M. WINGATE, D.D., N. C.; Rev. J. C. FURMAN, D.D., S. C.; Rev. JAMES P. BOYCE, D.D., LL.D., S. C.; Rev. A. J. BATTLE, D.D., Ga.

Nashville Advisory Committee.

Rev. T. G. JONES, D.D., Tenn.; Rev. WILLIAM SHELTON, D.D., Tenn.; Rev. W. D. NELSON, Tenn.; Rev. W. A. INMAN, Tenn.; Rev. S. SANDERSON, Tenn.; Rev. CHARLES MANLY, D.D., Tenn.; N. K. DAVIS, LL.D., Ky.; Rev. T. RAMBAUT, LL.D., Mo.; Rev. I. T. TICHENOR, D.D., Ala.; Rev. THEODORE WHITFIELD, Miss.; Rev. W. E. PAXTON, La.; Rev. R. C. BURLESON, D.D., Texas.

The Corresponding Secretary was elected by the Board of Councillors, according to the provisions of the Constitution, at a meeting of the Board held immediately after the adjournment of the Convention.

THE EXCURSION TO CROZER THEOLOGICAL SEMINARY.

In accordance with the vote accepting the invitation (see page 26), the Convention visited Crozer Theological Seminary, distant about fifteen miles from Philadelphia, on Thursday afternoon, May 30th. A train of cars had been placed at the service of the Convention by Mr. Samuel P. Crozer, and a very brief ride brought the delegates to the village of Chester, on the border of which, on elevated and beautiful grounds, stands the Seminary. The public buildings of the institution are the principal edifice, used for lecture-rooms and dormitories, and the Library; the latter erected by Mr. William Bucknell, in memory of his deceased wife, who was a daughter of the late Mr. John P. Crozer, from whom the institution takes its name. Besides the public buildings, there are commodious dwellings for Professors, and cottages for students having families. The examination of grounds and buildings, and of the library, already containing many works which are rare and valuable, gave great satisfaction to the visitors, and an ample collation closed the delightful occasion. The institution is young, but has sprung rapidly into maturity of life; its course of studies, its Professors, the character of its work, and the number of its students, giving it equal rank with its elder sisters. It consecrates wealth to sacred and enduring purposes, and enters on its career with universal benedictions.

THE BREAKFAST IN FAIRMOUNT PARK.

The following is the response to the invitation on page 85:

Philadelphia, May 29th, 1872.

MESSRS. HORATIO GATES JONES, WILLIAM RUFUS BUCKNELL, W. W. KEEN, *Committee, &c.*

Gentlemen: I have sincere pleasure in acknowledging the receipt of your kind note of this date, in which you extend a cordial invitation to the Convention over which I have the honor to preside, to partake of a breakfast at Fairmount Park on Friday next.

By a unanimous vote of the Convention, I am instructed to convey to you both its grateful acceptance of your generous invitation, and its high appreciation of the kindness which has inspired it.

With sentiments of high regard, I am

Your obedient servant,

FRANCIS WAYLAND,

President of the Baptist Educational Convention.

In a train of cars provided for the purpose, the members of the Convention left the city for the Park at about fifteen minutes before nine o'clock. The Park was in the extremest beauty of spring, and the day, whether in sun-shine, breeze or shade, so lovely and inspiring, that it could not be surpassed. Besides the members of the Convention, other guests were present by invitation, among whom, accompanying Mr. George H. Stuart, were Father Gavazzi and the Rev. Dr. Thompson of the Free Church of Italy. The breakfast was spread in the Pavilion or Banqueting Hall, a light and tasteful structure, and was in every respect in keeping with the beaut of exterior nature, the generous intentions of the host, and the character of the assemblage. The Hon. Francis Wayland, President of the Convention, presided. On his right were William Bucknell, Esq., the host; President E. G. Robinson, D.D., LL.D.; President Alvah Hovey, D.D.; Rev. S. S. Cutting, D.D., and President James P. Boyce, D.D., LL.D. On the left of the President were the Rev. Barnas Sears, D.D., LL.D.; Father Gavazzi; the Rev. A. C. Kendrick, D.D., LL.D.; George H. Stuart, Esq., and the Rev. Dr. Thompson.

The divine blessing was invoked by the Rev. Dr. Sears.

After the ample and elegant repast, the President introduced the speaking by a felicitous welcome on behalf of Mr. Bucknell, and called up successively several speakers to respond to sentiments. The first, "Philadelphia: her generous hospitality to the delegates of this Convention is proof that she deserves to be called the City of Brotherly Love," was responded to by W. E. Littleton, Esq., President of the Select Council of the City. Then "The Philadelphia Baptists: their brethren from all parts of the country will long remember their kindness and courtesy," responded to by the Rev. J. Wheaton Smith, D.D., "Italy, redeemed, regenerated, disenthralled," responded to by Father Gavazzi; "The Crozer Theological Seminary," responded to by the Rev. Lemuel Moss, D.D.; "The Baptist Clergy of Philadelphia; worthy of their denomination, they can have no higher praise," responded to by Rev. P. S. Henson, D.D.; "The American Baptist Educational Commission: Tithonus is young again, and Aurora rejoices" (see page 175); responded to by Rev. S. S. Cutting, D.D.; "Our Presbyterian Brethren," responded to by Rev. Alexander Reed, D.D., and George H. Stuart, Esq.; "The University of Rochester, represented by philologist and philosopher, poet and divine," responded to by Rev. A. C. Kendrick, D.D., LL.D.; "The Religious Press an important Auxiliary of the Pulpit," responded to by Rev. Edward Bright, D.D.; "Our Southern Colleges and Theological Schools: may they be as prosperous as their sisters of the North," responded to by Rev. James P. Boyce, D.D., LL.D.; "The Protestant Episcopal Church," responded to by Rev. D. R. Goodwin, D.D.

Though no speakers had spoken long, the speeches had been so many that the last moment of possible time had been consumed, and the assemblage broke up with very great reluctance, singing with unusual ferv[illegible] the hymn:

"Blest be the tie that binds
Our hearts in Christian love,"

and taking the hand of Mr. Bucknell, as they departed for the returning train.

Taking into account the character of the persons present, the beauty of the day and of the place, the elegance of the repast, and the sustained excellence of the speaking, creating no regrets, and obliterating, in a manner most memorable, some which had arisen in the flush of earnest debate in the Convention, the "Bucknell Breakfast" will abide in the recollection of those present as among the most delightful incidents of the social experiences of a life-time.

ERRATA.—Page 48, second line from bottom, for "keep" read "help." Page 51, line 18, for "totally" read "totality."

INDEX.

PAGE.

www.ingramcontent.com/pod-product-compliance
Lightning Source LLC
LaVergne TN
LVHW011212110826
845150LV00006B/1409